THE INDIAN CONSTITUTION—

A Case Study of Backward Classes

THE INDIAN CONSTITUTION—
A Case Study of Backward Classes

RATNA G. REVANKAR

RUTHERFORD ● MADISON ● TEANECK
Fairleigh Dickinson University Press

Associated University Presses, Inc.
Cranbury, New Jersey 08512

ISBN 0-8386-7670-7
Printed in the United States of America

CONTENTS

PREFACE

The problem of Backward Classes in the Indian Constitution embodied in this book is so current and growing that it has assumed new dimensions, necessitating a restatement. The term "Backward Classes" is a comprehensive one comprising four sections of Indian society: Scheduled Castes, Scheduled Tribes, Other Backward Classes, and Denotified Communities. These sections constitute the underprivileged classes of the country, for whom special treatment is accorded in the Indian Constitution. The present study examines the relevant provisions of the Constitution relating to Backward Classes. The scope of the study is so defined because the problem is largely a Constitutional one. It is based on the analysis and observations of the committees constituted in India to investigate the problem.

ACKNOWLEDGMENTS

THE PRESENT WORK IS A REVISION OF MY PH.D. DISSERTATION submitted to Karnatak University, Dharwar, India. I am greatly indebted to Professor G. S. Halappa, Chairman, Political Science Department, K.U.D., for his encouragement and the University for giving me the permission to publish this work. My grateful thanks are also due to Professor Norman D. Palmer, Professor of Political Science and South Asian Studies, University of Pennsylvania, for the critical review of this work.

I also wish to take this opportunity to thank my husband, Dr. Ganapathi Revankar, without whose active cooperation this book could not have been published.

Bangalore, India   Ratna Revankar

THE INDIAN CONSTITUTION—

A Case Study of Backward Classes

1
CASTE AND BACKWARD CLASSES

Introduction

CASTE SYSTEM IN INDIA IS SO UNIVERSAL THAT NO STUDY OF
Indian social, economic and political institutions would be
complete without a reference to it. Besides, caste constitutes the very basis of the structure of Backward Classes.
The problem of Backward Classes, viz. "The Scheduled Castes," "The Scheduled Tribes," "Other Backward
Classes," and "Denotified Communities," has arisen chiefly
from the social structure of Hindu society. Hence a brief
review of the caste system from different angles is imperative.

A caste in India is fairly definable as an endogamous
group or even as a collection of endogamous groups,
bearing a common name, whose members follow traditionally a single occupation or certain cognate occupations, have by fact or fiction a common origin and are
generally deemed to form a homogeneous unit, whose
constituent parts are more closely allied to one another
than to any other section of society.[1]

A. L. Kroeber defined caste as "an endogamous and
hereditary subdivision of an ethnic unit occupying a posi-

1. *Encyclopaedia Britannica*, Vol. 4, 1910, p. 977.

tion of superior or inferior rank or social esteem in comparison with other such subdivisions."[2]

A caste is an organism of a lower type; it grows by fission, and each step in its growth detracts from its power to advance or even to preserve the art which it professes to practice.[3]

Caste has been variously defined by both Indian and European scholars. The factors emphasized by scholars in their definitions center round endogamy, hereditary professions, exclusive social classes with codified social distance, ritual ranking of society, etc. However, there is no unanimity among the scholars as regards the definition of the term "caste" and its genesis. This is because the complexity of the problem defies an impartial treatment of the subject.

Of late, Taya Zinkin has arrived at the conclusion that caste is not class, it is not color, it is not Aryan or non-Aryan, and it is not occupation. But then what is it? She very aptly remarks, "It is much easier to say what caste is not, than what caste is."[4]

Origin of the Caste System

Origin of the caste system is a much discussed problem. Innumerable theories are advanced and the most outstanding among them are:

1. Code of Manu or Manu Dharmashastra;
2. Nesfield's Functional theory of caste;
3. Ibbetson's theory of caste;
4. Senart's theory of caste;
5. Risley's explanation of caste; and
6. Modern theories of caste by Ghurye and Dutt.

In tracing the origin of caste, people are greatly influenced by the facts recorded about this institution in the

2. *Encyclopaedia of the Social Sciences*, Vol. 3, 1935, p. 254.
3. *The Imperial Gazetteer of India*, Vol. 1, 1907, p. 343.
4. Taya Zinkin, *Caste Today*, 1963, p. 1.

ancient sacred works such as Vedas, Upanishads, Puranas, and Dharmashastras.[5] The commonly known theory of caste is "Chathurvarna" or the fourfold division of society into Brahman, Kshatriya, Vaishya, and Shudra. This ideal of Chathurvarna is mentioned in Purushasūkta, a hymn in Rigveda. The names of the four orders are given as Brahman, Kshatriya, Vaishya, and Shudra, who were created by the Supreme Soul for the prosperity of the worlds. Brahman was supposed to have been originated from the mouth of the Creator, Kshatriya from His arms, Vaishya from His thighs, and Shudra from His feet. Just as all the organs are indispensable for the proper functioning of the human body, so also the four divisions of society were indispensable for social harmony. Besides, the Brahman was entrusted to study, teach, perform sacrifice for the general good, and receive alms for livelihood. Kshatriya was bound to protect the people. Vaishya had to undertake business, cultivate land, etc. Shudra was destined to render service to the other three groups. This functional classification was considered important for the smooth running of administration.

Caste system in its original form—Chathurvarna—was dynamic, liable to change according to the corresponding change in the traits of individuals. According to the Varna theory, "Guna" or character was chiefly responsible for the classification of castes. But the Varna theory cannot be interpreted in the strict sense of color theory. Physical color was not so much emphasized as the intrinsic qualities of the people. The intrinsic qualities were symbolized in color. The "Satvaguna" of Brahmans was symbolized in white color; "Rajas" or passion was symbolized with the red color of valor for which stood the Kshatriyas; the Vaishyas were attributed to yellow color, the lust for wealth; and the Shudras were supposed to be of a "tamasic"

---

5. *Manu Samhita:* III. 151. VIII. 1, 2.

nature of dark.[6] This fourfold division of society was referred to in the Bhagavad Gita as:

> The four orders of society (viz., the Brahman, the Kshatriya, the Vaishya and the Shudra) were created by Me classifying them according to their prenatal qualities and apportioning corresponding duties to them; though the author of this creation, know Me the immortal Lord, to be a non-doer.[7]

Brahmans were exalted to the highest social status for the presence of virtues like self-sacrifice, self-control, selfless motives, and profound thought. Then came the Kshatriyas for their heroic venture to put down antisocial elements. Next in order were the Vaishyas to maintain the moral standards in business, as wealth constituted the social trust of the country. Likewise, the menial service of the Shudras was never degraded but viewed mainly from the angle of spirituality.

Coming to the critical theories of caste, Nesfield was of the firm conviction that "Function and function only, as I think was the foundation upon which the whole caste system of India was built up."[8] His theory runs as follows:

> Each caste or group of castes represents one or other of those progressive stages of culture which have marked the industrial development of mankind, not only in India, but in every other country in the world wherein some advance has been made from primeval savagery to the arts and industries of civilized life. The rank of any caste as high or low depends upon whether the industry represented by the caste belongs to an advanced or backward stage of culture; and thus the natural history of human industries affords the chief clue to the graduations as well as to the formation of Indian castes.[9]

---

6. G. H. Mees, *Dharma and Society*, Gravenhage: N. V. Servire, 1935.
7. *The Bhagavad Gita*, Chap. 4, 12.
8. Extract taken from *The Imperial Gazetteer of India*, p. 338.
9. *Ibid.*

Sir Denzil Ibbetson's hypothesis of caste centered around tribal division, functional guilds, and religion. To quote his theory in brief:

Thus, if my theory be correct, we have the following steps in the process by which caste has been evolved in the Punjab:

(1) The tribal divisions common to all primitive societies;

(2) The guilds based upon hereditary occupation common to the middle life of all communities;

(3) The exaltation of the priestly office to a degree unexampled in other countries;

(4) The exaltation of the Levitical blood by a special insistence upon the necessarily hereditary nature of occupation;

(5) The preservation and support of this principle by the elaboration from the theories of the Hindu creed or cosmogony of a purely artificial set of rules, regulating marriage and intermarriage, declaring certain occupations and foods to be impure and polluting, and prescribing the conditions and degree of social intercourse permitted between the several castes. Add to this the pride of social rank and the pride of blood which are natural to man, and which alone could reconcile a nation to restrictions at once irksome from a domestic and burdensome from a material point of view; and it is hardly to be wondered at that caste should have assumed the rigidity which distinguishes it in India.[10]

Senart emphasized the family or gentile theory as the basis of "caste." According to him the functional theory of caste system was superficial, because dislocation of the functional division, where members of the different communities performing functions contrary to their allotment by the caste rigidity, was widely seen in the country. He opined that "It would be an exaggeration to imagine

10. *Ibid.* pp. 336–37.

Hindu society as enclosed according to the occupations of its members in a chessboard of unchangeable and impassable squares."[11] His theory of caste was based on usage and tradition. He remarked: "The social organism of India, the play of its motive forces, is moreover regulated infinitely more by custom, varying according to locality and baffling in its complexity, than by legal formulae laid down in authentic and easily accessible texts."[12] He argued that caste was but a normal development of ancient Aryan institutions adjusting itself to the conditions prevailing in India. The parallelism put forward in the development of his theory was the close correspondence between the social organization of the Hindus and that of the Greeks and Romans. He further observed that the caste system

> . . . by the domination it claimed for the Brahmans, it preserved a rigidity concerning religious scruples which was reflected in the severity of the caste rules; it served as a basis for that hierarchy which has become an integral part of the system and facilitated its establishment by lending peculiar force to the ideas of purity which, generally speaking, determine the levels of the social scale.[13]

Sir Herbert Risley presented his theory of caste on "a basis of fact and a superstructure of fiction." The basis of fact was the invasion of a country by another instills the principle of racial distinction. So caste system started with the fact of racial distinction after the Aryan invasion of the indigenous Dravidians.

> Once started in India, the principle was strengthened, perpetuated, and extended to all ranks of society by the fiction that people who speak a different language, dwell

---

11. Emile Senart, *Caste in India*, 1930, p. 33.
12. *Ibid.*, p. 2.
13. *Ibid.*, p. 197.

in a different district, worship different gods, eat different food, observe different social customs, follow a different profession, or practice the same profession in a slightly different way must be so unmistakably aliens by blood that intermarriage with them is a thing not to be thought of.[14]

The peculiar characteristics of the Indian intellect which contributed to the growth of the caste system, according to Risley, were:

Its lax hold of facts, its indifference to action, its absorption in dreams, its exaggerated reverence for tradition, its passion for endless division and subdivision, its acute sense of minute technical distinctions, its pedantic tendency to press a principle to its furthest logical conclusion, and its remarkable capacity for imitating and adapting social ideas and usages of whatever origin.[15]

Modern theories of caste attribute racial factors to the genesis of caste system. The theory developed by G. S. Ghurye reads as follows:

Basing my calculation on some of the physical measurements taken by anthropologists and using one of the statistical devices to gauge the nearness of distance of one caste from another in the totality of these measurements, I have established a general correspondence between finer physical type and high position in the caste hierarchy.[16]

The physical affinities of high castes and their marked separation from low castes are further illustrated in the caste hierarchy of Uttar Pradesh, Punjab, Bihar, Bengal, and Bombay. He further observes: "This racial origin of

14. Herbert Risley, *The People of India*, 1915, p. 275.
15. *Ibid.*, pp. 275–76.
16. G. S. Ghurye, *Caste and Class in India*, 1957, p. 176.

the principal feature of the caste system is further supported by the early term 'Varna' meaning color, used to specify the orders in society."[17]

Similar ideas are expressed by N. K. Dutt[18] as regards the origin of the caste system. But in the course of his argument he paves the way for the conclusion that caste is a function of more than one variable, race, occupation, language, residence, and religion.

Thus a number of theories have been advanced on the genesis of the caste system. But unfortunately there is no unanimity among the scholars as regards its origin and nature. The complexity of the problem has influenced the scholars to emphasize one-sided views. From the Varna theory of caste system to the modern critical theories of caste, there is great divergence of views. Some authors emphasize the religious aspect of caste, some describe caste as the functional division of society, while others rely on racial factors, custom and usage, tradition, tribal divisions, etc. The conclusion arrived at by Herbert Risley after a detailed study of the problem is:

> The origin of caste is from the nature of the case an insoluble problem. We can only frame more or less plausible conjectures, derived from the analogy of observed facts. The particular conjecture now put forward is based, firstly, upon the correspondence that can be traced between certain caste gradations and certain variations of physical type; secondly, on the development of mixed races from stocks of different color; and thirdly, on the influence of fiction.[19]

An intensive study of the social institution of caste points to the direction that a number of factors have contributed to the genesis and growth of this institution at different

---

17. *Ibid.*, pp. 178–79.
18. N. K. Dutt, *Origin and Growth of Caste in India,* 1931.
19. Risley, *The People of India,* p. 277.

intervals. Since the institution was subject to several influences, the basis once accepted as the origin ceased to be the sole factor with the transformation of the social institution. For instance, "Guna" or character was emphasized in the Varna theory of caste, which is incidentally the oldest and the widely accepted theory. But with the lapse of time, we find references being made to the factor of "birth" as the sole determinant of caste in Mahabharata about 700 B.C. With the Aryan invasion of the indigenous Dravidians, we find several theories springing up emphasizing the functional division and racial distinction constituting the origin of the caste system. Modern practice has traveled very far from the early origins. Hence, from the above analysis it could be safely concluded that the genesis of the caste system is attributable to a number of factors: "Guna" or character, birth, occupation or guild, tribal division, racial distinction, tradition, and usage. To emphasize a single factor would be to err on the origin of the caste system. The only consolation that the study of the caste system has offered to the social scientist, in the words of Herbert Risley, is: "The search for origins, like the quest of the Sangreal, possesses endless fascination, and if it does not yield any very tangible results, it at least has the merit of encouraging research."[20]

Caste System—An Analysis

Caste system is not a peculiar phenomenon found only in India. Analogous institutions are found in almost all the major civilizations of ancient times, even though they may vary in intricate details. Stratification of society is found even in the advanced countries of the world. Social distinctions and social distance are common in all societies. In a democracy, egalitarian ideology holds good in theory. It may even sound a basic reality before the court of law.

---

20. *Ibid.*, p. 258.

But in actual practice inequality is an accepted social order in all countries. Inequalities in income, wealth, social prestige, social standing, political power, intellectual abilities, and so on, do exist and they cannot be ruled out absolutely. Ranking is therefore a common feature in all societies. But the social stratification of society in India stands out distinct because the basis of stratification is heredity rather than individuality.

Institutions similar to the caste system were found in the primitive societies of Egypt, Japan, China, Persia, Greece, Rome, Ceylon, Siam, South Africa, Burma, Germany, and England. In Egypt, the society was divided into three classes: landowners, serfs, and slaves. Occupations were traditional and hereditary; the artisans particularly were prevented from professing any occupation other than their hereditary trade. Likewise, sacerdotal literature of ancient Persia makes a reference to the division of society into four classes: priests, warriors, cultivators, and artisans. In China, society was divided into four orders: gentility, farmers, artisans, and merchants. In Japan the five distinct social divisions were: hereditary soldiers (the Samurai), farmers, artisans, traders, and Etas. The Etas of Japan compare favorably with the Untouchables living in the outskirts of the cities and villages. Roman society was divided into patricians, plebeians, and slaves. Similarly, Anglo-Saxon English society was marked with three social groups—the nobleman, the common free man, and the slaves. In Europe, occupations involving manual labor were rated very low in social estimation. But here, the option was given to the goldsmiths who, in spite of being grouped under the artisan class, were rated high, as their work involved brain work more than manual labor. German society of the eighteenth century was marked with five divisions: princes, nobles, burghers, peasants, and serfs.

A brief review of the social divisions which prevailed in

different parts of the world helps us to demarcate the distinct features of the caste system. The notable distinction is that the term "caste" is not found in any social stratification. Instead we come across the term "class." This poses another problem as to whether "caste" can be equated with "class." Are they synonymous? But this is only a hypothesis. Caste stands altogether on a different plane and it has very remote comparison or correspondence to class. Yet another distinct trait is that the caste organization as found in India is very comprehensive and all-in-all. It regulated not merely the vocational set-up of different social orders but even catered to their moral behavior. Apart from this there was a social injunction, that the failure to observe caste rules would render people to be out-castes. On the contrary, the scope of class organization was limited in the sense that it regulated only the professional behavior of the people. It left untouched the social life of the people. Moreover, class distinctions in Western societies were based on race, language, rank, and social status. But under the caste hierarchy "birth" was made the determinant for social stratification. Social isolation among the people professing the same religious faith was the glaring feature of the caste system as contrasted with the class organization. It is true that in both class and caste organization public service ranked high and the menial jobs were rated low. Class hierarchy was found in all medieval civilizations, so also social stratification and certain taboos concerning eating, marriage, etc. But the practice of "untouchability" based on ceremonial purity was a peculiar trait found only in the Indian caste organization.

A Survey of the Caste System

Caste as conceived by the Varna theory had flexibility. Even though there was fourfold classification of society, it rested on the basis of intrinsic qualities of individuals. There was some spirituality behind the caste structure rather than absurd rigidity. "Guna" or character gave way to "birth" as the determinant of caste during the time of *Mahabharata* (700 B.C.). With the Aryan invasion, functional classification became marked. But there was mobility of occupation. Even Johann Bühler (1837-98) remarked[21] that occupations were not hereditary in Vedic or Buddhist times. The functional classification emphasized more the spirit of cooperation. But gradually there was functional disintegration with every fresh invasion of the country. The result was, a number of castes professing varied occupations came into existence. From the original fourfold division there were as many as fifty-seven mixed castes which were ethnic or functional in origin.[22] But still the caste system aimed at a synthesis of the diverse social and cultural elements in the country. It was a sort of social security for racial groups of different types. It illustrated the comprehensive synthesis characteristic of the Hindu mind with its faith in the collaboration of races and the cooperation of cultures. "Paradoxical as it may seem, the system of caste is the outcome of tolerance and trust."[23]

Later, the stamping of occupation to particular caste of a specific region became the order of the day. This specific allotment of functions was necessitated by the self-sufficiency principle. Every village was a self-sufficient unit, and so, to avoid competition, caste groups on functional basis were formed. Rural India with agricultural economy was able to maintain an autonomous and compact system of functional division of society. The most important thing to be noticed in this context was that castes acted as occupational guilds. There was united action on the part

21. *Sacred Books of the East*, Vol. XXV.
22. *Manu Samhita*, X, 8., pp. 48–49.
23. S. Radhakrishnan, *The Hindu View of Life*, 1948, p. 93.

of the caste groups because of their dual membership to the caste on the one hand and occupation on the other. Thus caste system acted not only as a political stabilizer but also was responsible for the preservation of the cultural heritage of our hoary past. As Taya Zinkin has observed:

> In the long turmoil that was Indian history, caste held together the fabric of society; the integrity of the village was built round the framework of caste; the survival of Hinduism under Muslim and Christian onslaughts might well have been impossible without the devotion of peasant and scholar alike to caste-customs and caste-ritual.[24]

Yet another unique feature to be noted is, the people opted social security and solidarity rather than equality. This was the keynote for the survival of functional classification of society. The lower castes were impressed by the Hindu philosophy that whatever may be one's caste, Brahman or Shudras, one can attain perfection by doing well the duties assigned to him and remaining within the fold of his caste. People were not induced to aspire for higher social status. The performance of duties rather than the demand for rights was emphasized. The sense of unity and social harmony regulated society. Functional classification of castes worked well for centuries chiefly because the social divisions were more conscious of their responsibilities and duties rather than rights and privileges.

Gradually caste system, begun by the principles of endogamy and traditional occupation, culminated in the vivisection of society with the ideas of purity and impurity. It sowed the seeds of segregation and exclusiveness in short the "touch-me-not-ism" in Hindu society. In due course, the caste structure deteriorated beyond repair. It

24. Zinkin, *Caste Today*, p. 10.

sealed society into water-tight social divisions isolated from each other by imposing taboos on food, matrimony, social get-togethers, and the like. The social distance between the sub-castes of the same caste was made so great, that a person born in a particular caste (subdivision) had no mobility in occupation nor could he mingle with other subdivisions for purposes of marriage. The only mobility was found in the violation of caste rules which meant social boycott and extermination. A. R. Wadia has commented on this malady as "the high metaphysics of the Upanishads and the ethics of the Gita have been reduced to mere words by the tyranny of caste."[25] Thus, at a time when artisans and cultivators breathed in an air of freedom and liberty in Western countries their Indian counterparts were imprisoned within the folds of the rigid caste system.

The perverted motives of caste system which later took hold of Hindu society were: the rigid concept of social hierarchy, the theory and practice of pollution, birth as the lever for selecting profession, and static social structure. Primary importance was given to a man's "birth" in a particular caste for deciding his "be-all" and "end-all." As J. H. Hutton remarked:

> From the point of view of the individual member of a caste, the system provides him from birth with a fixed social milieu from which neither wealth nor poverty, success nor disaster can remove him, unless of course he so violates the standards of behaviour laid down by his caste that it spews him forth—temporarily or permanently.[26]

The climax of the perverted motive of caste system culminated in propounding the theory of pollution to ex-

---

25. A. R. Wadia, *Contemporary Indian Philosophy*, p. 368.
26. J. H. Hutton, *Caste in India*, 1961, p. 111.

tremities. This social malady of India brought in its train a Pandora's box. As A. R. Wadia rightly pointed out: "Worst of all, she has become the home of untouchability and unapproachability which have branched her with the curse of Cain."[27]

The theory and practice of pollution was exalted to the maximum. It was asserted that the touch and even sight of the untouchables caused pollution to members of high castes, particularly the Brahmans. The untouchables were deprived of all services of the community—use of public wells, entry to temples, schools, medical aid, and other facilities, for fear of contamination. Brahmanism was in due course attacked for creating rigid social distinctions. B. R. Ambedkar pointed out: "Inequality is the official doctrine of Brahmanism and the suppression of the lower classes aspiring to equality has been looked upon by them and carried out by them without remorse as their bounden duty."[28] "Dharma," the keynote of the Hindu social organization, gave way to "Artha," and "Kama" subsequently. Caste system, started with the spirit of social harmony, turned out a sort of plague hampering the progress of Hindu society. It was incessantly felt by the intelligentsia of the country that the eradication of caste system was inevitable for the integration of society. B. R. Ambedkar emphatically stated: "The outcaste is a by-product of the caste system. There will be outcastes as long as there are castes."[29]

Thus, the caste system which was the outcome of trust and tolerance, cooperation, and consolidation became an institution of discrimination and segregation repugnant to the spirit of Hinduism. As Radhakrishnan pointed out: "Though it has now degenerated into an instrument of

---

27. Wadia, *Contemporary Indian Philosophy*, p. 368.
28. Quoted in Dhananjay Keer, *Dr. Ambedkar: Life and Mission*, 1954, p. 220.
29. *Ibid.*

oppression and intolerance, though it tends to perpetuate inequality and develop the spirit of exclusiveness, these unfortunate effects are not the central motives of the system."[30]

The notions of caste discrimination and social exclusiveness were repudiated from time immemorial. The principles of unity of the human race and the brotherhood of mankind were taught by the great religious thinkers from Buddha down to Vivekananda. Each of these thinkers bequeathed the message of universal brotherhood. Indian history is replete with social and religious movements starting with the Upanishads and followed by a number of isms (Buddhism, Jainism, Vaishnavism, Shaivism, Sikhism, etc.), working toward the eradication of caste system. These movements inspired in the people a liberal social philosophy preaching the gospel of equality. But it is our misfortune, that in spite of a rich cultural heritage and high ideals we fostered a rigid caste system.

Till the advent of British rule, the Brahmans enjoyed high social status in caste hierarchy. But gradually the caste structure started showing signs of decay and disintegration. With the rapid industrialization of the country, there was a further setback in the rigid observance of caste rules. The dwindling of cottage industries and handicrafts in the face of foreign competition and the destruction of village autonomy gave a rude shock to the caste structure, necessitating some modifications. The establishment of a uniform British law throughout the country undermined the integrity of the caste structure. It deprived caste councils of the power to decide civil and criminal cases concerned with the members of the particular castes. This put an end to legal inequalities arising out of the exercise of justice by different caste councils. Besides, they issued a warning to all educational institutions against the segregation of depressed class pupils. Grants

_____
30. Radhakrishnan, *The Hindu View of Life*, p. 93.

to schools which practiced segregation were withdrawn. The universalization of education by the British gave a setback to Brahmanical supremacy in the field of education. As a result of this the passive submission of the lower orders to higher castes ceased to operate. It stirred the intelligentsia of the lower castes to organize popular movements like the Non-Brahman Movement in South India, to cast off the domination of caste Hindus. The new class of intellectuals trained under the system of English education was chiefly responsible for weakening the rigidity of the caste system. The political writings of Rousseau, J. S. Mill, and others infused ideas of liberty and equality among the educated classes. Naturally the newly educated sections, who were denied the benefits of education for ages, felt the need for improving the social status of their communities. The emergence of a new class of intellectuals, imbued with the spirit of liberty spontaneously found in the writings of Western thinkers, realized the futility of Hindu orthodoxy. This influence of English literature on democracy was far reaching. The principle of popular sovereignty left a lasting impression on the minds of the younger generations. There developed in the country an urge to end caste superiority and substitute in its place the dignity of individual personality and the unity of the nation.

Here it is relevant to touch the debit side of the British impact on caste system. It is true that the British regime did many things to put down caste system. But they did not evince interest in shattering the caste institution root and branch. In the first place, the census enumeration on caste basis definitely produced opposite results. As remarked by the census superintendent, Mr. Middleton:

Caste in itself was rigid among the higher castes, but malleable amongst the lower. We pigeonholed everyone by caste, and if we could not find a true caste for them, labelled them with the name of an hereditary occupation. We deplore the caste system and its effects on social and economic problems, but we are largely responsible for the system we deplore.[31]

They encouraged caste-consciousness in states by way of reserving seats in the legislature on caste basis. Electorates were divided on the basis of religion. They further divided the separate electorates by reserving certain seats in each constituency to non-Muslims, as they were supposed to be underrepresented in the country's legislature. This method of reservation created cleavages between different communities, Brahmans versus non-Brahmans in Madras, Marathas with the rest of the population in Bombay, etc. Caste-consciousness was encouraged in a different way. Some vestige of this conflict is prevalent even to the present day. The conflict of Brahman vs. non-Brahman started during the British regime is continuing to operate, particularly in Madras State (Dravida Munnetra Kazagam Party). Thus, caste which was mainly a social institution entered the arena of politics during the British regime. In the course of time it became a problem to be tackled on the political and social plane at par. It would be no exaggeration if we remark that the caste element was revived rather than eliminated during the British regime. The caste system was seen in a new garb during British rule.

Coming to the mobility of occupations in the caste system, Brahmans had the option of going in for any trade other than their own and meanwhile retaining the same social status accorded to them. Mobility was absolutely restricted in the case of lower orders. Even thinkers who refused to accept the rigidity of the functional theory of caste admit that preferential treatment was given to Brahmans in the choice of occupation. J. N. Bhattacharya,

---

31. *Census Report*, 1921, *Punjab Report*, p. 434.

a firm believer in the social harmony of the caste system, admits: "caste is often described by European scholars as an iron chain which has fettered each class to the profession of their ancestors, and has rendered any improvement on their part impossible. This view may, to some extent, be regarded as correct so far as the lower classes are concerned."[32] Emile Senart also observed: "It is perhaps among the Brahmans that there occurs the most complicated mixture of occupations and confusion of trades."[33] By way of illustration he further remarked: "People who proudly bear the title of Brahman, and to whom everywhere this assures great respect, may be found engaged in all sorts of tasks; priests and ascetics, learned men and religious beggars, but also cooks and soldiers, scribes and merchants, cultivators and shepherds, even masons and chair-porters."[34]

The change of social status was visibly found among non-Brahmans in the course of the evolution of caste system. There were chances of the last three orders getting merged with each other by improving their social status. But birth was the sole criterion for classifying Brahmans. People born in non-Brahman castes had no chance of calling themselves Brahmans or raising their social status at par with Brahmans by any means, learning, or wealth. Birth as the chief determinant of caste was markedly found among Brahmans.

We may quote as typical of the movement for consolidation the desire of the artisan castes in many parts of India to appear under a common name; thus carpenters, smiths, goldsmiths and some others of similar occupations desired in various parts of India to be returned by a common denomination such as Viswakarma or Jangida, usually desiring to add a descriptive noun

32. J. N. Bhattacharya, *Hindu Castes and Sects*, 1896, Part I, p. 8.
33. Senart, *Caste in India*, p. 35.
34. *Ibid.*, pp. 35–36.

implying that they belonged to one of the two highest varnas of Hinduism, either Brahman or Rajput.[35]

The lower classes thus displayed the desire to rise in social estimation by attributing new designations to their caste groups.

The difficulties wrought by such community fancies in changing the nomenclature of their castes have been well stated by the Superintendent of Census operations for Madras, thus:

> Sorting for caste is really worthless unless nomenclature is sufficiently fixed to render the resulting totals close and reliable approximations. Had caste terminology the stability of religious returns caste sorting might be worthwhile. With the fluidity of present appellations it is certainly not. . . . 227,000 Ambattans have become 10,000 . . . , Navithan, Nai, Nai Brahman, Navutiyan, Pariyari claim about 140,000—all terms unrecorded or untabulated in 1921. . . . Individual fancy apparently has some part in caste nomenclature.[36]

Some new ranks claimed by old castes are recorded in Table 1-1.[37]

TABLE 1–1

Old Name	1921 Claims	1931 Claims
Kamar	Kshatriya	Brahman
Sonar	Kshatriya	Brahman
	Rajput	Vaishya
Sutradar	Vaishya	Brahman
Nai	Thakur	Brahman
Napit	Baidya	Brahman
Rawani (kahar)	Vaishya	Kshatriya
Muchi	Baidya Rishi	Kshatriya
Chamar	Baidya Rishi	Galhot Rajput

35. *Census Report*, 1931, Vol. 1, para. 182, p. 431.
36. *Ibid.*, p. 432.
37. *Ibid.*, p. 431.

Thus there was a tendency among lower castes to attribute Brahmanhood to their caste groups for purposes of social superiority. Such a tendency is visible even today and this social imitation of the lower caste groups has been termed by M. N. Srinivas as "Sanskritisation." The Brahmans are becoming more and more Westernized and the lower orders are aspiring to be Sanskritized. The lower orders of the caste hierarchy are adopting new customs and habits discarded by the Brahmans. Sanskritization is therefore supposed to be the preliminary step to Westernization. Economic advance, political leadership, and education are some of the relevant factors in Sanskritization. Sanskritization, in short, means cultural and structural changes in society. But at the same time, as M. N. Srinivas remarks: "Sanskritisation does not always result in higher status for the Sanskritised caste, and this is clearly exemplified by the untouchables."[38]

The nineteenth century marked a notable change in traditional Hinduism. The intelligentsia of the country sought to reorganize society on the basis of reason rather than faith. They attributed difference in wealth and educational attainments particularly to the unequal opportunities offered to the people. The emergence of a new middle class from among the lower orders who broke away the barrier of hereditary occupation and took to business was chiefly responsible for undermining the domination of Brahmanical supremacy. Hindu orthodoxy and religious conservatism were questioned by the lower orders. The lower orders not only entered educational institutions but also emerged as the ruling capitalists of the country by undertaking big enterprises and managing agencies. Hence birth and caste were made figments of fancy. On the contrary, wealth and education constituted the determinants of individual social prestige. The concept of equality was emphasized. A revision of the old social ideal

---

38. M. N. Srinivas, *Caste in Modern India*, 1962, p. 58.

in the context of social transformation was urged. These ideas found expression in a series of socio-religious movements—the Brahmo Samaj, Arya Samaj, Prarthana Samaj, Ramakrishna Mission, and others. These religious movements inspired in the people the value of universal brotherhood, rationality, liberalism, and the concepts of equality and justice. Eradication of caste was felt indispensable for the dynamic evolution of society. They aimed at the establishment of society on the twin principles of catholicity and cosmopolitanism. The fact that the caste system was a man-made institution rather than ordained by God was manifested to the people. These religious thinkers made a restatement of Hindu Scriptures and convinced the people to work for the salvation of mankind rather than to parade under the banner of high and low. Vivekananda appealed to the Brahmans:

> It is clearly the duty of the Brahmans of India to remember what real Brahmanhood is. As Manu says, all these privileges and honours are given to the Brahman because 'with him is the treasury of virtue.' He must open that treasury and distribute its valuables to the world.[39]

Likewise, Gandhiji's entry into politics constituted a landmark in the history of the caste system. To him goes the credit for averting the danger that would have befallen the country by mass conversion of untouchables to other religious beliefs. Commenting on the sin of untouchability, he remarked:

> Hinduism has sinned in giving sanction to untouchability. It has degraded us, made us the pariahs of the empire. Even the Mussulmans caught the sinful contagion from us, and in South Africa, in East Africa and

---

39. *Selections from Swami Vivekananda*, p. 22.

Canada the Mussulmans no less than the Hindus came to be regarded as pariahs. All this evil has resulted from the sin of untouchability.[40]

He convinced the people the philosophy of vedantha, that every man is eternally free. He appealed to the moral regeneration of society to break away the shackles of Hindu orthodoxy. He fervently criticized the caste system: "Caste today is in the crucible and only Heaven knows, or perhaps the Brahmans know the final result."[41]

Another outstanding personality who stood for the cause of untouchables was B. R. Ambedkar. He fought for their rights and carved for them a niche in the Republican Constitution of India. He emphatically stated: "In a changing society there must be a constant revaluation of old values and the Hindus must realize that if there must be standard to measure the acts of men there must also be readiness to revise these standards."[42] He vowed to wean away untouchability, and observed: "If I fail to do away with abominable thraldom and human injustice under which the class into which I was born has been groaning, I will put an end to my life with a bullet."[43]

The unflinching courage and daring efforts of a number of leaders of thought and action were chiefly responsible for the weakening of the caste system, if not its complete abolition. In the long run the caste system underwent radical changes in its structure. The caste system, begun with socio-religious motives, became a political issue under the British regime and finally assumed constitutional importance.

The next phase in the transformation of the caste system started with the framing of the Indian Constitution.

40. M. K. Gandhi, *Hindu Dharma*, 1950, p. 279.
41. M. K. Gandhi, *The Removal of Untouchability*, 1937, p. 50.
42. B. R. Ambedkar, *Annihilation of Caste*, 1937, p. 80.
43. Quoted in *Dhananjay Keer, Dr. Ambedkar: Life and Mission*, p. 446.

An increasing interest has been shown for helping the lower orders of the caste hierarchy. The downtrodden sections familiarly known as the "backward classes" received special attention of the constitution makers. The uplift of these sections has been recognized as an important responsibility of the government. The circumstances necessitating the incorporation of certain articles in the Constitution for backward classes have been explained by B. R. Ambedkar, the Chairman of the Drafting Committee, that: "The Indian Constitution must provide safeguards to prevent castes 'with their own interests' from doing mischief to other helpless castes."[44] He further explained the purpose behind this constitutional safeguard:

> Where the spirit which actuates the various social groups is only non-social, their existence may not be taken into account in framing a constitution. There is no cause for danger in a group which is only non-social. But where a group is actuated by an antisocial spirit towards another and to which alien is synonymous with enemy, the fact must be taken into account in framing the constitution and the class which has been the victim of antisocial spirit must be given protection by proper safeguards.[45]

Independent India has realized that freedom would be futile if the fruits of freedom are not equally shared by all sections of society. The democratic ideal emphasizes a footing of equality for all citizens irrespective of their caste affiliations. The aim is to bring about radical social and economic changes, to correct the imbalance in society caused by the caste structure. The aim is reflected in the Preamble:

---

44. B. R. Ambedkar, *What Congress and Gandhi have done to the Untouchables*, 1946, p. 193.
45. *Ibid.*, pp. 193–94.

JUSTICE, Social, Economic and Political;
LIBERTY of thought, expression, belief, faith and worship;
EQUALITY of status and of opportunity;
            and to promote among them all,
FRATERNITY assuring the dignity of the individual and the unity of the nation.[46]

Part III of the Constitution guarantees a series of fundamental rights to the citizens. Hence specific provisions have been made to safeguard the special rights and interests of Backward Classes. Part IV contains the Directive Principles of State Policy, wherein a mention has also been made for protecting the weaker sections of society. Part XVI of the Constitution deals with Special Provisions for Backward Classes.

---

46. Preamble to the Constitution of India.

2

CONSTITUTIONAL PROVISIONS
FOR BACKWARD CLASSES

Basic Approach of the Constitution

The inception of the Indian Constitution on January 26, 1950, was a great event not only in the political history of India but also in the history of human rights. The Constitution has opened up new vistas of growth through an array of rights and privileges to the citizens in general and Backward Classes in particular. The object of the Constitution finds expression in the Preamble, which proclaims in unequivocal terms:

We, The People of India, having solemnly resolved to constitute India into a Sovereign Democratic Republic and to secure to all its citizens:
JUSTICE, social, economic and political;
LIBERTY of thought, expression, belief, faith and worship;
EQUALITY of status and of opportunity;
and to promote among them all
FRATERNITY assuring the dignity of the individual and the unity of the Nation. . . .

Justice, liberty, equality, and fraternity, time and again

proclaimed as the inalienable rights of man, are guaranteed by the Constitution. But an exploration of the constitutional meaning and significance of these terms constitutes the crux of the problem.

The term justice is currently used in two senses: as representing, on the one hand, the faithful realization of existing law as against any arbitrary infraction of it; and as representing, on the other, the ideal element in all law—the 'idea' which the law tends to subserve.[1]

"Liberty may be defined as affirmation by an individual or group of his or its own essence."[2] Liberty means therefore freedom, the negation of license. Article 19 deals elaborately with the freedoms granted by the Constitution. Liberty sounds very significant in the sense that, after centuries of foreign domination in the country, citizens cherish the idea of liberty. But mere cherishing of liberty would be meaningless if it does not cater to the full-fledged development of the individual and the nation. As Nehru remarked: "Civil liberty is not merely for us an airy doctrine or a pious wish, but something which we consider essential for the orderly development and progress of a nation."[3]

Similarly, "Equality," the keynote of democratic institutions, is assured under Art. 14 of the Constitution. Equality does not mean the leveling down of people, but only an equal treatment of citizens in the enjoyment of rights.

"Fraternity" postulates human values by respecting the dignity of human personality. Article 17 of the Constitution, which refers to the abolition of untouchability, is an illustration of the advocacy of the concept of fraternity.

---

1. Georges Gurvitch, *Encyclopedia of the Social Sciences*, Vol. 8, 1949, p. 509.
2. Harold J. Laski, *Encyclopedia of the Social Sciences*, Vol. 9, 1949, p. 444.
3. Jawaharlal Nehru, *The Unity of India*, 1948, p. 67.

Thus, the Preamble clearly illustrates that the Constitution has realized the importance of justice, liberty, equality, and fraternity for the success of democracy. It gives accent to justice in the social, economic, and political sphere. Social justice demands the eradication of social inequities based on caste, color, race, creed, etc. Economic justice rules out distinction from man to man from the point of view of economic values. Every man is rewarded according to his labor. Political justice refers to the absence of arbitrary treatment of citizens in the political sphere—the right to exercise franchise and enter legislatures without any caste distinctions. The Constitution makers have realized that political freedom alone would be futile in the absence of social and economic justice, and so they have guaranteed justice in all the three spheres. This idea of guaranteeing justice in the triple field was mooted in pre-independent India. Rabindranath Tagore very lucidly brought out the significance of creating such justice, for

. . . whatever weakness we cherish in our society will become the source of danger in politics. The same inertia which leads us to our idolatry of dead forms in social institutions will create in our politics prison-houses with immovable walls. The narrowness of sympathy which makes it possible for us to impose upon a considerable portion of humanity the galling yoke of inferiority, will assert itself in our politics in creating the tyranny of injustice.[4]

The Constitution of India has conferred on the citizens the right of "Adult Suffrage." Article 326 says:

The elections to the House of the People and to the Legislative Assembly of every state shall be on the basis of adult suffrage; that is to say, every person who is a

---

4. Rabindranath Tagore, *Nationalism*, 1920, p. 123.

citizen of India and who is not less than twenty-one
years of age on such date as may be fixed in that behalf
by or under any law made by the appropriate Legislature and is not otherwise disqualified under this constitution or any law made by the appropriate Legislature
on the ground of non-residence, unsoundness of mind,
crime or corrupt or illegal practice, shall be entitled to
be registered as a voter at any such election.

Franchise prior to independence was very much restricted. One of the recommendations of the "Constitutional proposals of the Sapru Committee" was the introduction of adult franchise for seats other than those
reserved for special communities. The question of introducing adult franchise was examined first by the Lothian
Committee in 1932. The impediments to the introduction
of adult suffrage according to the Franchise Committee
were: ". . . the huge numbers involved—numbers which
are far larger than have ever been made the foundation
for a democratically governed state in history—and the
fact that only 8 percent of these are literate (men literates
13.9 percent; women literates 2.1 percent).[5] Illiteracy was
stressed as an impediment to the intelligent exercise of
knowledge in casting vote. Besides, lack of facilities in the
villages to enlighten the illiterate masses regarding public
questions was another drawback in the introduction of
adult franchise.

But the Constitution of Independent India took a bold
step in introducing adult suffrage, in spite of the prevalence of an overwhelming population ignorant of the
three R's. The principle of popular sovereignty has not
only been enshrined in the Constitution as an ideal but
practiced as a basic reality. If the Preamble begins with a
ringing note of popular sovereignty, Art. 326 proceeds
with an enhancement of the worth and value of individual

5. *Report of the Indian Franchise Committee,* Vol. 1, 1932, para. 33,
pp. 17–18.

personality. Every individual is made to realize his importance in the country's national life through the exercise of franchise, irrespective of educational qualifications or social status. Citizens are placed on a footing of equality, called upon to join hands to make the venture of democracy a success in India. The introduction of adult franchise undoubtedly roused the curiosity of the world and planted doubts in many nations as to the success of adult franchise in a country like India with its huge illiterate population. But the four general elections of the country have left no scope for any such fears. The Report of the First General Elections observed:

> However backward and ignorant the common man in an "undeveloped" country may be, he possesses in his own way enough common sense to know what is good for him. Given a simple enough system of ballot which he understands, he can be trusted to cast his vote intelligently in accordance with his own free will in favour of the representative of his choice.[6]

But the two essential requisites for the smooth running of the system as recommended by the Report were:

> (1) the conduct of Elections must be strictly non-partisan or under neutral control, and
> (2) the Executive Government must sincerely desire free and fair Elections and actively work for the same.[7]

Speaking about adult suffrage, A. L. Mudaliar remarked in the Madras Legislative Council on August 9, 1950:

> Adult suffrage is a unique experiment in this country. No civilized country in the world has given adult suffrage to voters, 80 percent of whom are illiterate . . .

6. *Report of the First General Elections in India*, 1951–52, Vol. 1 (General) , p. 11.
7. *Ibid.*

the point I want to emphasise is that . . . you must be vigilant so that the avalanche of adult suffrage may not land you in a morass. For the sake of keeping abreast of the times and showing to the world on paper how enlightened we are, the Constituent Assembly rushed to the conclusion that adult suffrage was a good thing. It is very necessary to take steps to see that this adult suffrage does not prove to be like the "churning of the ocean" which resulted in producing not nectar but something else.[8]

It was Nehru who strongly advocated adult suffrage, for he always felt that the widest possible franchise was an essential requisite for the realization of "Fullest Democracy." He ruled out the fears that illiterate masses are not capable of casting their votes intelligently and vice versa.

Whatever the impediments in the introduction of adult suffrage and drawbacks in the smooth running of the system, it has come to stay in independent India. The Constitution, by conferring adult franchise on citizens, has not only postulated the equality of man and restored the dignity of human personality, but has also offered opportunities to the citizens for the development of their stature.

Part III of the Constitution deals with a series of fundamental rights guaranteed to the citizens. The first and foremost of these is "Equality before law." Article 14 states: "The state shall not deny to any person equality before the law or the equal protection of the laws within the territory of India."

This doctrine of natural equality first found its expression in the Declaration of Rights of Man, 1789, proclaimed by the National Assembly of France. It stated: "Men are born and always continue free and equal in respect of their rights." The same ideal was echoed in the American Declaration of Independence, which proclaimed: "We

---

8. Quoted in S. R. Maheswari, *The General Elections in India,* 1963, pp. 21–22.

hold these truths to be self-evident, that all men are created equal . . ." It got a further backing in the Declaration of Human Rights wherein Article 7 states: "All are equal before the law and are entitled without any discrimination to equal protection of the law. All are entitled to equal protection against any discrimination in violation of this Declaration and against any incitement to such discrimination."

Equality guaranteed in Article 14 of the Constitution is an extension of the principle ensured in the Preamble. The two phrases in the article—"equality before the law" and "the equal protection of the laws," may be better described as a harmonious fusion of the American Constitutional safeguard and the English law.

To interpret the meaning of these two phrases, "equality before the law" means that the state should not differentiate between the citizens either in the promulgation or application of law. In short, it means justice. It is the negation of differential treatment, impartiality at the altar of justice. The principle of equality before the law has been beautifully explained by Ivor Jennings: "Equality before the law means that among equals the law should be equal and should be equally administered, that like should be treated alike."[9] Similarly, "equal protection of the laws" means that equal treatment should be meted out in like circumstances irrespective of any considerations whatever. The law of the land should be the same to the highest and the lowest.

Interesting interpretations of Art. 14 have been given by judges in a series of cases where the said equality clause is presumed to be violated and the citizens are deprived of the fundamental right to equality.[10]

---

9. Ivor Jennings, *Law of the Constitution*, 3rd ed., p. 49.
10. See *Chiranjit Lal Chowdhuri* v *The Union of India and others,* 1950; *The State of Bombay* v *F. N. Balsara,* 1951; *The State of West Bengal* v *Anwar Ali; Kathi Raning Rawat* v *The State of Saurashtra,* etc.

The interpretation of Article 14 given by Mahajan, J. in the *State of West Bengal* v. *Anwar Ali,* reads:

> Equality of right is a principle of Republicanism and Article 14 enunciates this equality principle in the administration of justice. In its application to legal proceedings the article ensures to everyone the same rules of evidence and modes of procedure. In other words, the same rule must exist for all in similar circumstances. This principle, however, does not mean that every law must have universal application for all persons who are not by nature, attainment or circumstance in the same position.[11]

In *Kathi Raning Rawat* v. *The State of Saurashtra,* the concept of equality has been further interpreted by B. K. Mukherjea, J., that:

> Equality prescribed by the Constitution would not be violated if the statute operates equally on all persons who are included in the group, and the classification is not arbitrary or capricious, but bears a reasonable relation to the objective which the legislation has in view.[12]

The meaning and scope of Article 14 has been best brought out by Fazl Ali, J., in dealing with the case of the *State of Bombay and Another* v. *F. N. Balsara.* The principles summarized by him laid by the court in the case of *Chiranjit Lal Chowdhury* v. *The Union of India* and others were:

> (1) The presumption is always in favour of the constitutionality of an enactment, since it must be assumed that the legislature understands and correctly appreciates the needs of its own people, that its laws are

11. *A.I.R.* Vol. 39, 1952, para. 35, P.S.C. 85.
12. *A.I.R.* Vol. 39, 1952, para. 32, P.S.C. 131.

directed to problems made manifest by experience and its discriminations are based on adequate grounds.

(2) The presumption may be rebutted in certain cases by showing that on the face of the statute, there is no classification at all and no difference peculiar to any individual or class and not applicable to any other individual or class, and yet the law hits only a particular individual or class.

(3) The principle of equality does not mean that every law must have universal application to all persons who are not by nature, attainment or circumstance in the same position, and the varying needs of different classes of persons often require separate treatment.

(4) The principle (of equality) does not take away from the state the power of classifying persons for legitimate purposes.

(5) Every classification is in some degree likely to produce some inequality, and mere production of inequality is not enough.

(6) If a law deals equally with members of a well-defined class, it is not obnoxious and it is not open to the charge of denial of equal protection on the ground that it has no application to other persons.

(7) While reasonable classification is permissible, such classification must be based upon some real and substantial to distinction bearing a reasonable and just relation to the object sought to be attained, and the classification cannot be made arbitrarily and without any substantial basis.[13]

Judicial pronouncements from time to time have thrown sufficient light on the meaning of the equality clause of Article 14. The judicial interpretation of that clause seems to be largely influenced by the American interpretation of the "equal protection" clause in the

---

13. *The Supreme Court Report,* Vol. 2, 1951, Part VII, July 1951, pp. 708–9.

Fourteenth Amendment. That equal protection clause as interpreted by Justice Van Devanter reads:

(1) The equal protection clause of the Fourteenth Amendment does not take from the State the power to classify in the adoption of Police laws, but admits of the exercise of a wide scope of discretion in that regard, and avoids what is done only when it is without any reasonable basis and therefore is purely arbitrary.

(2) A classification having some reasonable basis does not offend against that clause merely because it is not made with mathematical nicety or because in practice it results in some inequality.

(3) When the classification in such a law is called in question if any state of facts reasonably can be conceived that would sustain it, the existence of that state of facts at the time the law was enacted must be assumed.

(4) One who assails the classification in such a law must carry the burden of showing that it does not rest upon any reasonable basis, but is essentially arbitrary.[14]

But Article 14 differs in scope from the "equal protection clause" in the Fourteenth Amendment to the Constitution of the United States. The scope of Article 14 is much wider, insofar as it refers to both resident aliens and citizens alike. The term 'State' in Art. 14 refers to the conduct of "the Government and Parliament of India and the Government and Legislature of each of the States and all local or other authorities within the territory of India under the control of the Government of India." (Art. 12.) On the contrary, the "equal protection clause" refers only to the conduct of the constituent states of the American Union.

In spite of these precise interpretations, the concept of

---

14. Quoted in Dowling and Edwards, *American Constitutional Law*, 1954, p. 372.

equality remains largely a controversy. In practical administration it calls for clarification at every step. For instance, the introduction of prohibition in certain States of India, to the exclusion of others, would definitely sound a discrimination on the part of the Government. Here comes the need for the clarification of the "equality clause." By equality is meant that any classification made for administrative convenience should be objective and rational. Inequalities being inherent abstract or mathematical equality constitutes only an ideal. In other words, as Venkatarama Ayyar, J., had remarked: "What Article 14 prohibits is the unequal treatment of persons similarly situated."[15] The concept of equality is made a specific Constitutional guarantee for the purpose of creating men equal even though they are born unequal.

Equality is further guaranteed in Art. 15:

(1) The State shall not discriminate against any citizen on grounds only of religion, race, caste, sex, place of birth or any of them.

(2) No citizen shall, on grounds only of religion, race, caste, sex, place of birth or any of them, be subject to any disability, liability, restriction or condition with regard to

(a) access to shops, public restaurants, hotels and places of public entertainment; or

(b) the use of wells, tanks, bathing ghats, roads and places of public resort maintained wholly or partly out of State funds or dedicated to the use of the general public.

(3) Nothing in this article shall prevent the State from making any special provision for women and children.

(4) Nothing in this article or in clause (2) of Art. 29 shall prevent the State from making any special

---

15. *Kishan Singh* v *State of Rajasthan, A.I.R.* Vol. 42, 1955, para. 3, P.S.C. 797.

provision for the advancement of any socially and educationally backward classes of citizens or for the Scheduled castes and the Scheduled Tribes.

Clause (4) has been incorporated by the Constitution (First Amendment) Act, 1951. The keynote of this clause is to ensure the reservation of seats for Backward Classes in educational institutions. Without the incorporation of this clause, reservations under Clause (1) of Article 15 would be a contradiction in terms.

In this connection we may raise the objection: Does not the Constitution guarantee rights on the one hand and snatch away from the other? Clause (1) of Article 15 proclaims that no discrimination should be done on grounds only of religion, race, caste, sex, place of birth or any of them and the subsequent Cl. (4) declares, that "nothing shall prevent the State from making any special provision for the advancement of any socially and educationally backward classes." Is not reservation of seats for Backward Classes an indirect discrimination? Besides, the term "Backward Classes" has not been precisely defined. It has been left so vague and obscure leaving sufficient room for exercising discretionary powers by the States in the matter of classifying communities as "Backward" or "Forward" for purposes of granting special privileges. The writ petitions which pile up in High Courts, specially in Mysore State, clearly demonstrate the difficulties caused by the failure of defining the term "Backward Classes" precisely. The scope of Art. 15, originally supposed to be much wider than Art. 14, seems to be restricted by the incorporation of Cl. (4) by the Constitution (First Amendment) Act, 1951.

But a deeper study of the Constitution justifies the incorporation of Cl. (4) in Art. 15. It is in keeping with the Resolution of the Constituent Assembly which reads: "Wherein, adequate safeguards shall be provided for minorities, backward and tribal areas, and depressed and other backward classes."[16] It is quite appropriate that the Backward Classes should look to the Constitution for special favors to redress the wrongs done in the past by creating social disabilities. It is equally justifiable that the Constitution should make special provision to safeguard the interests of Backward Classes. This special situation was explained by Dakshayani Velayudan as

> Neither Lord Pethic-Lawrence, the Secretary of State for India, nor even the Prime Minister, Mr. Attlee, nor even the Leader of the opposition, Mr. Churchill, is going to improve the condition of the Harijans. What we want is the removal, immediate removal of our social disabilities. Only an Independent Socialist Indian Republic can give freedom and equality of status to the Harijan. Our freedom can be obtained only from Indians and not from the British Government.[17]

Rightly so, free India alone was to provide safeguards for the advancement of Backward Classes.

Explaining the scope of Cl. (4) of Art. 15, V. G. Ramachandran observed:

> Since political power is apt to be misused, a safeguard in the limitation in Art. 15 (4) is to include the word "reasonable" before the words "special provision." The word "reasonable" will indeed provide judicial review in cases of abuse of this power of classification. It may be that if a classification is proved to be unreasonable and malafide and it is shown to the Court that it does not help the really backward classes but some others who are made to parade as backward, then the Court may be justified in treating such classification as ultra vires of Art. 15, particularly when the real object of

---

discrimination against other citizens is apparent. But to enable the Court to effectively go into the matter the word "reasonable" is necessary before the words "special provision."[18]

Art. 16 provides:

(1) There shall be equality of opportunity for all citizens in matters relating to employment or appointment to any office under the State.

(2) No citizen shall, on grounds only of religion, race, caste, sex, descent, place of birth, residence or any of them, be ineligible for, or discriminated against in respect of, any employment or office under the State.

(3) Nothing in this article shall prevent Parliament from making any law prescribing, in regard to a class or classes of employment or appointment to an office [under the Government of, or any local or other authority within, a State or Union Territory, any requirement as to residence within that State or Union Territory] prior to such employment or appointment.

(4) Nothing in this article shall prevent the State from making any provision for the reservation of appointments or posts in favour of any backward class of citizens which, in the opinion of the State, is not adequately represented in the Services under the State.

(5) Nothing in this article shall affect the operation of any law which provides that the incumbent of an office in connection with the affairs of any religious or denominational institution or any member of the governing body thereof shall be a person professing a particular religion or belonging to a particular denomination.

Clause (3) of the aforesaid article restricts the principle of equality of opportunity to all citizens in the matter of employment by making some exception to the privileges

18. V. G. Ramachandran, *Fundamental Rights and Constitutional Remedies*, Vol. 2, 1960, p. 1161.

guaranteed under clauses (1) and (2), respectively. As regards employment under the Union, the qualification of residence is not necessary. However, the Union Parliament is competent to make the qualification of residence a necessity in particular classes of employment under a State. This exception, it is argued, is devised for the purpose of maintaining the efficiency of the service. But even here, it is gratifying to note, the power to legislate on this matter is vested in the Union Parliament and the States are powerless to enjoy discretionary powers.

Defending the limitation of clause (3), B. R. Ambedkar observed:

> You cannot allow people who are flying from one province to another, from one State to another, as mere birds of passage without any roots, without any connection with that particular province, just to come, apply for posts and, so to say, take the plums and walk away. Therefore, some limitation is necessary.[19]

Clause (4) favors the policy of making reservation for certain sections of society who are backward. It appears that the absence of a definition of the term "backward" may lead to bitterness and misuse of the provision to obtain preferential treatment. Further, the expression "Backward Classes," referring to "the Scheduled Castes" and "Scheduled Tribes," is used in Article 335. But a different expression is used in the present clause which would lead to a different legal interpretation. It was observed by B. R. Ambedkar in the Constituent Assembly that if the State included a very large number of classes within the reservation permitted by this clause, an individual who is aggrieved may go to the court for a declaration that the reservation is ultra vires. In such cases, the court would be slow to interfere with the decision of the State, unless

---

19. Constituent Assembly Debates, p. 700.

it is an abuse of the power or a fraud on the Constitution. The Court would not, ordinarily, substitute its own view for that of the Legislature as to whether a class is "backward" or not.

Article 17 gets the special distinction in the Constitution for materializing Gandhiji's dream of doing away with untouchability. It proclaims: " 'Untouchability' is abolished and its practice in any form is forbidden. The enforcement of any disability arising out of 'Untouchability' shall be an offence punishable in accordance with law."

In accordance with this provision of the Constitution, " 'The Untouchability (Offences) Act, 1955' " came into force on June 1, 1955. The keynote of this Act is that it provides penalties for preventing a person on the ground of untouchability from entering a place of public worship, offering prayers therein, or taking water from a sacred tank, well or spring. Penalties are also provided for enforcing all kinds of social disabilities, such as denying access to any shop, public restaurant, public hospital/or educational institution, hotel/or any place of public entertainment, the use of any road, river, well, tank, water tap, bathing ghat, cremation ground, sanitary convenience, dharmashala, sarai, or musafirkhana, utensils kept in such institutions and hotels and restaurants. The Act also prescribes penalties for enforcing occupational, professional or trade disabilities, in the matter of enjoyment of any benefit under a charitable trust, in the construction or occupation of any residential premises in any locality or the observance of any social or religious usage or ceremony.[20]

Article 17 is unique in the sense that it has given a death blow to the century-old practice of untouchability. It reflects the spirit of the Constitution—the determination to restore the dignity of the individual and assure frater-

---

20. The Untouchability (offences) Act, 1955.

nity. Untouchability is not only prohibited but it is made punishable by law. The Parliament has assumed the power to legislate on this matter uniformly in all the States.

The principle of equality is further elaborated in Art. 18 thus:

1) No title, not being a military or academic distinction, shall be conferred by the State.

2) No citizen of India shall accept any title from any foreign State.

3) No person who is not a citizen of India shall, while he holds any office of profit or trust under the State, accept without the consent of the President any title from any foreign State.

4) No person holding any office of profit or trust under the State shall, without the consent of the President, accept any present, emolument, or office of any kind from or under any foreign State.

This Article by abolishing all titles which create superficial distinctions in society ensures the principle of equality in the Indian Constitution.

Article 19 (1) guarantees some of the Fundamental Rights essential for the restoration of the dignity of individual personality. It reads:

All citizens shall have the right —
(a)　to freedom of speech and expression;
(b)　to assemble peaceably and without arms;
(c)　to form associations or unions;
(d)　to move freely throughout the territory of India;
(e)　to reside and settle in any part of the territory of India;
(f)　to acquire, hold and dispose of property; and
(g)　to practice any profession, or to carry on any occupation, trade or business.

The fundamental rights guaranteed under Art. 19 are civil rights subject to the power of the State to restrict them. The State is authorized to impose restraints on the exercise of these rights, mainly to promote public welfare by discouraging the conflicting interests of the individual and society.

Art. 21 provides: "No person shall be deprived of his life or personal liberty except according to procedure established by law."

The right to freedom of religion is enshrined in Article 25 thus:

1) Subject to public order, morality and health and to the other provisions of this part, all persons are equally entitled to freedom of conscience and the right freely to profess, practice and propagate religion.

2) Nothing in this article shall affect the operation of any existing law or prevent the state from making any law —

(a) regulating or restricting any economic, financial political or other secular activity which may be associated with religious practice;

(b) providing for social welfare and reform or the throwing open of Hindu religious institutions of a public character to all classes and sections of Hindus.

Explanation I—the wearing and carrying of kirpans shall be deemed to be included in the profession of the Sikh religion. Explanation II—In sub-clause (b) of clause (2), the reference to Hindus shall be constructed as including a reference to persons professing the Sikh, Jaina, or Buddhist religion, and the reference to Hindu religious institutions shall be constructed accordingly.

Article 29 (1) confers on the citizens cultural and educational rights. It reads:

1) Any section of the citizens residing in the territory of India or any part there of having a distinct language, script or culture of its own shall have the right to conserve the same.

2) No citizen shall be denied admission into any educational institution maintained by the State or receiving aid out of State funds on grounds only of religion, race, caste, language or any of them.

Clause (2) of this Article came in for criticism when the Madras Government order refused admission of a candidate to Medical College solely on the ground that the candidate belonged to Brahmin Community. According to Madras G. O., out of every 14 seats, 6 were to be filled by non-Brahmin Hindus, 2 by Harijans, 1 by Anglo-Indians and Indian Christians and 1 by Muslims. The Supreme Court however invalidated the Madras G.O. as it was a violation of Article 29 (2).[21]

In the above-mentioned case, the Madras High Court held that the Madras G.O., which distributed seats in State educational institutions according to communities in certain proportions, was void on the ground of Arts. 15 (1) and 29 (2). The Supreme Court upheld this decision on the ground of contradiction of Art. 29 (2) while no decision was considered necessary in regard to Art. 15 (1).

The result was, Art. 29 (2) was amended by the Constitution (First Amendment) Act, 1951. The amendment laid down that "Nothing in clause (2) of Article 29 shall prevent the State from making any special provisions for the advancement of any socially and educationally backward classes of citizens or for the Scheduled castes and the Scheduled Tribes." Accordingly, the State is now empowered to reserve seats in State Colleges for any socially and educationally backward classes of citizens or for the Sched-

---

21. *State of Madras* v *Champakam Dorairajan, A.I.R.* 1951, sections 226, 228.

uled Castes and Scheduled Tribes. This amendment has validated the authority of States to make reservations for Backward Classes. The incorporation of clause (4) in Art. 15 brings Art. 16 (4), 46 and 340 in line to make constitutional the reservation of seats for Backward Classes in educational institutions and create special privileges for their advancement.

The welfare objective of the Constitution finds expression in Art. 38, which comes under the category of "Directive principles of State Policy," enshrined in Part IV of the Constitution. It says: "The State shall strive to promote the welfare of the people by securing and protecting as effectively as it may a social order in which Justice, social, economic and political, shall inform all the institutions of the national life."

Further, the Constitution of India has made education a special responsibility of the Union and State Governments. Art. 45 states: "The State shall endeavor to provide, within a period of ten years from the commencement of this Constitution, for free and compulsory education for all children until they complete the age of fourteen years."

Article 46 provides:

> The State shall promote with special care the educational and economic interests of the weaker sections of the people, and, in particular, of the Scheduled castes and the Scheduled Tribes, and shall protect them from social injustice and all forms of exploitation.

In this Article, the term "weaker sections" is used unlike other Articles, wherein we come across the term "Backward Classes." But as usual none of these terms have been precisely defined, as a result of which there is lot of confusion in the Constitutional interpretation of these terms in specific cases. Now the question may be raised, "After all, Article 46 constitutes only a Directive Principle unenforceable by the Judiciary, and what is the significance of incorporating this Article to confer special privileges to the Backward Classes? Directive principles are nothing more than mere directions to the States to undertake particular lines of action for the benefit of weaker sections of society. They serve as nothing more than a pointer to the humanitarian ideal of the Constitution. The Supreme Court of India has made clear how ineffective Directive Principles are, by invalidating the Madras G.O. in the famous case *State of Madras* v *Champakam Dorairajan.*[22]

In the above-mentioned case, Art. 46 was referred in defense of Madras G.O. But the Supreme Court held that no directive contained in Part IV of the Constitution could override any of the Fundamental Rights contained in Part III of the Constitution. This fact was stressed by B. R. Ambedkar when he interpreted:

> Directive Principles are nothing but obligations imposed by the Constitution upon the various Governments in the country, though if the Governments failed to carry them out, no one could ask for specific performance.
>
> Further,
>
> The State could only discharge them through legislation. It implied that the State, in regard to these matters, had the implied power to make a law.[23]

The Constitution of India thus reflects a social philosophy with Justice as the guiding principle. "The Preamble," "Fundamental Rights," and "Directive Principles" point toward the establishment of a "Just Society," upholding the concepts of liberty, equality and fraternity and safeguarding the unity of the country. Myron Weiner has aptly remarked:

---

22. *Ibid.*
23. *The Hindu,* May 19, 1951.

The Indian Constitution is more than a set of rules guiding behaviour; it is a kind of charter for her westernized leadership; a set of goals and expectations. It is almost as if the whole of this lengthy Constitution were a body of directives.[24]

When we consider the composition of India's population with a preponderance of underprivileged classes of various categories—"The Scheduled Castes," "The Scheduled Tribes," "Other Backward Classes," and "Denotified Communities," the Constitutional emphasis on justice, implying social, economic and political interests of the people, would be greatly appreciated. The Constitution of India forges a changed sense of unity, unity based on the egalitarian principle of justice. This unity is very significant in the sense that our society was hitherto based on caste—the authoritarian and undemocratic principle.

Special Provisions

Part XVI of the Constitution deals with the special provisions relating to Backward Classes.

Article 330 states:

1) Seats shall be reserved in the House of the People for —
   (a) the Scheduled Castes;
   (b) the Scheduled Tribes except the Scheduled tribal areas of Assam; and
   (c) the Scheduled Tribes in the autonomous districts of Assam.

2) The number of seats reserved in any State (or Union territory) for the scheduled Castes or the Scheduled Tribes under clause (1) shall bear, as nearly as may be, the same proportion to the total number of

---

24. Myron Weiner's paper, entitled "Some Hypotheses on the Politics of Modernization in India," in *Leadership and Political Institutions in India*, Richard L. Park and Irene Tinker (eds.), 1960, p. 29.

seats allotted to that State (or Union Territory) in the House of the People as the population of the Scheduled Castes in the State (or Union Territory) or of the Scheduled Tribes in the State (or Union Territory) or part of the State (or Union Territory), as the case may be, in respect of which seats are so reserved, bears to the total population of the State (or Union Territory).

Article 332 states:

1) Seats shall be reserved for the Scheduled Castes and the Scheduled Tribes, except the Scheduled Tribes in the Tribal areas of Assam, in the Legislative Assembly of every State.

2) Seats shall be reserved also for the autonomous districts in the Legislative Assembly of the State of Assam.

3) The number of seats reserved for the Scheduled Castes or the Scheduled Tribes in the Legislative Assembly of any State under clause (1) shall bear, as nearly as may be, the same proportion to the total number of seats in the Assembly as the population of the Scheduled Castes in the State or of the Scheduled Tribes in the State or part of the State, as the case may be, in respect of which seats are so reserved, bears to the total population of the State.

4) The number of seats reserved for an autonomous district in the Legislative Assembly of the State of Assam shall bear to the total number of seats in that Assembly, a proportion not less than the population of the district bears to the total population of the State.

5) The constituencies for the seats reserved for any autonomous district of Assam shall not comprise any area outside that district except in the case of the constituency comprising the cantonment and municipality of Shilong.

6) No person who is not a member of a Scheduled Tribe of any autonomous district of the State of Assam shall be eligible for election to the Legislative Assembly

of the State from any constituency of that district except from the constituency comprising the cantonment and municipality of Shilong.

The number of reservations in single-member constituencies for Scheduled Tribes in the States where the concentration of Scheduled Tribes was practically small, two-member constituencies were formed, one seat being reserved for the Scheduled Tribes. Thus the Scheduled Tribes were given adequate representation in Parliament and State Legislatures in the First General Elections. Out of a total reservation of 477 seats, in Legislative Assemblies for Scheduled Castes, 475 were reserved in two-member constituencies. Out of a total of 192 seats reserved for the Scheduled Tribes in Legislative Assemblies, 88 were reserved in single-member constituencies, and the remaining one in the Nasik-Igatpuri three-member constituencies.

But two-member constituencies are abolished today, with the passing of "The two-member constituencies (Abolition) Act, 1961." The object of the Act is:

> Members of the Scheduled Castes and Tribes generally favour small single-member constituencies which involve less expenditure and trouble. Double-member constituencies are inconvenient and cumbersome from the administrative point of view also. Hence, the act is amended to divide every two-member Parliamentary and Assembly constituency into two single-member constituencies, of which one should be reserved for the Scheduled Caste as the case may be, for the Scheduled Tribes.[25]

According to 1961 Census, the Delimitation Commission has redetermined the elective seats allotted to all the states (excluding Jammu and Kashmir and Nagaland) in

---

25. *The Gazette of India* (Extra), Part II—Section 1, No. 7, dated March 10, 1961/Phalguna 18, 1882.

the Lok Sabha. The total number of seats alloted to these States has now been determined as 490 as against 481. In addition, 27 seats have been allotted to Jammu and Kashmir, Nagaland, North East Frontier Agency, and the various Union Territories. The number of seats to be reserved for Scheduled Castes and the Scheduled Tribes in the Union Territories, has not yet been determined. For the Lok Sabha, Jammu and Kashmir are allotted 6 seats, North East Frontier Agency, 1, and 18 for the Union Territories. Out of this 18, 2 seats are reserved for the Scheduled Castes and 2 for the Scheduled Tribes.

Seats allotted to Scheduled Castes and Scheduled Tribes in the Lok Sabha, according to 1961 Census, are 75 and 33, respectively. Their representation in Vidhana Sabhas are 471 and 227.

The Territorial Councils have been replaced by Legislative Assemblies in the Union Territories.[26] The representation of Scheduled Castes and Scheduled Tribes to these Assemblies were 41 for Himachal Pradesh, 32 for Manipur, and 32 for Tripura up to 1961–63.

Article 334 reads:

Notwithstanding anything in the foregoing provisions of this Part, the provisions of this Constitution relating to —

a) the reservation of seats for the Scheduled Castes and the Scheduled Tribes in the House of the People and in the Legislative Assemblies of the States; shall cease to have effect on the expiration of a period of (twenty years) from the commencement of this Constitution:

Provided that nothing in this article shall effect any representation in the House of the People or in the Legislative Assembly of a State until the dissolution of the then existing House or Assembly, as the case may be.

---

26. The Government of Union Territories Act, 1963.

It was first stated that reservations would cease after the expiration of ten years from the commencement of the Constitution, viz., 1960. However, the time limit fixed for the reservation of seats in the House of the People and Legislative Assemblies has been extended for ten more years by an amendment of the Constitution—"The Constitution (Eighth Amendment) Act, 1959, making reservation of seats in the House of the People and Legislative Assemblies constitutional till 1970. On Dec. 9, 1969, Lok Sabha (Lower House of Parliament) passed the constitutional amendment bill seeking to extend the reservations in the House and State Assemblies for Scheduled Castes and Scheduled Tribes for a further period of 10 years— that is, up to 1980.

Article 335 ensures:

The claims of the members of the Scheduled Castes and Scheduled Tribes shall be taken into consideration, consistently with the maintenance of efficiency of administration, in the making of appointments to Services and Posts in connection with the affairs of the Union or of a State.

The Constitution of India has struck a balance in this article by giving a fair share in the administration of the country to the Scheduled Castes and Scheduled Tribes on the one hand, and at the same time insisting on the efficiency and integrity of the Services while making appointments.

Article 338 ensures:

1) There shall be a Special Officer for the Scheduled Castes and Scheduled Tribes to be appointed by the President.

2) It shall be the duty of the Special Officer to investigate all matters relating to the safeguards provided for the Scheduled Castes and Scheduled Tribes under

this Constitution and report to the President upon the working of those safeguards at such intervals as the President may direct, and the President shall cause all such reports to be laid before each House of Parliament.

3) In this article, references to the Scheduled Castes and Scheduled Tribes shall be constructed as including references to such other backward classes as the President may, on receipt of the report of a commission appointed under clause (1) of article 340, by order specify and also to the Anglo-Indian Community.

In compliance with this article, the commissioner for Scheduled Castes and Scheduled Tribes was appointed by the President on November 18, 1950. He is entrusted with the task of investigating and evaluating the progress made, as well as the measures needed to better the position of the Scheduled Castes and Scheduled Tribes. The Ministry of Home Affairs of the Government of India is in charge of the overall responsibility of executing the safeguards provided in the Constitution.

Article 339 reads:

1) The President may at any time and shall, at the expiration of ten years from the commencement of this Constitution, by order appoint a Commission to report on the administration of the Scheduled Areas, and the welfare of the Scheduled Tribes in the States.

The order may define the composition, powers and procedure of the Commission and may contain such incidental or ancillary provisions as the President may consider necessary or desirable.

2) The Executive Power of the Union shall extend to the giving of directions to [a State] as to the drawing up and execution of schemes specified in the direction to be essential for the welfare of the Scheduled Tribes in the State.

Accordingly "the Scheduled Areas and Scheduled Tribes

Commission" was appointed on April 28, 1960, to investigate and report on the problems of the Scheduled Tribes. The Report was submitted in October, 1961.

Article 340 provides for the appointment of a commission to investigate the problem of Backward classes. It says:

1) The President may by order appoint a Commission consisting of such persons as he thinks fit to investigate the condition of socially and educationally backward classes within the territory of India and the difficulties under which they labour and to make recommendations as to the steps that should be taken by the Union or any State to remove such difficulties and to improve their condition and as to the grants that should be made for the purpose by the Union or any State and the conditions subject to which such grants should be made, and the order appointing such Commission shall define the procedure to be followed by the Commission.

2) A Commission so appointed shall investigate the matters referred to them and present to the President a report setting out the facts as found by them and making such recommendations as they think proper.

3) The President shall cause a copy of the report so presented together with a memorandum explaining the action taken thereon to be laid before each House of Parliament.

Likewise, the President under Article 340 of the Constitution appointed "the Backward Classes Commission," on January 29, 1953, with the following terms of reference:

a) to determine the criteria to be adopted in considering whether any sections of the people in the territory of India (in addition to the Scheduled Castes and Scheduled Tribes specified by notifications issued under Articles 341 and 342 of the Constitution) should be

treated as socially and educationally backward classes;
and in accordance with such criteria, prepare a list of
such classes setting out also their approximate numbers
and their territorial distribution;

    b) to investigate the conditions of all such socially
and educationally backward classes and the difficulties
under which they labour.[27]

The Commission was thus entrusted with the difficult
task of finding out the criteria for determining backwardness. As regards the classification of Scheduled Castes and
Scheduled Tribes the Commission found it easy because
there is a well-defined test of "untouchability" in the former and "Tribal Organization" in the latter, respectively.
However, the report of the Commission was not unanimous. The list of Backward Classes prepared by the Commission included as many as 2,399 communities, out of
which 913 alone accounted for an estimated population of
115.1 millions. Though the report of the Commission was
rather disappointing, insofar as no solution was discovered
for the problem of Backward Classes, yet it served a very
useful purpose by demonstrating the general backwardness
of the country through facts and figures recorded in their
report, 1955.

Article 341 provides:

    1) The President [may with respect to any State (or
Union Territory) , and where it is a State, after consultation with the Governor thereof,] by public notification,
specify the castes, races or tribes or parts of or groups
within castes, races or tribes which shall for the purposes
of this Constitution be deemed to be Scheduled Castes
in relation to that State (or Union Territory, as the
case may be) .

    2) Parliament may by law include in or exclude from

---

27. Memorandum on the *Report of the Backward Classes Commission,*
1956, p. 1.

the list of Scheduled Castes specified in a notification issued under clause (1) any caste, race or tribe or part of or group within any caste, race or tribe, but save as aforesaid a notification issued under the said clause shall not be varied by any subsequent notification.

In compliance with this Article, the Constitution (Scheduled Castes) Order, 1950, the Constitution (Scheduled Castes) (Part C States) Order, 1951, the Scheduled Castes lists (Modification) Order, 1956, the Constitution (Jammu and Kashmir) Scheduled Castes Order, 1956, and the Constitution (Dadra and Nagar Haveli) Scheduled Castes Order, 1956, were passed, specifying the lists of Scheduled Castes throughout India, for purposes of conferring special concessions envisaged in the Constitution. Article 342 states:

1) The President may [with respect to any State (or Union Territory), and where it is a State, after consultation with the Governor thereof], by public notification, specify the tribes or tribal communities or part of or groups within tribes or tribal communities which shall for the purpose of this Constitution be deemed to be Scheduled Tribes in relation to that state (or Union Territory, as the case may be.)

2) Parliament may by law include in or exclude from the list of Scheduled Tribes specified in a notification issued under clause (1) any tribe or tribal community or part of or group within any tribe or tribal community, but save as aforesaid a notification issued under the said clause shall not be varied by any subsequent notification.

Accordingly, the Constitution (Scheduled Tribes) Order came into force in 1950. But it was subjected to bitter criticism. It was remarked that the list of Scheduled Tribes was not prepared on scientific lines, but was rather haphazard and vague. The attention of the Government was focused on the Census Reports of 1941 and 1951 which recorded a remarkable reduction in tribal population. The critics argued that a general increase in total population of the country would coincide with a corresponding increase in population of all categories. Hence, there was no reason for the decrease in tribal population. They argued that the decrease in tribal population was chiefly due to the negligence on the part of the Government.

Whatever the controversy, a memorandum was submitted to the President by H. N. Kunzru and fifteen other members of Parliament on December 17, 1950. The points dealt with in the Memorandum were:

> Firstly, no adequate reasons were furnished by the Government for the reduction of 33 percent of the total tribal population, if the general trend of increase of the Indian population as given in the Census of 1951 was taken into consideration. Secondly, it is impossible to agree that as compared to the figures of 1941, the strength of tribal population could be reduced by 6.3 millions in 1950, unless this was calculated in an arbitrary manner. For instance, in the figures given by the Government, the tribal population in Madhya Pradesh has been reduced from 4.44 millions to 2.46 millions, i.e., by nearly 50 percent. In the same manner, the tribal population of Rajasthan has been reduced from 1.55 millions to 0.45 millions or nearly 75 percent. Similarly, the tribal population in Assam, Bihar, Orissa, Hyderabad, West Bengal has been considerably reduced.[28]

In addition to the aforesaid order, the Constitution (Scheduled Tribes) (Part C States) Order 1951, the Scheduled Tribes Lists (Modification) Order, 1956, and

---

28. Extract of the memorandum submitted to the Backward Classes Commission, on behalf of Bharatiya Adimjati Sevak Sangh, Delhi, appeared in *Vanyajati*, Vol. III, No. 1, 1955, p. 33.

the Constitution (Andaman and Nicobar Islands) Scheduled Tribes Order, 1959, were passed.

Reservation Policy

Constitutional safeguards for minorities were heralded during the British regime. The Act of 1919 marks a landmark in the Constitutional history of India. This Act gave weight to the representation of minority communities not only in Provincial Legislature, but also provided adequate safeguards in Public Service, by reserving a certain percentage of posts by direct recruitment to the Indian Civil Service. Reservation of posts for minority communities was thus made intravires of the Constitution. The object behind these reservations was that the British Government wanted to pacify different sections of minorities in India, chiefly, to consolidate their position.

The Montagu-Chelmsford Report (Act of 1919) fully studied the problem of Communal electorates granted to minorities and realized its shortcomings. But they were forced to favor this measure of Communal electorates because the Muslims were already accorded the privilege of separate electorates by the Act of 1909. Besides, the famous "Lucknow Pact" concluded between the Congress and the Muslims League had secured some communal amity in the same direction. In compliance with the policy pursued by the British Government prior to 1919, the Montagu-Chelmsford Report favored political safeguard to Sikhs, Muslims, Depressed Classes, and other minorities.

The following Table illustrates the communal composition of Provincial Legislative Councils together with population and voting ratios of the minority communities:[29]

---

29. Quoted in *Speeches and Documents on the Indian Constitution* 1921–47, selected by Maurice Gwyer and A. Appadorai, Vol. I, 1957, pp. 128–29.

TABLE 2–1

NON-MUHAMMADANS (Inclusive of Depressed Classes)				
Province	Percentage of communal seats	Percentage of total seats	Population ratio (percent)	Voting ratio (percent)
Madras	79.0	73.3	90.0	93.0
Bombay	60.7	53.5	78.9	81.0
Bengal	50.0	47.9	45.1	53.0
United Provinces	65.7	58.6	85.4	86.0
Punjab	29.8	25.5	32.0	32.1
Bihar and Orissa	70.4	61.2	85.2	88.8
Central Provinces (including Berar)	85.0	78.0	95.4	91.6
Assam	63.6	47.1	65.9	69.8
Sikhs				
Madras	—	—	—	—
Bombay	—	—	—	—
Bengal	—	—	—	—
United Provinces	—	—	—	—
Punjab	17.9	15.9	11.1	24.1
Bihar & Orissa	—	—	—	—
Central Provinces (including Berar)	—	—	—	—
Assam	—	—	—	—
Muhammadans				
Madras	13.7	10.6	6.7	4.7
Bombay	34.2	25.4	19.8	17.7
Bengal	41.4	30.8	54.6	45.1
United Provinces	31.2	26.0	14.3	14.1
Punjab	47.7	40.4	55.2	43.7
Bihar & Orissa	25.3	18.5	10.9	10.9
Central Provinces (including Berar)	13.2	9.6	4.4	8.4
Assam	36.3	30.2	32.3	30.1
Indian Christians				
Madras	5.3	5.3	3.2	1.8
Bombay	1.3	0.9	1.1	nil
Bengal	1.1	0.7	0.2	nil

United Provinces	1.1	0.8	0.3	nil
Punjab	1.5	2.1	1.5	nil
Bihar & Orissa	1.4	1.0	0.7	nil
Central Provinces (including Berar)	nil	nil	0.3	nil
Assam	nil	nil	1.9	nil
Anglo Indians				
Madras	1.0	0.8	0.05	0.2
Bombay	1.3	0.9	0.05	nil
Bengal	2.1	1.4	0.05	0.4
United Provinces	1.1	0.8	0.02	nil
Punjab	1.5	1.1	0.02	nil
Bihar & Orissa	1.4	1.0	0.01	nil
Central Provinces (including Berar)	Shared with Europeans, 1.9	1.4	0.03	nil
Assam	nil	nil	0.01	nil
Europeans				
Madras	1.0	9.8	0.02	0.2
Bombay	2.5	19.3	0.2	1.3
Bengal	5.3	19.2	0.05	1.3
United Provinces	1.1	13.8	0.05	0.3
Punjab	1.5	14.9	0.1	nil
Bihar & Orissa	1.4	18.4	0.02	0.5
Central Provinces (including Berar)	Shared with Anglo Indians, 1.9	10.9	0.05	nil
Assam	nil	22.6	0.04	nil

Thus, Communal electorates became a regular feature of the Constitutional problem in India ever since the Act of 1919. The Communal electorates controversy figured very prominently in the various sessions of the Round Table Conference during 1929-32. "The Minorities Sub-Committee of the Round Table Conference," 1930, unanimously proposed that the new Constitution to be envisaged for India should contain provisions to assure minority communities that their interests would not be prejudiced. It was agreed by all that unless the minority groups are satisfied, constitutional problem in India would not be solved. But unfortunately the two sessions of the Round Table Conference ended in failure, as they could not reach any agreement on communal deadlock—the problem of percentage of representation in Legislature. It was during this time that the policy of separate electorates as a solution to communal deadlock was suggested.

Speaking at a meeting of the Minorities Committee on November 13, 1931, Gandhiji commented on the proposed policy of separate electorates as:

It will create a division in Hinduism which I cannot possibly look forward to, with any satisfaction whatsoever. I do not mind Untouchables, if they so desire, being converted to Islam or Christianity. I should tolerate that, but I cannot possibly tolerate what is in store for Hinduism if there are two divisions set forth in the villages.[30]

The failure of the second session of the Round Table Conference to reach any agreement on communal deadlock prompted Ramsay MacDonald, the then Prime Minister, to announce the British Government's Provisional Scheme of Minority representation the famous "Communal Award" on August 16, 1932. He remarked: "We never wished to intervene in the communal controversies of India. We made that abundantly clear during both the sessions of the Round Table Conference, when we strove hard to get Indians to settle this matter between themselves."[31]

Under "Communal Award," Depressed Classes—the so-called Scheduled Castes of today—were considered as a minority community and were given thereby the benefit of separate electorates. The circumstances which contrib-

---

30. *Ibid.,* p. 259.
31. *Ibid.,* p. 259.

uted to the introduction of separate electorates were clearly explained by Ramsay MacDonald:

> For many years past, separate electorates, namely the grouping of particular categories of voters in territorial constituencies by themselves has been regarded by minority communities as an essential protection for their rights. In each of the recent stages of Constitutional development, separate electorates have consequentially found a place. However much Government may have preferred a uniform system of Joint electorates, they found it impossible to abolish the safeguards to which minorities still attach vital importance.[32]

But "Communal Award" raised a lot of heat and dust in the Indian political circles. Ambedkar, the leader of the "Depressed Classes," felt that "Communal Award" by creating separate electorates would help the untouchables to improve their status in society, by means of fair representation in Legislatures. It was his opinion that untouchables forsaken by Hindu orthodoxy could take refuge only under the British protection of separate electorates. In his frenzy, he overlooked the shortcomings of separate electorates and the havoc it would cause to Hindu society and to India's political future. Separate electorates meant not only the division of Hindu society but also estrangement between different sections of society. As a protest to this measure, Gandhiji, who was then serving a term of imprisonment at Yeravada jail, undertook a "fast unto death." The result was that Ambedkar was forced to fall in line with Gandhiji's way of thinking, of abolishing separate electorates for Depressed Classes. This understanding between the two great leaders culminated in the "Poona Pact," which came into effect on September 25, 1932. Instead of separate electorates, the Depressed Classes gained the advantage of an increased number of reserved

---

32. *Ibid.,* p. 260.

seats in the Legislature by virtue of the "Poona Pact."
Besides, "Poona Pact" formed the basis of representation
in the Act of 1935, as far as the Depressed Classes were
concerned.

The text of the Poona Pact was:[33]

1. There shall be seats reserved for the Depressed
classes out of the general electorate seats in the Provincial Legislatures as follows:

Madras	30
Bombay with Sind	15
Punjab	8
Bihar & Orissa	18
Central Provinces	20
Assam	7
Bengal	30
United Provinces	20
Total	148

These figures are based on the total strength of the
Provincial Councils announced in the Prime Minister's
(Ramsay MacDonald) decision.

2. Election to these seats shall be by Joint Electorates,
subject, however, to the following procedure:

All the members of the Depressed Classes, registered
in the general electoral roll in a constituency, will form
an Electoral College, which will elect a panel of four
candidates belonging to the Depressed Classes for each
of such reserved seats, by the method of the single vote;
the four getting the highest number of votes in such
Primary election, shall be candidates for election by the
General Electorate.

3. Representation of the Depressed Classes in the
Central Legislature shall likewise be on the principle
of Joint Electorates and reserved seats by the method of
Primary election in the manner provided for in clause

33. Quoted in B. R. Ambedkar, *States and Minorities*, 1947, Appendix
II, pp. 54–55.

(2) above, for their representation in the Provincial Legislatures.

4. In the Central Legislature, eighteen per cent of the seats allotted to the General Electorate for British India in the said Legislature shall be reserved for the Depressed Classes.

5. The system of Primary Election to a panel of candidates for Election to the Central and Provincial Legislatures, as herein before mentioned, shall come to an end after the first ten years, unless terminated sooner by mutual agreement under the provision of clause (6) below.

6. The system of representation of the Depressed Classes by reserved seats in the provincial and Central Legislatures as provided for in clause (1) and (4) shall continue until determined by mutual agreement between the communities concerned in the settlement.

7. Franchise for the Central and Provincial Legislatures for the Depressed Classes shall be as indicated in the Lothian Committee Report.

8. There shall be no disabilities attaching to anyone on the ground of his being a member of the Depressed Classes in regard to any elections to Local Bodies or appointment to the Public Services. Every endeavour shall be made to secure fair representation of the Depressed Classes in these respects, subject to such educational qualifications as may be laid down for appointment to the Public Service.

9. In every Province, out of the educational grant, an adequate sum shall be earmarked for providing educational facilities to the members of the Depressed Classes.

The Poona Pact was, however, welcomed with mixed feelings. Ambedkar was none too happy about the proposals. He commented on the Poona Pact:

If the Poona Pact increased the fixed quota of seats,

it also took away the right to the double vote given to them. This increase by the "Communal Award" in seats can never be deemed to be a compensation for the loss of double vote. The second vote given by the "Communal Award" was a priceless privilege. Its value as a political weapon was beyond reckoning.[34]

He made it very clear that the Poona Pact was accepted only because of Gandhiji's "Coercive fast" and not that it could secure for Depressed Classes a better representation in the Legislature.

The next phase in the history of minority representation was the Act of 1935. There was no major change in the communal reservation policy for minorities, in allocating seats to the Federal Legislature in 1935.

The Act of 1935 carried forward the principle of communal reservation much farther than that envisaged in the Act of 1919. The only change was, separate electorates for Depressed Classes was withdrawn in consonance with the terms of the Poona Pact, while it continued for other communal minorities. Under this Act, Hindus who formed more than 70 percent of the population were given only 105 general seats in the Federal Assembly, which included 19 seats reserved for Depressed Classes. On the contrary, Muslims, Sikhs, Europeans, Indian Christians, and Anglo-Indians, who formed less than 30 percent, were given almost equal number of seats. Communal minorities were thus given greater political safeguards.

The Constituent Assembly of India following the footsteps of earlier Acts, accepted the proposal to guarantee certain political safeguards to minorities. "The Advisory Committee on Minorities," 1947, recommended certain percentage of reservation in Legislatures to minorities. Minorities were accordingly grouped into three categories on population basis.

---

34. B. R. Ambedkar, *"What Congress and Gandhi have done to the Untouchables,"* 1946, p. 90.

Group A—Population less than ½ percent in the Indian Dominion, omitting States.
  i)   Anglo-Indians
  ii) Parsees
  iii) Plains tribesmen in Assam.
Group B—Population not more than 1½ percent.
  iv) Indian Christians
  v) Sikhs.
Group C—Population exceeding 1½ percent.
  vi) Muslims
  vii) Scheduled Castes.

Parsees and Anglo-Indians were not given any reservation of seats in Legislatures. It was assured that if these minorities failed to secure adequate representation their claim for reservation would be considered by the Government. However, Indian Christians, Muslims, and Scheduled Castes were given reservation of seats in the Central and Provincial Legislatures on the basis of their population.

The recommendations made by the Report of the Advisory Committee on Minorities, Fundamental Rights, etc., 1947, as regards the political safeguards to minorities were as follows:[35]

  i) That all elections to the Central and Provincial Legislatures will be held on the basis of Joint electorates with reservation of seats for certain specified minorities on their population ratio. This reservation shall be for a period of ten years at the end of which the position is to be reconsidered. There shall be no weightage. But members of the minority communities for whom seats are reserved shall have the right to contest general seats;
  ii) That there shall be no statutory reservation of seats for the minorities in cabinets, but a convention on

35. *Constituent Assembly Debates*, Vol. 8, 1949, Appendix B, para. 2, p. 313.

the lines of Paragraph VII of the Instrument of Instructions issued to Governors under the Government
of India Act, 1935, shall be provided in a Schedule to
the Constitution;

iii) That in the All-India and Provincial Services,
the claims of minorities shall be kept in view in making
appointments to these services consistently with consideration of efficiency of administration; and

iv) That to ensure protection of minority rights an
officer shall be appointed by the President at the Centre
and the Governors in the Provinces to report to the
Union and Provincial Legislatures respectively about
the working of the safeguards.

But the partition problem created some difficulties, particularly in East Punjab and West Bengal. A special sub-
committee with Sardar Vallabhbhai Patel, as Chairman,
was appointed by the Advisory Committee on Minorities,
Fundamental Rights, etc., in 1948. The most important
problem dealt with by this special subcommittee was the
problem of the Sikhs. The demands made by the Sikhs
were:

i) that the Sikhs should have the right to elect representatives to the Legislature through a purely communal
electorate;

ii) that in the Provincial Legislature of East Punjab,
50 percent of the seats and in the Central Legislature
5 percent should be reserved for the Sikhs;

iii) that seats should be reserved for them in the
U.P., and Delhi;

iv) that Scheduled Caste Sikhs should have the same
privileges as other Scheduled Castes; and

v) that there should be a statutory reservation of a
certain proportion of places in the Army.[36]

But it was felt that, though Sikhs constituted a minority
on the basis of their population ratio, yet they were not

---

36. *Ibid.*, para 3, p. 314.

subjected to any social disabilities like the Scheduled Castes. Moreover, the demands made by the Shromani Akali Dal, on behalf of Sikhs, was anathema to the successful working of democracy. It meant a revival of communalism which was dangerous to national solidarity. Hence, the demands of the Sikhs were turned down without any consideration. The special subcommittee explained very clearly the reason for not conceding the demands that: "We feel convinced that to accede to the demands of the Shromani Akali Dal will lead, by an inevitable extension of similar privileges to other communities, to a disrupting of the whole conception of the Secular State which is to be the basis of our new Constitution."[37]

Commenting on the policy of Communal reservation, Nehru observed:

> Reason No. 1 was that we feel that we could not remove that without the goodwill of minorities concerned. It was for them to take the lead or to say that they did not want it. For a majority to force that down their throats would not be fair to the various assurances that we had given in the past, and otherwise, too, it did not look the right thing to do. Secondly, because in our heart of hearts we were not sure about ourselves nor about our own people as to how they would function when all these reservations were removed, we agreed to that reservation, but always there was this doubt in our minds, namely, whether we had not shown weakness in dealing with a thing that was wrong.[38]

The report of the Advisory Committee on Minorities, Fundamental Rights, etc., came up for consideration on December 30, 1948. Some of the members of the Committee were of the opinion that, since the position had greatly changed after 1947—that is, after the recommendations made by the Advisory Committee—it was of utmost impor-

---

37. *Ibid.*, para 6, p. 315.
38. *Ibid.*, p. 329.

tance to discontinue reservations on religious grounds for Muslims, Christians, Sikhs, etc. Reservations on religious grounds was dangerous as that would gradually lead to separatism in the body politic.

Incidentally, Mukerjee moved a motion in the Constituent Assembly in May, 1949, for the dropping of the clause on communal reservation of seats in the Legislature on population basis. The Sikhs voluntarily agreed to the dropping of reservation benefits. But Muniswamy Pillai moved an amendment in favor of continuing the reservation benefits to Scheduled Castes for a period of ten years. The Advisory Committee unanimously agreed to accept Muniswamy Pillai's amendment and thereby discontinued reservation policy for other minorities altogether. Accordingly, on May 11, 1949, the Advisory Committee, with one dissenting voice, passed the said resolution, as amended by Muniswamy Pillai, in the following form: "That the system of reservation for minorities other than Scheduled Castes in Legislatures be abolished."[39]

The object behind the Government Reservation policy was lucidly explained by Sardar Vallabhbhai Patel as:

> Even if today any concession is made it is with the sole object of easing the suspicions of even the smallest group in this House, because I think that a discontented minority is a burden and a danger and that we must not do anything to injure the feelings of any minority so long as it is not unreasonable.[40]

To trace a few important phases, minority representation under the Act of 1919 resulted in the creation of communal electorates. The Act of 1919 favored communal electorates because the Muslims who were offered the privilege of separate electorates as far back as 1909 had to be appeased by offering similar political safeguards. More-

---

39. *Ibid.,* Appendix A, para. 5, p. 311.
40. *Ibid.,* p. 352.

over, the "Lucknow Pact" concluded between the Congress and the Muslims League had secured some communal amity which had to be kept up.

Likewise, the Simon Commission appointed in 1927, to go through the Constitutional Reforms in India, suggested the continuation of the policy of communal electorates advocated by the Act of 1919.

But the Nehru Committee in 1928 exhibited a departure from the British policy of separate electorates for minorities. For the first time in the Constitutional history of India, this committee advocated the introduction of Joint Mixed electorates both for the House of Representatives and the Provincial Legislature. In Central Legislature, Muslims who formed the minority community in certain specific provinces were to be given reservation of seats in accordance with population ratio. In North West Frontier Province reservation benefits were proposed to be given to non-Muslims.

The next stage in the evolution of minority representation was the Round Table Conference, during 1929-32. The problem of communal representation figured very prominently in the two sessions of the Round Table Conference. But the failure of the Conference to reach any agreement on the subject of communal representation prompted Mr. Ramsay MacDonald to announce the Government Policy of "Communal Award," which meant separate electorates for minorities. Ambedkar welcomed the proposal of Communal Award, as it meant special safeguards to Depressed Classes. But such a measure spelled danger to Hinduism and national solidarity, as it was likely to estrange relationship between sections of Hindus instead of reconciling their differences. Hence, Gandhiji undertook "fast unto death" and averted the danger of separate electorates. As a result of Gandhiji's fast, separate electorates were abolished for Depressed Classes and Joint electorates were substituted by the Poona Pact in 1932.

With the ushering in of the Poona Pact, the idea of separate electorates cherished by Depressed Classes and conferred by the British Government was outdated. The era of joint electorates with reservation of seats for Depressed Classes became the order of the day.

However, the policy of communal reservation was pursued by the British Government even much later. The Act of 1935 gave greater political safeguards to communal minorities, particularly Muslims, Sikhs, Anglo-Indians, and Europeans, at the expense of the Hindu population including the Depressed Classes, who formed three fourths of the total population.

The departure of the British from the Indian political scene since 1935 marked a setback in the policy of communal representation. The Constituent Assembly of India, though favored the validity of communal representation in the initial stages, realized in course of time the drawbacks of the system. Very wisely indeed, in the year 1949, the Advisory Committee on Minorities, Fundamental Rights, etc., appointed by the Constituent Assembly passed the resolution to discontinue communal reservation of seats in the Legislature with the exception of the Scheduled Castes. Since 1949, reservation of seats in the Legislature on communal basis was given up once for all, as communalism was sure to harbor ill feelings among different communities, undermining the national solidarity and integration.

The Constitution of Independent India, heralded on January 26, 1950, although it makes provision for reservation of seats in the House of the People and the Legislatures to the Scheduled Castes and Scheduled Tribes, it is gratifying to note that a time limit has been placed for the discontinuation of reservation benefits. By the Constitution (Eighth Amendment) Act, 1959, reservation would cease to have effect on expiration of a period of twenty years from the commencement of this Constitution, viz., 1970.

Reservation in Legislatures and Parliament

Articles 330 and 332 make provision for the reservation of seats in the Lok Sabha and Legislative Assemblies in States, for the Scheduled Castes and Scheduled Tribes. The number of seats reserved for the Scheduled Castes and Scheduled Tribes in Lok Sabha were 75 and 33, respectively, out of the total of 500 seats, according to the 1961 Census. As regards Legislative Assemblies, 470 and 221 are reserved for the Scheduled Castes and Scheduled Tribes, respectively. These classes have shown commendable improvement in their representation in political institutions of the country, insofar as a good number of persons belonging to these classes have been elected to the Legislative Assemblies and Lok Sabha, against unreserved seats during the last general elections.

Table 2-2 shows the number of the Scheduled Castes and Scheduled Tribes members elected against unreserved seats in the State Legislative Assemblies:[41]

TABLE 2–2

Name of the State	LEGISLATIVE ASSEMBLIES	
	Scheduled Castes	Scheduled Tribes
Andhra Pradesh	—	—
Assam	—	2
Bihar	—	1
Kerala	1	—
Madhya Pradesh	—	5
Madras	1	—
Maharashtra	—	1
Mysore	—	—
Orissa	1	—
Punjab	1	—
Uttar Pradesh	4	—
West Bengal	4	—
TOTAL	12	9

41. *Report of the Commissioner for Scheduled Castes and Scheduled Tribes*, 1961–62, Part II, Appendix XXVII, para. 18.4, p. 75.

The representation of the Scheduled Castes and Scheduled Tribes in the Territorial Councils is given in Table 2-3.[42]

Commenting on the representation secured by the Scheduled Castes and Scheduled Tribes in the Legislatures, the Commissioner for Scheduled Castes and Scheduled Tribes, 1961-62, has observed:

> If in course of time, a sufficiently large number of Scheduled Castes/Scheduled Tribe persons get elected to the Lok Sabha and the Vidhana Sabhas from general constituencies, there will be no need for continuing the reservation of seats for them and the Constitutional provisions in this regard can be allowed to lapse. To bring about such a situation, it is necessary that all the political parties in the country should consider this problem very carefully and endeavour to set up as many suitable Scheduled Caste/Scheduled Tribe persons, as possible, from their parties for the general seats in Lok Sabha and the Vidhana Sabhas.[43]

The number of the Scheduled Caste persons appointed as Ministers, Deputy Ministers, and Parliamentary Secretaries in the Union Cabinet has gone up from three in 1960-61 to five in 1961-62. As regards the Scheduled Tribe persons, the number increased from one to two. In the States, the number of the Scheduled Caste Ministers, Deputy Ministers and Parliamentary Secretaries increased from 26 in 1960-61 to 28, after the last General Election, in 1961-62. While the number of the Scheduled Tribe Ministers, Deputy Ministers and Parliamentary Secretaries decreased from 15 to 11.[44]

The greatest landmark in the history of the Union Public Service Commission is that a woman member belonging

---

42. *Ibid.*, para. 18.8, p. 76.
43. *Ibid.*, Part I, para. 18.5, pp. 124–25.
44. *Ibid.*, para. 18.10, pp. 125–26.

TABLE 2-3

Name of the Union Territory	Total number of members	No. of Scheduled Caste Members			No. of Scheduled Tribe Members		
		Elected against reserved seats	Elected against unreserved seats	Nominated	Elected against reserved seats	Elected against unreserved seats	Nominated
Himachal Pradesh	41	12	—	†	—	1	†
Manipur	32*	—	1	—	—	9	1
Tripura	32*	—	2	†	—	10	†

* Including 2 nominated members.
† Nominations yet to be made.

to the Scheduled Tribes has been appointed to membership in the Union Public Service Commission. This honor goes to Mrs. Vonnily Khongman, Chairman of the Assam Public Service Commission and a former member of Parliament.

The Scheduled Castes and Scheduled Tribes have also been given representation in local bodies—Gram Panchayats, Panchayat Samities, and Zila Parishads. There is a proposal to absorb them in Nyaya Panchayats, the judicial bodies in village administration. It is felt that the representation of these classes in local bodies would foster friendly relations and gradually undermine social barriers.

Reservation in Services

In pursuance of the provisions contained in Articles 16 (4) and 335, the Government of India has made reservations for the Scheduled Castes and Scheduled Tribes in services since January 26, 1950.

The rules governing the reservations are:

a) *Scheduled Castes*—$12\frac{1}{2}$ percent of vacancies filled by direct recruitment on all-India basis by open competition, i.e., through the Union Public Service Commission or by means of Open Competitive tests held by any other authority. Where recruitment is made otherwise than by open competition, the reservation is $16\frac{2}{3}$ percent.

b) *Scheduled Tribes*—Both for recruitment by open competition and otherwise than by open competition, the reservation is 5 percent of the vacancies filled by direct recruitment.

The reservation orders apply to vacancies filled by direct recruitment, and also to vacancies filled by limited competitive test open to departmental candidates.

A person is held to be a member of a Scheduled Caste or Scheduled Tribe, as the case may be, if he belongs to a caste or a tribe which has been declared to be a Scheduled Caste or a Scheduled Tribe for the area in which he or she is resident under one of the following orders:

i) The Constitution (Scheduled Castes) Order, 1950, The Constitution (Scheduled Castes) (Part C States) Order, 1951,

The Constitution (Scheduled Tribes) Order, 1950, The Constitution (Scheduled Tribes) (Part C States) Order, 1951, as amended by the Scheduled Castes and Scheduled Tribes Lists (Modification) Order, 1956;

ii) The Constitution (Jammu and Kashmir) Scheduled Castes Order, 1956;

iii) The Constitution (Andaman and Nicobar Islands) Scheduled Tribes Order, 1959;

iv) The Constitution (Dadra and Nagar Haveli) Scheduled Castes, Order, 1962;

v) The Constitution (Dadra and Nagar Haveli) Scheduled Tribes, Order, 1962.

The relaxations allowed are:

1) *Age limit*—The maximum age limit prescribed for appointment to a service or post is increased by five years in the case of candidates belonging to Scheduled Castes and Scheduled Tribes.

2) *Standards of Suitability.*

a) *Direct recruitment by Examination.*

If, according to their normal positions in the competition or selection, candidates belonging to Scheduled Castes or Scheduled Tribes obtain less vacancies than the number reserved for them, candidates of such castes or tribes who have secured lower positions but who have qualified at such examination may be selected by the appointing authority at his discretion to make up the deficiency.

b) *Direct recruitment other than by Examination.*

The appointing authorities are authorised to se-

lect candidates from the Scheduled Castes and
Scheduled Tribes of a lower standard than that of
others, provided they possess the prescribed minimum educational and technical qualifications.

3) *Promotion to Non-selection posts:*

Where promotions are made on the basis of senior-
ity, subject to fitness, cases of persons belonging to
Scheduled Castes and Scheduled Tribes are judged in
a sympathetic manner without applying too rigid
standard of suitability. Cases of supersession of such
candidates, if any, are decided at a high level.

4) *Promotion to selection posts:*

The assessment of merit of a candidate belonging
to Scheduled Castes and Scheduled Tribes for promotion to Selection posts and the determination of his
position on the select panel is done sympathetically on
the basis of a relaxed standard. Such a candidate need
not be excluded from the select list unless he is considered unsuitable for promotion even on the basis of
relaxation.

5) *Fees:*

The fees prescribed for admission to any Examination or selection to the service or posts are reduced to
one fourth in the case of candidates belonging to
Scheduled Castes and Scheduled Tribes.

Formerly, the rule followed by the Government of India
in filling up the vacancies was, if sufficient number of
candidates belonging to Scheduled Castes were not available for vacancies reserved for them, the unfilled vacancies
were treated as reserved for the Scheduled Tribes and vice
versa, subject to future adjustments. But now, the rules
stand revised on the recommendations of the Scheduled
Areas and Scheduled Tribes Commission. The recommendations were:

i) At the moment, if a vacancy reserved for a Scheduled Tribe is not filled owing to the nonavailability of a suitable candidate, the vacancy is kept open for a period for which the vacancy may be kept open, if the State Government can get a candidate who is near enough the prescribed qualification, he may be given coaching for a time, reexamined and recruited if he is found to have made satisfactory progress.

ii) The existing orders of the Union Government which permit the appointment of Scheduled Caste candidates in the vacancies reserved for Scheduled Tribes, where suitable qualified Scheduled Tribe candidates are not available, should, in our opinion, be rescinded. The presence of such a permissive order makes for the complacency. The recruiting authorities should make all possible efforts to find the Scheduled Tribe candidates.[45]

At this juncture, reference must be made to CARRY FORWARD RULE pursued by the Government of India as a new policy of reservation.

The Government of India has revised the "carry forward rule" in respect of vacancies in Central Services reserved for Scheduled Castes and Scheduled Tribes.

It has now been decided that if sufficient number of suitable candidates eligible for reserved vacancies is not available on any occasion of recruitment, such vacancies would not be treated and filled as unreserved vacancies but shall be carried forward for subsequent occasions of recruitment.

For subsequent occasions the number of normal reserved vacancies and the "carried forward" reserved vacancies together should not exceed 45 percent out of the total number of vacancies. If there are only two vacancies, one would be treated as reserved. But if there is only one vacancy, it will be treated as unreserved.

The allocation of the "carried forward" vacancies within

---

45. *Report of the Scheduled Areas and Scheduled Tribes Commission,* Vol. I, 1960–61, para. 27.39, p. 340.

TABLE 2-4

Category of posts	Scheduled Castes				Scheduled Tribes		
	Total No. of posts	No. of posts due	No. of candidates available	No. of posts actually filled	No. of posts due	No. of candidates available	No. of posts actually filled
Class I	5,751	958	Information not available	20	287	Information not available	6
Class II (Gazetted)	5,653	942		50	282		18
Class II (non-Gazetted)	3,103	517		63	155		3
Class III	549,300	91,550		24,819	27,465		2,548
Class IV	789,027	131,504		161,958	39,451		14,512

this limit among the Scheduled Caste-Scheduled Tribe candidates will be in proportion to the total "carried forward" reserved vacancies of the two classes.

The surplus above 45 percent will be carried forward to the subsequent occasion of recruitment—subject, however, to the condition that the particular vacancies carried forward do not become time-barred due to their becoming more than two years old.[46] But the carry forward rule of reservation with regard to vacancies and posts in State services has been struck down by the Supreme Court of India as unconstitutional.[47]

The actual representation of the Scheduled Castes and Scheduled Tribes in the Central Government Services, in 1953, is recorded in Table 2–4:[47a]

The number of the Scheduled Castes and Scheduled Tribe employees in the Central Government services, as of January 1, 1963, is shown in Table 2-5:[48]

The representation of the Scheduled Castes and Scheduled Tribes in the I.A.S. cadre from 1948 to 1960, is shown in Table 2-6:[49]

Further details regarding the representation of the Scheduled Castes and the Scheduled Tribes in the I.C.S./ I.A.S., I.P./I.P.S., I.F.S. (A) and I.F.S. (B) are recorded in Table 2-7:[50]

Table 2-8 records the representation of the Scheduled Castes in the Armed Forces of the country in 1952 and 1953.[51]

---

46. *The Hindu*, December 25, 1963.
47. Devdas *v* The Union of India, A.I.R. 1964 Sc. 179.
47a. *Report of the Backward Classes Commission*, Vol. I, 1956, para. 277, p. 134.
48. *Report of the Commissioner for Scheduled Castes and Scheduled Tribes*, 1962–63, Part I, para. 20.2, p. 154.
49. *Journal of the National Academy of Administration*, Vol. 5, No. 2, July 1960, Table XII, p. 75.
50. Compiled from the *Reports of the Commissioner for Scheduled Castes and Scheduled Tribes* 1961–62, and 1962–63, pp. 133, 158.
51. *Social Welfare in India*, 1955, Appendix II, Table A, pp. 466–67.

TABLE 2-5*

Class of Service	Total no. of employees including Scheduled Castes/ Scheduled Tribes on 1-1-1963	Number of the Scheduled Caste employees on 1-1-1963		Number of Scheduled Tribe employees on 1-1-1963	
		Permanent			
I	8,632	113	(1.30%)	13	(0.15%)
II	14,339	330	(2.30%)	31	(0.21%)
III	620,580	46,366	(7.47%)	5,310	(0.85%)
IV (excluding sweepers)	646,720	150,806	(16.36%)	21,873	(3.38%)
		Temporary			
I	5,930	105	(1.77%)	17	(0.28%)
II	9,969	322	(3.23%)	20	(0.02%)
III	240,625	23,768	(9.87%)	3,305	(1.36%)
IV (excluding sweepers)	152,250	27,937	(18.34%)	6,283	(4.12%)

* The figures given in the table do not include information in respect of the Ministries of Defence, Labour and Employment, Works, Housing and Rehabilitation. (Dept. of Rehabilitation), Transport and Communication (Dept. of Transport) and the Dept. of Defence Production, as it has not been made available so far.

TABLE 2-6

Year	Total no. of probationers	Scheduled Caste	Per cent	Scheduled Tribe	Per cent
1948	33	—	—	—	—
1949	33	—	—	—	—
1950	35	1	2.9	—	—
1951	29	1	3.6	—	—
1952	38	—	—	—	—
1953	32	—	—	—	—
1954	42	—	—	—	—
1955	49	—	—	1	2.0
1956	57	1	1.8	1	1.8
1957	77	5	6.5	—	—
1958	64	2	3.2	—	—
1959	54	2	3.7	2	3.7
1960	72	1	1.4	5	6.9

TABLE 2-7

Services	Number of Scheduled Caste Officers as on						
	1-1-57	1-1-58	1-1-59	1-1-60	1-1-61	1-1-62	1-1-63
I.C.S./I.A.S.	18	29	35	38	39	46	68
I.P./I.P.S.	10	14	16	20	22	29	39
I.F.S. (A)	N.A.	N.A.	3	4	4	N.A.	7
I.F.S. (B)	N.A.	N.A.	29	30	47	N.A.	60

Services	Number of Scheduled Tribe Officers as on						
	1-1-57	1-1-58	1-1-59	1-1-60	1-1-61	1-1-62	1-1-63
I.C.S./I.A.S.	3	6	8	10	15	20	23
I.P./I.P.S.	5	5	7	6*	5†	6	11
I.F.S. (A)	N.A.	N.A.	—	1	1	N.A.	3
I.F.S. (B)	N.A.	N.A.	6	7	8	N.A.	6

* One joined the Indian Frontier Service during the year 1959.
† One officer resigned from the service during the year 1960.

Table 2-9 indicates the position of the Scheduled Castes and Scheduled Tribes in the Armed Forces up to December 31, 1962:[52]

The fact that the Government of India has given ample opportunities to the members of the Scheduled Castes and Scheduled Tribes to shoulder the country's services is crystal clear from the aforesaid tables. But the general impression regarding the Government's reservation policy is rather disappointing. The Commissioner for Scheduled Castes and Scheduled Tribes has made the following observation on this matter:

An assessment of the progress made during the last several years, since the Government of India announced their policy decision to reserve certain percentage of vacancies for the Scheduled Castes and the Scheduled Tribes, shows that the position as regards the actual

52. *Report of the Commissioner for Scheduled Castes and Scheduled Tribes*, 1962–63, Part I, para. 20.18, p. 161.

TABLE 2–8

Rank	1952	1953
Army		
Majors	3	5
Captains	27	29
Lieutenants	8	6
Second lieutenants	2	0
J.C.O's	601	435
N.C.O's	3,273	2,533
Other ranks	22,288	18,666
Recruits	3,435	2,831
Noncombatants (enrolled)	5,616	7,177
Noncombatants (unenrolled)	4,530	—
Civilians employed in lieu of military	961	—
Civilian personnel	13,279	—
Navy		
Lieutenants	—	1
Ratings	—	260
Air Force		
Commissioned officers (Pilot officers)	—	1
Flight sergeants	5	2
Sergeants	23	3
Corporals	79	24
Aircraftsmen	112	48
Recruits	—	19

representation of the Scheduled Castes and the Scheduled Tribes in services and posts under the various Ministries of the Government of India and their attached and subordinate offices is not satisfactory. There is no doubt that their numbers are, generally, increasing from year to year in the Central Government Services, but the rate of progress is very slow.[53]

Statistical data recorded in the preceding Tables 2-6 and 2-7 show that the representation of the Scheduled

53. *Ibid.*, 1961–62, para. 19.3, p. 129.

TABLE 2-9

Arm of Service	Officers/ ORs/ Ratings/ Airmen/ Civilians	Percentage of increase/ decrease in the number of persons as on 12–31–62, as compared to the number of persons as on 12–31–1961	
		Scheduled Castes	Scheduled Tribes
Army	Officers	+6.82	0.00
	JCOs/WOs & OR civilians*	+17.83	+11.26
	Civilian gazetted	+40.00	+100.00
	Civilian non-gazetted†	+0.68	+9.26
Navy	Officers	0.00	0.00
	Sailors	+36.00	+8.00
	Civilians gazetted	0.00	−100.00
	Civilians non-gazetted	+29.00	−2.60
Air Force	Commissioned officers	+100.00	+100.00
	Other commisisoned officers	+43.00	+14.00
	Civilians gazetted	+0.00	+0.00
	Civilians non-gazetted	+18.07	+54.54

* Includes civilians of regular and non-regular establishments.
† Includes NCSU.

Castes and Scheduled Tribes in All India Services falls short of Government expectations. The average representation recorded by these two classes in competitive examinations—I.A.S., I.P.S., and I.F.S.—are 2.5 and 1.1, respectively, as against 12½ and 5 percent of the total reservation, as envisaged in Government notifications.

The Union Public Service Commission records the poor recruitment of the Scheduled Castes and Scheduled Tribes candidates in key services for reserved posts. In the circumstances, it could be presumed that the poor recruitment in Class I and Class II services might be due to the fact that the Union Public Service Commission is keeping an eye on the suitability of candidates. This fact has been referred by the Constitution, in Article 335, which lays down:

> the claims of the members of the Scheduled Castes and the Scheduled Tribes shall be taken into consideration consistently with the maintenance of efficiency of administration, in the making of appointments to services and posts in connection with the affairs of the Union or of a State.

The fact that the efficiency factor should be given preference is not disputed by any authorities concerned. But, it has been stated, poor representation of the Scheduled Castes and Scheduled Tribes in these services is chiefly due to their bad scoring in viva voce or personality test. It has been argued that the judgment of suitability cannot be based on the results of the personality test alone. As pointed out by the Scheduled Areas and Scheduled Tribes Commission, viva voce tests are conducted by persons who may not have adequate knowledge of the conditions in the tribal areas and, therefore, of the handicaps under which the tribe is working, and this is one of the causes for deficiency in recruitment.

To improve the representation of the Scheduled Castes and Scheduled Tribes in All India Services, some measures are taken by the Government. To mention them, Pre-Examination Training Centers have been sponsored by the Government of India at the Universities of Allahabad and Bangalore, to provide special coaching to candidates coming from these communities. They are given free tuition, free boarding, and lodging facilities. With all these facilities, we hope that the Scheduled Caste and Scheduled Tribe candidates race up to reach the mark set for them by the recruiting authorities.

Even in lower services, it is felt that the Scheduled

Castes and Scheduled Tribes are not adequately represented. To overcome this shortcoming, the Government of India has issued instructions to the appointing authorities to select members of these communities, even if they possess a lower standard than others, provided they have minimum qualifications. The suggestion made by the Commissioner for Scheduled Castes and Scheduled Tribes is:

> It would be of very much help if the Ministry of Home Affairs make arrangements to scrutinise, in detail, the results of each examination and test held by appointing authorities, other than the Union Public Service Commission, with a view to discovering the possibilities of appointing even those who did not come to the expectations of the appointing authorities, by imparting them special training, if necessary. It is also desirable that the appointing authorities are not allowed to fill the reserved vacancies by members of other communities, unless and until the Ministry of Home Affairs are satisfied that all efforts needed to secure persons belonging to the Scheduled Castes or the Scheduled Tribes have been made.[54]

To give proper effect to the reservation decided upon, model rosters of 40 posts each have been prescribed for recruitment by open competition and otherwise. If the vacancies in a service or cadre are too few for the purpose, all corresponding posts are to be grouped together. Annual reports are required to be submitted by the employing authorities for scrutiny by the Government. To bring about a great awareness for ensuring effective implementation of the special representation orders, liaison officers have been appointed in the different Ministries of the Union Government.

The information regarding the position of the Sched-

---

54. *Ibid.*, para. 19.5, p. 131.

uled Castes and Scheduled Tribes in State services is not forthcoming from all the States and Union Territory Administrations. From the reports received from a few States, it is clear that these classes have not fared well in key posts of the State services. Only in Class III posts they have made satisfactory progress. It has been widely felt that the State Governments should take steps to collect requisite information about the placement of the Scheduled Castes and Scheduled Tribes in the various categories of State services. Besides, the State Government has been asked to issue brochures regarding reservation in their services in favor of the Scheduled Castes and Scheduled Tribes. It is gratifying to note that the Governments of Rajasthan and Maharastra have issued some instructions to the appointing authorities catering to the well-being of the Scheduled Castes and Scheduled Tribes. These instructions refer mainly to the forwarding of the applications of subordinate officers of the Scheduled Castes and Scheduled Tribes by the heads of the Departments, brooking no delay, waiving of the requirements of experience in absorbing Scheduled Castes and Scheduled Tribes, granting of study leave with arrangement to pay them scholarships to make up the general deficiency in their educational background, appointment of Backward Class candidates with minimum qualifications, and non-retrenchment of Backward Class personnel.

An Analysis of Constitutional Provisions

A survey of Constitutional Provisions for Backward Classes shows that two opposing trends are put into operation. These opposing trends are the concepts of "equality" and "special preference." Discrimination on grounds of caste, creed, sex, etc., is ruled out on the one hand, while on the other hand, special provisions have been made for Backward Classes under Articles 15 (4), 16 (4),

29 (2) , 330, 332, and 335. Special treatment for Backward Classes is accorded in the triple field: education, government service, and political representation. But political privilege by way of reservations in the Parliament and Legislatures is conferred only on the "Scheduled Castes" and "Scheduled Tribes." The "Other Backward Classes" and "Denotified Communities" are excluded from this benefit. It is felt that historical factors have created special circumstances, hence political privilege for "Scheduled Castes" and "Scheduled Trbes" could not be discontinued for these sections.

But in practical application, the concepts of "equality" and "special treatment" have created a tense situation. The Non-Backward Classes feel discriminated against by the special treatment policy. The tense situation has been clearly explained by Nehru:

> We come up against the difficulty that, on the one hand, in our Directive Principles of Policy we talk of removing inequalities, of raising the people in every way, socially, educationally and economically, of reducing the distances which separate the groups or classes of individuals from one another; on the other hand we find ourselves handicapped in this task by certain other provisions in the Constitution.[55]

M. N. Shrinivas comments on this dilemma of the Constitution that "the provision of Constitutional safeguards to the backward sections of the population, especially the Scheduled Castes and Tribes, has given a new lease of life to Caste."[56]

A. R. Wadia further observes:

Our Constitution aims at a casteless and classless so-

---

55. *Jawarharlal Nehru's Speeches* 1949–53, Extract of his speech on "Equality and the Backward Classes," pp. 517–18.
56. M. N. Srinivas, *Caste in Modern India*, 1962, p. 15.

ciety. But it has not seriously affected the solidity of caste except that it leaves any individual Hindu free to defy any rule of Caste without any fear of legal punishment or social ostracism.[57]

The tangle of equality and special treatment has been pictured by Nehru:

> We arrive at a peculiar tangle, namely, that we cannot have equality because in trying to attain equality we come up against certain principles of equality laid down in the Constitution. That is a very peculiar position. We cannot have equality because we cannot have non-discrimination, for if you are thinking of raising those who are down, you are somehow affecting the status quo, undoubtedly. You are thus said to be discriminating because you are affecting the status quo.[58]

But to attain changes in the status quo, people should be prepared to forego absolute equality in the larger interests of the community for a temporary period.

Traditional Hindu society was marked by "social haves" and "social have-nots" by way of caste system. As a consequence of this we are faced with a dilemma today. The special provisions envisaged for Backward Classes in the Constitution presents a tangle between "Backward Classes" and "Non-Backward Classes." But such conflicts are commonly found in all societies having class distinctions. "The encroachment of class upon class, of the underprivileged upon the privileged is not a tale of one era only or one region of the earth."[59]

But it could be said in favor of Constitutional Provisions for Backward classes that they are both justifiable and inevitable. The social conditions in India are such

57. A. R. Wadia, *Democracy and Society,* 1966, p. 84.
58. *Jawaharlal Nehru's Speeches,* 1949–53, p. 518.
59. Quoted in O'Malley, *Modern India and the West,* 1941, pp. 183–84.

that they necessitate the incorporation of special treatment for Backward Classes. Some sort of special assistance has to be given to those sections of society that are backward. A look into our historical past, a society based on the authoritarian principle of caste, which stood in the way of social and educational advancement of lower social orders, would justify the special treatment of these sections. Besides, the principle of equality enshrined in the Constitution cannot operate in a vacuum. To create equality, special facilities for Backward Classes are necessary. To transform a social order based on absolute inequality—caste system, special concessions to those sections that were the victims of absolute inequality are important. Moreover, special concessions guaranteed under Articles 330 and 332 are of a temporary nature. The continuance or discontinuance thereby depends on the changed conditions of Scheduled Castes and Scheduled Tribes in the political field. Though Art. 335 makes provisions for reservation in services, emphasis has been laid on "efficiency." Articles 15 (4), 16 (4) and 29 (2) are not mandatory but only enabling provisions of the Constitution.

The satisfactory solution for the juxtaposition of "equality and special preference" would be, as Myron Weiner suggests:

> If the Indian people are to accept democratic institutions, some of the community associations' demands must be met. It will require considerable skill to satisfy these demands without destroying the merit system.[60]

To sum up: "Constitutional problems are not solved like mathematical equations, for they are part of the problems of social life which do not conform to any mathematical formulae or rigid logic. The interpretation of the Constitutional law of a people living under an old and complex

---

60. Myron Weiner, *The Politics of Scarcity*, 1963, p. 77.

civilization like ours demands, when solving problems like the present, compromises and skilful adjustments which may not be strictly logical but which will make the Constitution workable."[61]

61. *Moinuddin* v *State of U.P. A.I.R.*, 1960, Vol. 47, para. 75, pp. 498–99.

3

SPECIAL PROBLEMS OF
BACKWARD CLASSES

BACKWARD CLASSES PRESENT COMPLEX PROBLEMS WHICH DE-
mand separate treatment. While educational and economic backwardness is a common feature of these underprivileged sections, they differ in their social disabilities.
Hence, the social disabilities of Backward Classes are dealt
with in this chapter in the light of the Constitutional guarantee of "social justice." Now, what is social justice? It is
difficult to give a precise definition of the term "social justice." William K. Frankena has defined it as follows: "Social justice is any system of distribution and retribution
which is governed by valid moral principles."[1] Social justice therefore refers to moral and legal justice. For purpose
of clarity, the Constitutional guarantee of social justice
to Backward Classes is studied under the following heads:
1) Emancipation of Scheduled Castes;
2) Elevation of Scheduled Tribes;
3) Enumeration of other Backward Classes; and
4) A brief note on Denotified Communities.

Emancipation of Scheduled Castes

The origin of the term "Scheduled Castes," as it is

---

1. Quoted in *Social Justice*, Richard B. Brandt (ed.), 1962, p. 3.

understood today, can be traced back to the latter part of the eighteenth century. Since then, the term has undergone great changes both in its definition as well as Constitutional import. The meaning and definition of the term were discussed in Legislative Councils, Franchise Committees, Statutory Commission, and Indian Central Committee. The terms coined by the several committees to denote "Scheduled Castes" were: "Depressed Classes," "Exterior Castes," "Excluded Castes," and "Backward Classes". The term "Scheduled Castes" came into vogue only with the Government of India Act of 1935, and this term is retained in the Constitution of India up to the present day.

It is necessary to examine the legal and Constitutional meaning of the term "Scheduled Castes" as understood at various phases of transformation.

The definition of the term "Depressed Classes" was discussed in the Indian Legislative Council as far back as 1916. It was decided in the council that the term "Depressed Classes" should include:

a) Criminal and wandering tribes,
b) Aboriginal tribes, and
c) Untouchables.

In 1917, Sir Henry Sharp, Educational Commissioner, Government of India, prepared a list of Depressed Classes in which he included:

a) Aboriginal or hill tribes,
b) Depressed Classes, and
c) Criminal tribes.

The explanation of the term "Depressed Classes," according to Sir Henry Sharp, reads:

. . . the depressed classes form the unclean castes whose touch or even shadow is pollution. But a wider significance is often attached to the expression, so that it includes communities which though not absolutely outside the pale of caste, are backward and educationally poor and despised and also certain classes of Muhammadans. Some have interpreted it as simply educationally backward. The task of defining is made difficult by doubt as to where the line should be drawn and the elastic differences of such classes dwell on the borderland of respectability. Sometimes the whole community declares itself to be depressed with a view to reaping special concessions of education or appointment.[2]

In the above explanation of Sir Henry Sharp, we find that diverse groups—aborigines, depressed classes, and criminal tribes—were grouped under one head "Depressed Classes." The term was rather vague and comprehensive, dealing with all sections of society who were downtrodden socially, educationally, and economically. However, the criterion for classifying the "Depressed Classes" is hinted in the explanation that those who pursue "unclean profession" or those who belong to "unclean castes" whose touch or even shadow is pollution. But the main drawback was the combining of other two Backward Classes in the same terminology without precise definition.

The Southborough Committee, 1919, the Statutory Commission and the Indian Central Committee, however, took a different stand from that of Sir Henry Sharp. They accepted the test of "untouchability" as the criterion for classifying "Depressed Classes." The Indian Franchise Committee stated that "the term 'Depressed Classes' should not include primitive or aboriginal tribes, nor should it include those Hindus who are only economically poor and in other ways backward but are not regarded as untouchables."[3]

The test of "untouchability" to classify "Depressed Classes" was accepted by the Census of 1911. Only those

2. Quoted in *the Report of the Indian Franchise Committee,* Vol. 1, 1932, para. 279, p. 109.
3. *Ibid.,* para. 282, p. 109.

who are untouchables and who " (7) are denied access to the interior of ordinary Hindu temples; (8) cause pollution, (a) by touch, (b) within a certain distance"[4] were included in the term "Depressed Classes."

The 1921 Census does not specify any criterion for classifying "Depressed Classes."

Later, B. R. Ambedkar found the need for substituting the term "Depressed Classes," by some other term like "Exterior Castes" or "Excluded Castes," until a better term was coined. In his note of dissent in the Report of the Indian Franchise Committee he observed:

> This designation has many advantages. It defines exactly the position of the Untouchables who are within the Hindu religion but outside the Hindu Society, and distinguishes it from Hindus who are economically and educationally depressed but who are both within the pale of Hindu religion and Hindu Society.[5]

Commenting on the precise definition of untouchables by the term "Exterior Castes," he further remarked: "The term has two other advantages. It avoids all the confusion that is now caused by use of the vague term "Depressed Classes" and at the same time is not offensive.[6]

B. R. Ambedkar's suggestion found expression in the 1931 Census. The reason for substituting the term "Exterior" for outcastes was given by the Census Commissioner for India thus:

> Outcaste correctly interpreted seems to mean no more than one who is outside the caste system and is therefore not admitted to Hindu Society, but since in practice the "Exterior Castes" also contained those who had been cast out from the Hindu Social body for some breach of

4. *Ibid.,* para. 285, p. 110.
5. *Ibid.,* para. 14, p. 211.
6. *Ibid.*

caste rules. "Outcaste" and "out cast" were in some cases synonymous and the derogatory implications of obliquity attaching to the latter term have unjustly coloured the former, a taint which is not conveyed by the substitution of the word "Exterior," which may connote exclusion but not extrusion.[7]

The term "Exterior Castes" was further defined by the Provincial Superintendent of Assam as follows:

By this expression I mean castes recognised definitely as Hindu castes whose water is not acceptable and who, in addition, are so deficient as castes in education, wealth and influence, or for some reason connected with their traditional occupations are so looked down upon that there seems little hope of their being allowed by Hindu Society to acquire any further social privileges within— at any rate—the next decade.[8]

The tests applied in classifying untouchables for purpose of Census enumeration of 1931 were:

(1) whether the caste or class in question can be served by clean Brahmans or not,

(2) whether the caste or class in question can be served by the barbers, water-carriers, tailors, etc., who serve the caste Hindus,

(3) whether the caste in question pollutes a high caste Hindu by contact or by proximity,

(4) whether the caste or class in question is one from whose hands a caste Hindu can take water,

(5) whether the caste or class in question is debarred from using public conveniences, such as roads, ferries, wells or schools,

(6) whether the caste or class in question is debarred from the use of Hindu temples,

---

7. *Census Report 1931*, Vol. 1, Part I, Appendix I, p. 471.
8. Ibid., p. 495.

(7) whether in ordinary social intercourse a well-educated member of the caste or class in question will be treated as an equal by high caste men of the educational qualifications,

(8) whether the caste or class in question is merely depressed on account of its own ignorance, illiteracy or poverty and but for that would be subject to no social disability,

(9) whether it is depressed on account of the occupation followed and whether but for that occupation it would be subject to no social disability.[9]

Thus, the term "Exterior Castes" was suggested as the satisfactory substitute for connoting the Depressed Classes. "Untouchability" was the chief test for classifying Depressed Classes. Socio-religious disabilities thrust on certain sections of society, as a consequence of which they suffered social exclusiveness and separateness, were given prime importance in any classification of Depressed Classes.

The term "Scheduled Castes" to connote Depressed Classes was coined by the Government of India Act, 1935. The term was defined as follows: "The 'Scheduled Castes' means such castes, races and tribes, corresponding to the classes of persons formerly known as 'the depressed classes' as His Majesty in council may specify.[10]

The Indian Independence Act, 1947, defined the term as:

The "Scheduled Castes" means such castes, races or tribes or parts or groups within castes, races or tribes, being castes, races, tribes, parts or groups which appear to the Governor General to correspond to the classes of persons formerly known as the "Depressed Classes" as the Governor-General may by order specify.

---

9. *Ibid.,* p. 472.
10. *Act of 1935,* Section 24 of First Schedule, Part I.

After Independence, the term "Scheduled Caste" is used in the Constitution to specify the untouchables. Article 341 (1) reads:

(1) The President may with respect to any State or Union Territory, and where it is a State, after consultation with the Governor thereof, by public notification specify the castes, races or tribes or parts of or groups within castes, races or tribes which shall for the purposes of this Constitution be deemed to be Scheduled Castes in relation to that State or Union territory, as the case may be.

(2) Parliament may by law include in or exclude from the list of Scheduled Castes specified in a notification issued under clause (1) any caste, race or tribe or part of or group within any caste, race or tribe, but save as aforesaid a notification issued under the said clause shall not be varied by any subsequent notification.

The term "Scheduled Castes" is defined in Art. 366 (24) as follows: " 'Scheduled Castes' means such castes, race or tribes or parts of or groups within such castes, races or tribes as are deemed under Article 341 to be Scheduled Castes for the purposes of this Constitution."

The criterion for specifying "Scheduled Castes" is precise and simple. The stigma of untouchability is the declared criterion for classifying Scheduled Castes.

From the point of view of the state the important test is the right to use public convenience—roads, wells, and schools, and if this be taken as the primary test, religious disabilities and the social difficulties indirectly involved by them may be regarded as contributory only. Some importance must be attached to them, since obviously if the general public regards the persons of certain groups as so distasteful that concerted action is resorted to in order to keep them away, persons of those groups do suffer under a serious disability.[11]

Socio-religious disabilities associated with the caste system have been made the basis for classifying Scheduled Castes. Accordingly, the Constitution (Scheduled Castes) Order, 1951, the Scheduled Castes lists (Modification) Order, 1956, were issued by the President in consonance with Art. 341. In spite of having a specific criterion for classifying Scheduled Castes—the test of untouchability, some ambiguities have been pointed out in the formulation of Scheduled Caste lists. The need for careful examination of these lists has been greatly felt by the Commissioner for Scheduled Castes and Scheduled Tribes.

The population of Depressed Classes as estimated by different committees prior to Independence is given in Table 3–1.[12]

According to the 1941 Census, the population of Scheduled Castes was 43,843,000. The population of Scheduled Castes according to the 1951 Census was 55,327,021, that is, 15.32 percent of the total population of the country. The 1961 Census recorded an increase in the population figures of Scheduled Castes, that is 64,504,113; 14.64 percent of the total population.

Social Disabilities of Scheduled Castes

Untouchability, the greatest social disability of the Scheduled Castes, is a blot on Hinduism. In the name of untouchability gross injustice was done to myriads of our unfortunate brethren, who were reduced more or less to a bestial position in society. What is meant by untouchability and who are untouchables? Untouchability is the

---

11. *Report of the Commissioner for Scheduled Castes and Scheduled Tribes,* 1951, pp. 8–9.

12. Quoted in *Report of the Indian Franchise Committee,* Vol. 1, para. 300, p. 119.

TABLE 3–1

The Depressed Classes (figures in millions)

PROVINCE	South Borough Committee	Sir Henry Sharp 1917	Census Commissioner 1921	Simon Commission	Census Commissioner 1931	Provincial Govt. 1932	Provincial Committee 1932	Remarks
Madras	6.4	5.7	6.4	6.5	7.0	7.1	7.1	
Bombay	0.6	1.6	2.8	1.5	1.8	1.7	1.7	
Bengal	9.9	6.7	9.0	11.5	—	11.2	0.07	0.7 by some 11.2 by the others.
United Provinces	10.1	8.4	9.0	12.0	12.6	6.8	0.6	9.2 Mr. Blunt's estimate
Punjab	1.7	2.1	2.8	2.8	1.3	1.3	1.3	
Bihar and Orissa	9.4	1.2	8.0	5.0	3.7	5.8	4.3	
Central Provinces	8.8	8.0	3.3	3.3	2.9	2.9	2.9	
Assam	0.3	2.7	2.0	1.0	1.9	0.65	0.65	
Total	42.2	31.5	43.3	43.6	31.2	37.45	18.62	

result of the theory and practice of pollution, fostered by the high castes or Brahmans, for whom the touch and even sight of a member of low caste, particularly the Harijans, caused pollution. It simply means the touch-me-not attitude of the Hindu society towards the Harijans. The untouchables were the outcastes of Hindu society who formed the fifth group popularly called Panchamas.

The theory regarding the origin of untouchables is a controversial one. Divergent views have been propounded which contradict one another. One of the theories is that untouchables constituted the most backward sections of the indigenous population conquered by the Aryans. The shudras are supposed to be the original inhabitants of Hindustan and the untouchables form a part of shudras. After their subjection they became "Dasyas" or "Dasyus" at the hands of the Aryans. It has been further observed that among the shudras who surrendered without any resistance came to be known as "touchables," and those who refused to surrender and offered stiff resistance became "untouchables." Another theory states that the untouchables were secluded because they were outside the scheme of creation. That is the reason why they were termed "Antyajas." But Ambedkar interprets the meaning of the term "Antya" not as the end of creation, but as the end of the village. The untouchables usually lived outside the village, so they came to be called "Antyajas." He traces the origin and development of the theory and practice of untouchability to factors historical, social, and religious. There is also a notion that mixed unions between high caste females with low caste males rendered them "chandalas." Thus, ideas of ceremonial purity, pursuit of unclean professions, eating habits (meat of dead animals, beef eating, etc.), mixed unions, and conquest of the Aryans are some of the factors attributed to the genesis of untouchability.

Whatever the controversy regarding the origin of untouchables, the fact that a certain section of society was kept in social isolation—a position similar to that of the institution of slavery in Western countries, is crystal clear. The untouchables lived on the outskirts of the villages, remote from the hustle and bustle of city life, mostly in penury. They were deprived of the basic necessities of life, such as access to wells, tanks, schools, temples, cremation grounds, bathing ghats, free movement, residence along with other sections of society, etc. They suffered social exclusiveness and degradation for the sin of being born in a caste, rated the lowest caste by Hindu orthodoxy. As B. R. Ambedkar observed:

> The outcaste is a by-product of the caste system. There will be outcastes as long as there are castes. Nothing can emancipate the outcaste except the destruction of caste system. Nothing can help Hindus and ensure their survival in the coming struggle except the purging of Hindu faith of this odious and vicious dogma.[13]

Eradication of untouchability was one of the basic objectives of the socio-religious movements of the nineteenth and twentieth centuries. Even earlier, dating back to Upanishads 1000 to 500 B.C., Buddhism, Jainism, Vaishnavism, Shaivism, Sikhism, Arya Samaj, Prarthana Samaj, Brahmo Samaj, and Ramakrishna Mission, refuted the practice of untouchability as alien to the spirit of Hinduism, which believed in fraternity and the unity of mankind. The idea that the "divine element" is present in all human beings irrespective of caste was proclaimed time and again by the great religious thinkers of the country. But in spite of vehement criticism of untouchability by social reformers and religious thinkers, Hindu society committed the sin of treating our own people as untouch-

---

13. Quoted in Dhananjay Keer, *Dr. Ambedkar: Life and Mission*, 1954, p. 220.

ables. Mere accident of birth prevented a fraction of Hindus from enjoying the civic rights and amenities of life, who gradually formed the most inarticulate group agitating for self-assertion.

The need for eradicating untouchability was felt by the British administration. But since this social disability was interrelated with religious practice, the Government hesitated to introduce any legislation. As the Joint Committee on Indian Constitutional Reform pointed out:

> In no other sphere, as all thoughtful Indians recognise, is the need for social reform more urgent and vital; yet Government is debarred, by the considerations we have stated, from effective interference in such matters as child marriages or the appalling problem of the untouchables.[14]

The British evinced interest in ameliorating the lot of untouchables not through Government interference but by encouraging the natives, or rather Indian reformers, to take the initiative in bettering their lot. As they observed: "There are fetters which only Indian hands can strike off; and we can do no more than give Indian reformers the opportunity themselves of attempting the task."[15]

Prior to Independence, the problem of untouchables was not only social and religious but also a political one. Tired of basking in perpetual subjection, they looked eagerly to the British administrators for the elevation of their position. They even sought refuge in Christianity, Islam, Buddhism, and other religious beliefs. Such mass conversion of untouchables to different religious beliefs was a serious threat to national solidarity. Luckily for the country, Gandhiji's* political acumen detected the danger

---

14. *Joint Committee on Indian Constitutional Reforms—1933–34,* Vol. I, Part I, Chairman's Draft Report, p. 54.

15. *Ibid.,* pp. 54–55.

* The affix "ji" to any name connotes respect to the man in India. Thus, the form *Gandhiji* connotes that he is highly respected in the country.

that would befall the country by such mass conversions. To avert this danger, he launched "the anti-untouchability" drive throughout the country for the eradication of this social evil. He became the champion of their cause and struggled hard to give the Harijan Movement an impetus on All India basis. The term "Harijan," which means people who are dear to Hari, coined by Narasi Mehta, was used by Gandhiji to connote the untouchables. It marked a great change in the nomenclature of untouchables who were referred to as "Adi Dravidas," "Antyajas," "Ati shudras," "Avarnas," "Bhangis," "Pariahs," "Panchamas," etc. Gandhiji made Harijan uplift an integral part of the struggle for Swaraj. He brought to light the political implications that would emerge from the socioreligious evils of untouchability. The year 1917 marked an important landmark in the history of the Harijan Movement, for it marked the recognition of the uplift of Harijans as an integral part of the Congress Program. Gandhiji undertook an intensive tour in 1933 to popularize the Harijan Movement. The twin objectives of the Harijan Movement were the breaking down of the century-old practice of untouchability and, secondly, the integration of Hindu society under the common banner of nationalism and freedom. The unremitting labor of Mahatma Gandhi was chiefly responsible for ameliorating the lot of untouchables. He identified the cause of untouchables with his life and fought to the last breath for their rights and privileges.

With the advance of education, some leaders of Scheduled Castes rose to prominence and organized parties to demonstrate their grievances and expose the injustice done to them in the name of religion. The two important organizations which gave publicity to their grievances were the All-India Depressed Classes Association and the All India Depressed Classes Federation. Ambedkar was the Architect of the All-India Depressed Classes Federation, which did laudable service for Harijan uplift. He awakened the Harijans from a long slumber to a life of activity. He infused in them a spirit to liberate themselves from the rigidities of the caste system. He created in them an urge to agitate for self-assertion at par with other sections of society. He warned a death knell to the political structure of democracy, if social inequalities like untouchability were entertained. Political equality and social inequality were contradiction in terms, and unless political equality was followed by social equality, democracy would not thrive. Like Gandhiji, he made Harijan uplift his mission in life, and remarked: "As between the country and myself, the country will have precedence; as between the country and the Depressed Classes, the Depressed Classes will have precedence—the country will have no precedence.[16]

Constitutional Safeguards for the Eradication of Untouchability

Since Independence, the eradication of untouchability has been made a Constitutional guarantee. The preamble to the Constitution proclaims in unequivocal terms the establishment of a just society. It guarantees:

> Justice, social, economic and political; Liberty of thought, expression, belief, faith and worship; Equality of status and of opportunity; and to promote among them all Fraternity assuring the dignity of the individual and the unity of the Nation; . . .

The Congress Party (ruling party), has embraced the ideal of "Ethical Socialism" to realize the objective of a classless and casteless society through social transformation. As Ambedkar remarked: "Democracy is incomplete and inconsistent with isolation and exclusiveness, resulting in

---

16. Quoted in Dhananjay Keer, *Dr. Ambedkar: Life and Mission*, p. 317.

the distinction between the privileged and unprivileged—privileges for a few and disabilities for the vast majority."[17] The Constitution of India has ushered in an era of rights and privileges for the Scheduled Castes in particular. A time has come now to set the house in order, by redressing the wrongs done in the name of religion through Constitutional means. Eradication of social disabilities has been made the responsibility of the Government, by incorporating Art. 17 in the Constitution.

Article 17 deals with the abolition of untouchability. It reads:

> Untouchability is abolished and its practice in any form is forbidden. The enforcement of any disability arising out of "untouchability" shall be on offence punishable in accordance with law.

This article corresponds with Art. 11 of the Draft Constitution of India, 1948. Untouchability is made not only antisocial, but a crime anathema to the concept of democracy. The removal of untouchability is felt inevitable for the restoration of Human Rights, to keep alive the brotherhood of mankind. Article 17 gets special distinction in the Constitution for visualizing Gandhiji's dream of doing away with untouchability. It reflects the spirit of the Constitution, the intention of the Constitution makers to restore the dignity of the individual and to establish fraternity. Untouchability, a social disability chiefly responsible for creating misfits in society, is not only prohibited but made cognizable. The Parliament has assumed the power to legislate on this matter uniformly in all the States.

Further, untouchability is made an offense under the Government of India, in compliance with "The Untouchability (offences) Act, 1955." This Act, which came into

---

17. *Ibid.*, p. 374.

force on June 1, 1955, provides penalties for enforcing social disabilities by denying access to wells, tanks, places of entertainment, temples, etc.; for enforcing occupational, professional or trade disabilities; and any other disability on the ground of untouchability. The punishment for the first offense is imprisonment extending to six months or a fine to the tune of Rs.500, or both. For subsequent offenses there is a provision in the Act for imposition of both imprisonment and a fine. Besides, the trying court may impose, if necessary, any other form of punishment.

Speaking about the Untouchability Offences Bill, which later became an Act in 1955, the then Home Minister, G. B. Pant, observed:

> This cancer of Untouchability has entered into the very vitals of our society. It is not only a blot on the Hindu religion, but it has created intolerance, sectionalism fissiparous tendencies. Many of the evils that we find in our society today are traceable to this heinous monstrosity. It was really strange that Hindus with their sublime philosophy and merciful kind-heartedness even towards insects should have been party to such intolerable dwarfing of manhood. Yet, Untouchability has been there for centuries and we have now to atone for it. The idea of Untouchability is entirely repugnant to the structure, spirit, and provisions of the Constitution.[18]

But Art. 17 and The Untouchability (offences) Act, 1955, face a legal dilemma, for both suffer for want of definition in the Constitution. The term "untouchability" is very familiar in our social system and it can be described at length, but still it is not defined in the Constitution; why? In the absence of a precise definition of the term "untouchability" either in Art. 17, or The Untouchability (offences) Act, 1955, the Constitutional guarantee for its abolition is vague. The loopholes resulting from

18. Quoted in M. V. Pylee, *India's Constitution*, 1965, p. 89.

the failure of the Constitution makers to define the term "untouchability" have been clearly illustrated in *Devarajiah* v. *Padmanna*. In this case, it has been observed by N. Sreenivasa Rau, J., that:

The Untouchability (offences) Act, 1955, does not define the word "Untouchability." This Act is obviously a law passed by Parliament in accordance with the provisions of Art. 17 of the Constitution of India, which abolishes "Untouchability" and forbids its practice in any form and provides for punishment, according to law of the enforcement of any disability arising out of "Untouchability."[19]

Elaborating this remark, he further points out:

There is no definition of the word "Untouchability" in the Constitution also. It is to be noticed that that word occurs only in Art. 17 and is enclosed in inverted commas. This clearly indicates that the subject-matter of that Article is not Untouchability in its literal or grammatical sense but the practice as it had developed historically in this country.[20]

In the above-mentioned case, it has been observed that the cases that are usually filed under the section of the Untouchability (offences) Act, 1955, amount only to social boycott and thus they very rarely come under the purview of the Act.

Whatever the drawbacks, the Act is not without some merits. The one interesting feature of The Untouchability (offences) Act, 1955, is that it is applicable not merely to Hindus but to all communities in India. In this context, G. B. Pant remarked:

---

19. *Devarajiah* v *Padmanna*, *A.I.R.*, 1958, Vol. 45, Mysore Section, para. 4, p. Mysore State 85.
20. *Ibid.*

This Bill does not apply to Hindus alone. It applies to all. . . . It will apply not only to Scheduled castes, but probably to Christians in the South who are not allowed to enter churches by those who consider themselves as belonging to higher classes. There are certain Muslims who are treated in the same manner by the followers of Islam. They will have the benefit of this provision. It is for their benefit that the word "untouchability" has been left undefined. So far as the Scheduled Castes are concerned, the Act makes it clear that they are entitled to the benefit of the provisions of this Act in any case.[21]

The cases registered under the Untouchability (offences) Act, 1955, are given in Table 3-2:[22]

TABLE 3–2

Year	No. of cases registered with the police		Position of disposal of cases at the end of each year			
	Total	Challenged	Convicted	Acquitted	Compounded	Pending
1955	180	180	80	12	12	76
1956	693	599	149	106	156	188
1957	492	415	87	35	85	208
1958	550	477	127	83	92	175
1959	481	401	105	70	82	144
1960	502	438	89	74	122	153
Total:	2,898	2,510	637	380	549	944

The incidence of untouchability prevailing in the country is quite high as recorded in Table 3-2. The figures of cases filed with the police, convictions, acquittals, and pending cases of 1955 stand in marked contrast with the figures for 1960. The cases registered under The Untouchability (offences) Act, 1955, are showing an upward curve

21. *Lok Sabha Debates,* April 27, 1955, Columns 6,545; 6,672.
22. *Report of the Commissioner for Scheduled Castes and Scheduled Tribes,* 1961–62, Part I, p. 7.

rather than deterioration. This shows that legislative enactment against untouchability has not proved very effective. Untouchability has struck its roots deep in the Indian soil, resisting all attempts to unearth it. More than legislative measures, what is needed today is a change of heart. People should realize that the removal of untouchability is not only a social problem but a national necessity. As Ambedkar stated: "The salvation of the Depressed Classes will come only when the caste Hindu is made to think and is forced to feel that he must alter his ways. I want a revolution in the mentality of the caste Hindus."[23] So, there should be a moral revolution not only among the higher classes but even among the untouchables themselves who practice untouchability among their own groups, for eradicating this social evil, root and branch, from Hindu society.

The field study conducted by "the Study Team on Social Welfare and Welfare of Backward Classes," reveals the discrimination that is still practiced in public life against the Harijans. The report reads:

(a) As many as 56.75 percent Harijan respondents experienced discrimination in public life particularly in regard to seating arrangements and use of common utensils;

(b) 56.8 percent of Harijan respondents expressed hesitation in visiting public places because of resentment of caste-Hindus;

(c) 32.4 percent respondents would not visit public places because of their economic dependence on the caste-Hindus;

(d) the religious isolation of Harijans still persists in a considerable degree which is obvious from the comparatively smaller percentage of non-Harijans associating with Harijans in religious activities:

(e) the degree of awareness of Untouchability (of-

---

23. Quoted in Dhananjay Keer, *Dr. Ambedkar: Life and Mission*, p. 214.

fences) Act, 1955, has been found to be higher among
the non-Harijan respondents, that is 77.7 percent as
compared to the Harijan respondents among whom it
was found to be 66.6 percent; and

(f) the evil of Untouchability exists among the Untouchables themselves and 18.3 percent respondents
admitted practising Untouchability against lower
castes.[24]

Untouchability no doubt stands abolished in the Constitution. But we hear cases being filed one after another,
particularly in rural areas. It has been realized that legislative enactments are of no avail to the moral reconstruction of society. Caste-consciousness and caste prejudices
are deep-rooted in villages and the only way to eradicate
unsocial habits is through moral appeal and public opinion. Gandhiji's dogma that "the purification required is
not of untouchables but of the so-called superior castes"
goes a long way in the removal of untouchability. It is
rather disheartening to state that caste clashes are frequently reported. To mention one such recent incident,
the Silambanur case of rioting, following a clash between
caste Hindus (Padayachis) and Harijans at Silambanur
village, Jayankondam Taluk, Tiruchirapalli district, of
April 16, 1964.[25] Incidents of such kind occur in most of
the villages in north and south India even today.

Apart from social legislation and legislative enactment,
the Government of India has realized the necessity to in-
tensify the work of voluntary or nonofficial agencies, working towards the removal of social disabilities. These voluntary agencies have been given a fillip by the Central as
well as the State Governments by way of financial assistance (grants-in-aid) to undertake the work of ameliorating the lot of Scheduled Castes. The First Five Year Plan

24. *Report of the Study Team on Social Welfare and Welfare of Backward Classes,* Vol. 1, 1959, Part III, para. 9, p. 189.
    25. *The Hindu,* May 14, 1964.

allocation for this work was to the tune of Rs. 2.3 millions. The Second Plan provision was Rs. 20.8 millions. The States' contribution to local voluntary organizations was estimated at Rs. 986,000 in 1956-57, and Rs. 1,323,000 in 1957-58. The contribution of the Ministry of Home Affairs was Rs. 786,000 in 1956-57 and Rs. 674,000 in 1957-58 to All India Voluntary Organizations. The Third Plan allocations for State Voluntary Organizations were Rs. 4.7 millions. Allocations made for the year 1961-62 were to the tune of Rs. 390,000. The expenditure incurred for the year 1961-62 was Rs. 0.3 millions. It has been desired by the Government of India that these voluntary agencies should concentrate not only on the eradication of untouchability, but also extend the scope of their work to new fields. In this direction, the Commissioner for Scheduled Castes and Scheduled Tribes recommends:

If the policy of encouraging and aiding voluntary agencies in taking up these various activities is to be pursued effectively, there is an urgent need that the State Governments, Union Territory Administrations, should make a study of the existing agencies in these areas, their experience, present performance and potentialities for different types of work. This study should also enquire into the procedure and terms and conditions under which grants are being given at present and the changes that will be needed, if their activities are to be expanded. On the basis of this assessment, a systematic programme should be drawn up, specifying the various fields in which these organisations should work according to their particular suitability and competence.[26]

Some of the important voluntary organizations working for the amelioration of Scheduled Castes are: the All India

---

26. *Report of the Commissioner for Scheduled Castes and Scheduled Tribes,* 1961–62, Part I, para. 6.12, p. 33.

Harijan Sevak Sangh; the Bharatiya Depressed Classes League; the Iswar Saran Ashram, Allahabad; the Bharat Dalit Sevak Sangh, Poona; the Indian Red Cross Society; the Ramkrishna Mission; and the Hindu Sweepers Sevak Samaj, Delhi.

The All India Harijan Sevak Sangh is unquestionably the oldest and the biggest voluntary organization which has rendered memorable service for the uplift of Harijans. The object of this organization is "eradication of untouchability in Hindu society with all its incidental evils and disabilities suffered by the so-called untouchables in all walks of life and to secure for them absolute equality of status with the rest of the Hindus." The Harijan Sevak Sangh was established in 1932, with Ghanashamdas Birla as the president and Amritlal Thakkar as the secretary. This Sangh is carrying on effective propaganda for the removal of untouchability by opening up wells, temples, restaurants, performance of religious functions in the houses of Harijans by Brahmin priests, convening of conferences among the villages to discuss the problem of eradicating untouchability, etc.

Similarly, the other voluntary organizations give much publicity to the cause of improving the position of untouchables. They run cosmopolitan hostels; render medical aid; impart training in handicrafts; observe Harijan days and Harijan weeks; distribute pamphlets on untouchability, etc.

In addition to these voluntary organizations, the Ministry of Information and Broadcasting is doing valuable service by producing documentary films and feature films. They also publish articles on untouchability in popular magazines, publish reports of the Conferences of State Ministers, Central Advisory Boards, and All India Backward Classes. Besides, they run mobile units for screening films and holding discussions through display of posters and the like. A chapter on untouchability has also been included in Indian reference annuals compiled by the Research and Reference Division.

The grants-in-aid made to non-official organizations during 1956–1963 are recorded in Table 3–3.[27] The State-wide allocation of grants-in-aid to voluntary organizations during the Second and Third Plan is given in Table 3–4.[28]

To assess the intensity of untouchability prevailing in the country, the States have been asked to maintain lists of villages which practice untouchability, on the recommendations of the Commissioner for Scheduled Castes and Scheduled Tribes. Many States have agreed to this proposal and lists are prepared with the cooperation of Assistant Commissioners for Scheduled Castes and Scheduled Tribes at State level and Gram Pracharakas of Voluntary Agencies at village level. Some States have instituted cash prizes to villages for non-practice of Untouchability. Madras State has instituted Gold Medals for maintaining cordial relations with Harijans in the social sphere, inter-caste marriages with Harijans, inter-dining, adoption of Harijan children by caste Hindus, etc. Mixed hostels and mixed colonies are advocated by many States as the means for the eradication of untouchability. It is widely felt that mixed hostels and mixed colonies foster the spirit of community living. Efforts are made by the Government of Bombay to give concessions to non-Backward Classes in purchasing sites in Harijan colonies and also joining the Backward Classes Cooperative society. Similarly, non-Backward students residing in Harijan hostels are also offered scholarships to maintain the expenses of the hostel. The All India Federation of Scheduled Castes, Tribes and

---

27. Compiled from the *Reports of the Commissioner for Scheduled Castes and Scheduled Tribes,* 1956–57, 1957–58, 1958–59, 1961–62, 1962–63.

28. *Report of the Commissioner for Scheduled Castes and Scheduled Tribes,* 1961–62, Part II, Appendix II, p. 4.

TABLE 3-3

Grants-in-aid to Non-official Organizations
for the Removal of Untouchability and Welfare of Scheduled Castes in Rs.

Name of the Organization	1956-1957		1957-1958		1958-1959		1961-1962	
	Grant-in-aid sanctioned	Expenditure incurred	Grant sanctioned	Expenditure incurred	Grant sanctioned	Expenditure incurred	Grant-in-aid sanctioned	Expenditure incurred
All India Harijan Sevak Sangh, New Delhi	359,400	336,218	324,000	318,883	293,000	290,347	381,500	343,081
Bharatiya Depressed Classes League, New Delhi	266,115	278,531	225,000	221,076	222,300	221,586	167,948	120,166

Iswar Saran Ashram, Allahabad	90,000	87,232	77,000	73,650	48,880	62,104	153,110	48,360
Bharat Dalit Sevak Sangh, Poona	48,000	44,585	47,700	58,801	78,940	N.A.	85,367	85,367
Indian Red Cross Society	—	—	—	—	—	—	52,650	39,855
Ramakrishna Mission, Narendrapur, 24 Parganas	—	—	—	—	—	—	32,470	32,470
Hind Sweepers Sevak Samaj, Delhi	—	—	—	—	—	—	27,970	N.A.

Other Backward Classes has proposed the establishment of "an inter-caste, inter-religious marriage bureau."[29]

Some of the recommendations made by the State Minis-

TABLE 3–4

Name of the State or Union Territory	Expenditure incurred during Second Five Year Plan	Provision made for Third Five Year Plan	Allocation made during 1961–62	Expenditure incurred during 1961–62
Andhra Pradesh	4.12	3.00	0.50	0.50
Assam	5.03	8.30	0.45	0.42
Bihar	2.81	2.00	0.40	0.38
Gujarat	2.50	—	—	—
Jammu & Kashmir	—	—	—	—
Kerala	0.50	—	—	—
Madhya Pradesh	3.36	5.00	1.00	0.33
Madras	1.40	—	—	—
Maharashtra	—	—	—	—
Mysore	0.44	—	—	—
Orissa	13.84	2.00	0.20	0.20
Punjab	—	—	—	—
Rajasthan	9.52	—	—	—
Uttar Pradesh	0.61	2.50	0.50	0.496
West Bengal	2.18	3.00	0.60	0.51
Andaman & Nicobar Islands	—	—	—	—
Delhi	0.14	1.00	0.20	0.154
Himachal Pradesh	0.57	—	0.063	0.063
Laccadive	—	—	—	—
Manipur	—	—	—	—
Pondicherry	—	—	—	—
Tripura	—	—	—	—
GRAND TOTAL	47.02	26.80	3.913	3.053

Organizations Working Among the Scheduled Castes, Rs. in Lakhs

---

29. Blitz, November 26, 1966.

ters Conference on Backward Classes, held in New Delhi, 1958, were:

(i) There would be no separate institutions, hostels or colonies exclusively for Harijans. In these at least 10 percent non-Harijans should be taken as far as possible, to give them a mixed character, Non-Harijans up to this number could be given the same facilities as are admissible to Scheduled Castes to encourage them to join such colonies or institutions.

(ii) The name 'Harijan' should be removed from the existing institutions, hostels or colonies wherever it exists.

(iii) In all general hostels controlled or assisted by the Government, at least 10 percent seats should be reserved for Harijans.

(iv) No assistance or loan should be given by the Government to General Housing Co-operative Societies unless they have 10 percent of their members from Scheduled Castes.[30]

To foster social habits among the people, "the study team on social welfare and welfare of Backward Classes" recommended:

(a) Steps may be taken which may lead to marriages between Harijans and non-Harijans. This should more be an indirect result of a congenial atmosphere that voluntary workers and organizations would have created rather than be the outcome of any direct campaign for this purpose.

(b) Social workers and voluntary organisations working in the field of Harijan welfare and social reform should persuade carefully selected caste-Hindu families to adopt Harijan children.[31]

---

30. *Report of the Commissioner for Scheduled Castes and Scheduled Tribes*, 1957–58, Part I, p. 23.
31. *Report of the Study Team on Social Welfare and Welfare of Backward Classes*, para. 13, p. 130.

Yet another device suggested for the removal of untouchability is to effect reforms in menial jobs like scavenging, to make these lowly professions attractive. As usual, the Government of Bombay took a pioneering lead in appointing a committee called "The Scavengers Living Conditions Enquiry Committee" to study and inquire into the working conditions of scavengers and suggest measures for improvement, as early as 1949. The recommendations of this committee chiefly dealt with better pay scales for scavengers, introduction of hygienic methods of carrying night soil, cleaning of streets, housing conditions, etc. The Government of India has taken some of the recommendations of this committee for implementation in other States to improve the lot of untouchables, who are mostly scavengers. Untouchability is based on unclean occupations, and it is because the sweepers and chamars pursue such unclean professions that they were rated very low in Hindu society. The idea of segregation emerged from the pursuance of unclean occupations by Harijans. So, to remove this evil, Harijans should give up these unclean professions and take up education to elevate their position in society. But this drastic step cannot be taken at once, for even though it may hold good with younger generations who are in their school-going stage, it is likely to affect Harijans who are already in service as scavengers. Likewise, the introduction of scientific methods in scavenging would do more harm than good, as it is likely to retrench most of the scavengers who are unable to take up any profession owing to illiteracy. So the only remedy for this problem, as suggested by the study team:

> If the prejudice of caste-Hindus against working in particular professions is removed by making the profession attractive both from the point of its content and returns, the stigma of untouchability involved in asso-

ciating with such a profession would diminish. It would be desirable, therefore, to invite caste-Hindus to work in these occupations.[32]

Another concession offered to the Harijans is the grant of legal aid. The Central Advisory Board for Harijan Welfare in the meeting held in October, 1957, suggested the scheme of introducing legal aid to Scheduled Castes by all States. In compliance with the recommendations of the Central Advisory Board, States chalked out a program for granting legal aid for the welfare of Scheduled Castes. The grants made by States during 1956-57 and 1957-58 are given in Table 3-5:[33]

TABLE 3–5

State	Grant-in-aid paid during		Plan provision
	1956–57	1957–58	
Andhra (Telengana Region)	—	3,000	24,000
Bihar	1,000	10,000	100,000
Bombay	—	2,000	N.A.
Mysore	—	2,500*	—
Rajasthan	5,300	2,500	40,000
Orissa	1,000	1,250	10,000
Delhi	200	1,600	9,000
Kerala	—	500	5,000
Madhya Pradesh	—	1,000	10,000

* Includes special health facilities and relief grants also.

But the Scheduled Castes are not able to utilize the free legal aid to fight discrimination in hotels, temples, public wells, Panchayat committee meetings, etc. Commenting on

32. *Ibid.*, para. 22, p. 195.
33. *Report of the Commissioner for Scheduled Castes and Scheduled Tribes,* 1957–58, para. 31, p. 22.

this situation, the committee of Congress members of Parliament says: "This indicates the dominating influence of the stronger sections and the terrible fear haunting on the Scheduled Castes to report and to take advantage of the free legal assistance benefits."[34] The fact that untouchability still prevails in India is no exaggeration. The problem of unifying the Harijans with other sections of society does not seem to be as easy as it has been thought. The Untouchability (offences) Act, 1955, has served to a certain extent in mitigating the evil of untouchability, but the major part of the Act appears to be nothing more than a comforting consolation to Harijans and a decorative piece of the Government. In the light of frequent Harijan clashes with caste Hindus (the Silambanur Case and the Sangrur Case), we have to admit that the Untouchability (offences) Act, 1955, is ineffective. To make it more effective, it has been suggested that six months' imprisonment or a fine of Rs. 500 will not be an effective measure to check untouchability. Punishment should be more rigorous if the act is to be effective. The caste system in Hindu society is still a powerful factor in determining social status and mere educative process would not be effective in stunting the rigidities of the caste system. The Commissioner for Scheduled Castes and Scheduled Tribes himself has admitted that untouchability is still found in many parts of India. He observes:

> But it is to be admitted that untouchability is still practised in many parts of the country, in some form or the other, the most common ones being:
> (i) denying access to public restaurants and hotels and the use of utensils kept in such places for general public;
> (ii) not allowing the use of wells, tanks, water taps and other sources of water;
> (iii) denial of service by barbers, *dhobie,* etc., and

---

34. *The Indian Express,* August 31, 1966.

(iv) denial of hired accommodation to Scheduled Caste persons when posted in the rural areas.[35]

Apart from these grievances, another interesting fact that has been brought to notice is that the temple entry is restricted to Harijans on the ground that the temples have been built by private people to counteract the effects of legislative enactment regarding temple entry for untouchables. Banaras and Kerala have demonstrated the ineffectiveness of legislative enactment against private institutions. Hence private institutions do not come within the ambit of legislative enactment. To make the Untouchability (offences) Act, 1955, more effective the Government should take steps to prevent discrimination against untouchables in private temples by similar legislation.

Facts recorded by the committee of Congress members of Parliament, the Registrar General of India, the Gokhale Institute of Politics and Economics, and the Untouchability Committee under the chairmanship of Mr. Eliyaperumal, throw light on the cases of discrimination against untouchables. According to the committee of Congress members of Parliament, "members of Panchayats belonging to Scheduled Castes are not allowed to sit on cots or on carpets in equality with other members."[36] The reports contain pathetic revelations about the separation of Scheduled Caste children from others in village schools, discrimination in hotels, denial of access to public wells, shameful treatment of the Scheduled Caste members of the Panchayats, etc.

Village surveys conducted by the Superintendent of Census operations in the States of Orissa, West Bengal, Punjab, and the Union Territory of Himachal Pradesh give information about the practice of untouchability in "Sample Villages." Poor knowledge of the law and attach-

---

35. *Report of the Commissioner for Scheduled Castes and Scheduled Tribes*, 1961–62, Part I, para. 3.2, p. 6.
36. *Indian Express*, August 31, 1966.

ment to time-old social status are the reported causes for the prevalence of untouchability.

So it has been felt, that the Ministry of Community Development and Cooperation should take measures to remove untouchability at the Block level. With the exception of the Gujarat Government, the other states so far have not evinced interest as regards this measure.

Accepting facts recorded by these impartial reports, it could be pointed out that education has not changed the basic social values of the caste-ridden society.

The mere passing of the Untouchability (offences) Act, 1955, is not enough. It should convince the untouchables, particularly in villages, that they are relieved of their shackles and they are in no way inferior to others. It is the failure of creating this confidence among the untouchables that is responsible for the prevalence of untouchability in the country. As Ambedkar observed:

> Untouchability as a touch-me-not-ism may be gradually vanishing in towns, although I am doubtful if this is happening in any appreciable degree. But I am quite certain Untouchability as a propensity on the part of the Hindus to discriminate against the Untouchables will not vanish either in towns or in villages within an imaginable distance of time.[37]

This observation, made prior to Independence, holds good even today. The reasons are not far to seek. In Ambedkar's words: "You cannot untwist a two-thousand-year twist of the human mind and turn it in the opposite direction."[38] Hence decades of social reform cannot untwist the century-old twist of the human mind. It has to be twisted by natural evolution and gradual social transformation.

We may now question that, in spite of legislative enact-

37. B. R. Ambedkar, *What Congress and Gandhi Have Done to the Untouchables*, 1946, p. 195.
38. *Ibid.*

ments, voluntary efforts, and Constitutional guarantee for the abolition of untouchability, it is still prevalent in the country (villages) defying all solutions. Why? There are certain reasons for this. First, efforts have been made to abolish distinctions between caste-Hindus and untouchables, but corresponding efforts to remove untouchability among the innumerable subdivisions of untouchables have not been made. Such a measure is very important for the rapid eradication of untouchability. This was pointed out by the president of the All-Cochin Rural Congress in a conference of Pulayas (untouchable caste) as early as 1939:

> The caste Hindus had been the targets of unsparing criticism for the social inequalities and disabilities of the depressed classes. But, nonetheless, there was the important fact, studiously hidden from the public, that the very social evils against which the depressed classes had chafed were rampant among the depressed classes themselves, for they were observing Untouchability and even unapproachability in their relations with those below them in the social scale.[39]

Commenting on the effects of untouchability, F. G. Bailey observes: "In this, its most rigid institution, the localized structure of caste-groups has failed entirely to adapt itself to changed economic conditions."[40] He proceeds: "The new economy demands social mobility: but untouchability is at once a cornerstone of caste and an insuperable obstacle to mobility. Localization and untouchability are the rocks against which beats the tide of the new economy."[41] Thus, the economic dependence of untouchables on other sections of society is also responsible for the prevalence of untouchability.

Some critics argue that caste as the sole identity for con-

39. Quoted in O'Malley, *Modern India and the West*, 1941, p. 381.
40. F. G. Bailey, *Caste and the Economic Frontier*, 1958, p. 272.
41. *Ibid.*, p. 275.

ferring special concessions to Scheduled Castes is responsible for the retention of untouchability. According to them, untouchability as the prime test for classifying Scheduled Castes is defective, as it contributes to the retention of untouchability by making people more caste-conscious. It is true that socio-religious disabilities were thrust on Harijans in the past, which are chiefly responsible for their degraded position in society. But apart from social disabilities there are other considerations to be given weight—economic conditions and educational advancement. Any concession to Scheduled Castes on the basis of untouchability does not produce lasting results. Economic facts should be given due weight for achieving fruitful results. Besides, scavengers are remaining scavengers, whereas the well-off among the Harijans are enjoying the special concessions. The ambiguities resulting from the caste criterion in classifying Scheduled Castes are reported in the specification of the lists of Scheduled Castes, under Art. 340 (1) and (2); the president issued the lists of Scheduled Castes through the Constitution (Scheduled Castes) Order, 1950, and the Constitution (Scheduled Castes) (Part C States), Order, 1951. There was confusion about the wrong inclusion and exclusion of castes in these lists of Scheduled Castes. Hence, suggestions were made by the Commissioner for Scheduled Castes and Scheduled Tribes for the revision of the lists. Accordingly, the lists were again amended by passing the Scheduled Castes and Scheduled Tribes Order (Amendment) Act, 1956. The President accordingly issued the Scheduled Castes Lists (Modification) Order, 1956, specifying the Scheduled Castes under the reorganized States. The Government of India also issued a list of Scheduled Castes in respect of the State of Jammu and Kashmir, in the Constitution (Jammu and Kashmir) Scheduled Castes Order, 1956. The Commissioner for Scheduled Castes and Scheduled Tribes has pointed out the necessity for further examination of these lists, as there are ambiguities in them. He pointed out:

It appears that there is a possibility of certain persons belonging to some non-Scheduled "Communities" and having surnames similar to those of some of the Scheduled Castes, trying to avail of benefits provided specially for Scheduled Caste persons. For instance, a person belonging to the Pasi community, which is a group within Khatri caste of Punjab, may claim that he is a Scheduled Caste because Pasi caste is included in the list of the Scheduled Castes for that State.[42]

In view of the ambiguities arising out of caste, sub-caste complications, and synonymous caste names, critics urge for the emphasis on "occupational test" and "economic test."

Presuming that difficulties may arise by making caste the prime consideration for classifying Scheduled Castes, Mahavir Tyagi insisted on substituting the term "class" for "caste" in the course of the Constituent Assembly Debates. He observed:

I therefore submit, Sir, that the Scheduled Castes should now go and in place of Scheduled Caste, the words "Scheduled Classes" be substituted so that we may not inadvertently perpetuate the communal slur on our Parliaments. . . . I do not believe in the minorities on community basis, but minorities must exist on economic basis, on political basis, and on an ideological basis and those minorities must have protection.[43]

Here the assertion is that if caste is the test for classification, the more articulate among the caste group will assert themselves. But if class is made the basis of classification,

---

42. *Report of the Commissioner for Scheduled Castes and Scheduled Tribes,* 1961–62, Part I, para. 2.2, p. 5.
43. *Constituent Assembly Debates,* May–June 1949, pp. 344–45.

the interests of the weaker sections would be represented. This idea has been expressed by different Committees appointed time and again to probe into the problem of Backward Classes. The study team on social welfare and welfare of Backward Classes pointed out:

> However, the ultimate objective would be to entirely eliminate criteria other than economic so that backwardness would be judged only on the basis of economic considerations. It is envisaged that the economic basis of need would then constitute the nucleus of a system of social security which can be extended in proportion to the expanding national resources.[44]

It is further argued that "occupation" or the unclean professions constitute the basis of untouchability. Hence, occupation forms the cause and untouchability is the effect. It is appropriate therefore to make the cause—"the pursuit of unclean occupations"—which rendered pollution and accorded inferior social position, the criterion for classifying Scheduled Castes. But unfortunately, the effect—untouchability, which resulted from pollution—is made the test for classifying Scheduled Castes. This provision enables the most articulate sections of Scheduled Castes to enjoy Constitutional privileges. If occupation is made the criterion, the chances of people among the Scheduled Castes with higher economic standards to come under the list of Scheduled Castes would be faint. Those who are economically and educationally advanced would be eliminated from the lists of Scheduled Castes, who would otherwise be included by the test of "caste" or the application of "untouchability" only. Such a policy would be rational and just. It is reasonable to differentiate between the advanced and the backward, even among the Sched-

---

44. *Report of the Study Team on Social Welfare and Welfare of Backward Classes,* 1959, para. 12, p. 126.

uled Castes, by the application of economic test and occupation. Those who are advanced should compete with the rest of the population and take their rightful place among the advanced classes. It is the duty of the nation to render assistance to the weaker sections of society in consonance with the establishment of a classless and casteless society. Such a policy would not only minimize the number of people getting included in the list of Scheduled Castes, but also facilitate the scanty resources at the disposal of the country, to be utilized for the betterment of weaker sections and provide them social security. The shortcomings of the criterion of untouchability have been amply illustrated by the Study Team:

> It was observed that 24% of the scholarship-holders in Assam, 32% in Bihar, 20% in Madhya Pradesh and 25% in Orissa, belonged to families having an income of Rs. 1501 and above per annum. The percentage of scholarship-holders in the lower income groups were found to be proportionately much less. Similarly with regard to financial assistance for housing, it was found that among those who get assistance, persons having comparatively higher incomes are found to be relatively numerous.[45]

Besides, untouchability has economic basis in the same degree as social basis. The only way to improve their economic status is by creating a new occupational structure by means of education. Lack of education is responsible for their poverty and low economic position. Once their economic position improves, they would automatically be improving their social position. So the abolition of untouchability rests chiefly on the evolution of a new socio-economic status for them through special concessions in the field of education, public service, and representation in legislatures and Parliament.

---

45. *Ibid.*, para. 14, p. 126.

Elevation of Scheduled Tribes

The problem of Scheduled Tribes is peculiar, as they were subjected not only to social ostracism but also segregation from the rest of the population. As a result of this segregation, the problem of classifying the Scheduled Tribes and specifying Scheduled Areas have become imperative. For this purpose, a historical perspective as to the origin of the terms "Scheduled Tribes" and "Scheduled Areas" is necessary.

Origin of the term Scheduled Tribes

The term "Scheduled Tribes" is of recent origin, which came into being with the birth of the Republican Constitution of India on January 26, 1950. Prior to that, Scheduled Tribes were variously termed as "Aboriginals," "Adivasis," "Forest Tribes," "Hill Tribes," and "Primitive Tribes." Up to 1919, they were included along with other categories of Backward Classes under the head of "Depressed Classes." It was decided in the Indian Legislative Council discussions, 1916, that the term "Depressed Classes" should include:

a) criminal and wandering tribes,
b) aboriginal tribes and
c) untouchables.

Similarly in 1917, Sir Henry Sharp, Educational Commissioner, Government of India, prepared a list of Depressed Classes, wherein he included aboriginal or hill tribes, depressed classes, and criminal tribes all in one. The need for separating "aboriginal tribes" from "Depressed Classes" was felt by the Indian Franchise Committee in 1919. Since then, the tribals were accorded a separate nomenclature. In the 1931 Census, we come across the term "Primitive Tribes" to specify the tribal population of India, who were till then termed "Forest Tribes" or "Hill Tribes."

The 1941 Census just mentions "tribes," all adjectives for the first time being dropped to qualify the tribes. Today, under the Constitution of India, the tribals are Scheduled and are popularly termed "Scheduled Tribes." The term "Scheduled Tribes" is defined under Art. 336 (25) as: " 'Scheduled Tribes' means such tribes or tribal communities or parts of or groups within such tribes or tribal communities as are deemed under article 342 to be Schedulued Tribes for the purpose of this Constitution."

In consonance with Art. 342 (1), the President issued the lists specifying Scheduled Tribes. These lists are contained in the Schedule appended to the following orders:

1. The Constitution (Scheduled Tribes) Order, 1950.
2. The Constitution (Scheduled Tribes) (Part C States) Order, 1951.
3. The Scheduled Tribes Lists (Modification) Order, 1956.
4. The Constitution (Andaman and Nicobar Islands) Scheduled Tribes Order, 1959.

Some discrepancies have arisen as regards the classification of Scheduled Tribes. The observations made by the Tribal Welfare Committee of the Indian Conference of Social Work, 1950, were: "The present schedule of tribes in India is not considered satisfactory by the committee, for it does not take into consideration an overall view of all the features that distinguish the tribes from other sections of the population."[46] The committee therefore recommended: " (1) that the habitat, (2) economic life, (3) social organization, (4) religious beliefs, (5) mode of life and (6) the art and folk-lore and the dialect be taken into consideration while drafting the amending bill to revise The Constitution (Scheduled Tribes) Order, 1950."[47]

It was felt that the tribal population was remarkably re-

46. *Report of the Commissioner for Scheduled Castes and Scheduled Tribes,* 1951, Appendix I, p. 54.
47. *Ibid.*

duced in the list of Scheduled Tribes prepared in consonance with the Constitution (Scheduled Tribes) Order,
1950. A memorandum was submitted to the President by
H. W. Kunzru and fifteen other members of Parliament
on December 17, 1950. The points dealt with in the
Memorandum were:

> Firstly, no adequate reasons were furnished by the
> Government for the reduction of 33 percent of the total
> tribal population, if the general trend of increase of the
> Indian population as given in the Census of 1951 was
> taken into consideration. Secondly, it is impossible to
> agree that as compared to the figures of 1941, the
> strength of tribal population could be reduced by 6.3
> millions in 1950, unless this was calculated in an arbi-
> trary manner. For instance, in the figures given by the
> Government, the tribal population in Madhya Pradesh
> has been reduced from 4.44 millions to 2.459 millions,
> i.e., by nearly 50 percent. In the same manner, the tribal
> population of Rajasthan has been reduced from 1.551
> millions to 0.442 millions or nearly 75 percent. Simi-
> larly, the tribal population in Assam, Bihar, Orissa, Hy-
> derabad, West Bengal has been considerably reduced.[48]

Now, the question arises as to the criteria to be adopted
in classifying Scheduled Tribes. Of all the categories of
Backward Classes, the Scheduled Castes is the only category having a precise criterion to classify them. But all
other categories of Backward Classes suffer for want of
precise criteria. The tribal Welfare Committee of the Indian Conference of Social Work, 1950, divided the tribal
population into four main discernible divisions:

> (i) Tribals who confine themselves to original forest
> habitats and are still distinctive in their pattern of life.

48. Extract of a Memorandum submitted to the Backward Classes
Commission, on behalf of Bharatiya Adimjati Sevak Sangh, Delhi, appeared in *Vanyajati* (Journal), Vol. 3, No. 1, 1955, p. 33.

These may be termed as tribal communities;

(ii) Tribals who have more or less settled down in rural areas taking to agriculture and other allied occupations. This category of people may be recognised as semitribal communities;

(iii) Tribals who have migrated to urban or semi-urban and rural areas and are engaged in "civilized" occupations in industries and other vocations and who have discriminatingly adopted traits and culture of the other population of the country. These may be classed as Acculturated Tribal Communities;

(iv) Totally assimilated tribals.[49]

By tribals is usually meant those who pursue hunting and fishing as their primary occupation. The classification of tribes becomes difficult as the tribes of India do not present a homogeneous ethnic stock. The tribes present complex diversity in cultural patterns, social set-up, language, etc. As a result of this, it is difficult to prescribe uniform standards for classifying tribes throughout the country. If we take tribal organization as the criterion, difficulties arise, as the tribal organization varies from tribe to tribe. Some tribes are more advanced, while others are below average. The Todas and Onges present very peculiar social structure and are extremely backward.

Under the auspices of the Bharatiya Adimjati Sevak Sangh, a conference was held on April 23, 1956, at Chhindwara to discuss the problems of the Scheduled Tribes. B. H. Mehta defined the tribals as follows: "Real tribals have as their characteristics hunting and fishing as their chief occupations. Their social organization is also peculiar. They have a chief as their head and a tribal assembly guides them in all matters."[50] M. Narasinga Rao further suggested: "The Scheduled Tribes should be classified

---

49. *Report of the Commissioner for Scheduled Castes and Scheduled Tribes*, 1951, p. 54.
50. Extract appeared in *'Vanyajati'* (Journal) Vol. 4, July, 1956, p. 57.

according to the degree of backwardness, and facilities should be given to them according to the degree of backwardness of each group."[51]

As the Commissioner for Scheduled Castes and Scheduled Tribes, 1951, pointed out:

> No such uniform test has, however, been evolved for classifying Scheduled Tribes with the result that in view of divergent opinions held by Census authorities and public men from time to time, difficulties have been experienced in determining as to which tribe can rightly be included in or excluded from the Schedule of tribes. I consider that some definite criterion for this purpose must also be devised so that full justice is done at the time of respecification of the "Scheduled Tribes."[52]

The common features found in tribes in various States are:[53]

"1. Tribal origin.

"2. Primitive way of life and habitation in remote and less easily accessible areas.

"3. General backwardness in all respects."

The Scheduled Areas and Scheduled Tribes Commission, 1960-61, further pointed out the anomalies that existed in the preparation of the list of the Scheduled Tribes.

> The old State of Hyderabad did not recognise Yenadis, the Yerukulas and Sugalis as Scheduled Tribes, whereas the old Andhra State recognised them as such and with abundant justification. The Yenadis and Yerukulas belong to that category of tribals who have emerged from the hills but not yet taken roots in the plains. They are more or less wandering without a place for rest and without occupation. Similar is the case of

---

51. *Ibid.,* p. 29.

52. *Report of the Commissioner for Scheduled Castes and Scheduled Tribes,* 1951, p. 9.

53. *Ibid.*

Gaddis who are found in the Himachal Pradesh and the adjoining Punjab Hills. In Himachal Pradesh they are recognised as Scheduled Tribes only in the Scheduled Areas where they do not live.[54]

It is also pointed out that because of territorial test some tribes are excluded from the lists.

Another observation made by the Commission was, as regards the stratification of tribes among the four discernible divisions of tribals, in compliance with the degree of backwardness prevalent among them. The Commission pointed out:

> We feel that at the base of these four layers is the class of tribals which is in an extremely underdeveloped stage and at the topmost level amongst the tribals is a layer that can very well afford to forgo any further help. We feel that this lowest layer needs the utmost consideration at the hands of the Government.[55]

For illustrative purpose, a list of non-vocal section of tribes in various States is furnished in Table 3-6:[56]

TABLE 3-6

1. Andhra Pradesh	Abuj Madia	Kotia-Khind
Lingadhari Koya	(Bastar)	Hill Bhuiya of
Chenchu	Birhor	Bhuiya Pirth
Yenadi	Sehariya	Lanjia Saora
2. Assam	Binjhwar	Koya
Mikir	6. Madras	Paidi Bhuiya
Abor	Kadar	of Bonai
3. Bihar	Irular	10. Rajasthan
Birhor	Paniyan	Schria
Asur	Malyali	11. West Bengal
Korwa	7. Maharashtra	Asur
Kharia	Katkari	Birhor

54. *Report of the Scheduled Areas and Scheduled Tribes Commission,* Vol. 1, 1960–61, Chairman's foreword to the President.
55. *Ibid.*
56. *Ibid.,* p. 3.

Sauria Paharia
4. Kerala
   Kadar
   Irrular
   Paniyan
   Kattunayakam
   Vishavan
5. Madhya Pradesh
   Pahadi Korwa
   Baiga in
      Baigachuk

Hill Goud
   (Chanda Dist.)
8. Mysore
   Kadu-Kuruba
   Senu-Kuruba
   Koraga
   Irular
9. Orissa
   Birhor
   Bonodo Proraja
   Juang

Sauria Paharia
Toto
Rabha
Lepcha
12. Andaman and
    Nicobar Islands
Jarawa
Onge
Sentinelese
Shom Pen.

Total population of the "Primitive Tribes" in 1931 was 24,613,848. The main figures of distribution are recorded in Table 3-7:[57]

TABLE 3–7

Ajmer-Merwara	18,904
Andamans and Nicobar	10,405
Assam	1,678,419
Bengal	1,927,299
Bihar and Orissa	6,681,228
Bombay	2,841,080
Central Provinces	4,065,277
Coorg	1,089
Madras	1,262,369
United Provinces	400,184
Provinces	21,092,610
States	3,521,238
Baroda	313,273
Central India	1,342,081
Cochin	1,048
Gwalior	281,033
Hyderabad	222,806
Rajputana	802,178
Travancore	21,728
Western India States	495,834
Total	24,613,848

57. *Census Report 1931*, Appendix II, p. 503.

According to 1941 Census, the tribal population was 24,712,000. The largest tribal groups were as in Table 3-8:[58]

TABLE 3-8

Tribe	Number	States where chiefly found
Gond	3,201,004	Andhra Pradesh, Bihar, Madhya Pradesh, Maharashtra, Orissa.
Santal	2,732,266	Bihar, Orissa, West Bengal.
Bhil	2,330,270	Andhra Pradesh, Gujarat, Madhya Pradesh, Maharashtra, Rajasthan.
Oraon	1,122,926	Bihar, Madhya Pradesh, Orissa, West Bengal.
Khond	744,904	Andhra Pradesh, Madhya Pradesh, Orissa.
Munda	706,869	Bihar, Madhya Pradesh, Orissa, West Bengal.
Boro Kacharis	594,979	Assam, West Bengal, Tripura.

According to the 1951 Census, the tribal population was 22,525,477, that is, 6.23 percent of the total population. The 1961 Census records the tribal population at 29,846,300, that is, 6.80 percent of the total population.

Evolution of the term "Scheduled Areas"

The administration of tribal areas was totally neglected by the British. It was only in 1874 that some measures were taken for the protection of tribal interests, by classifying the areas populated by tribals as Scheduled tracts. The Government of India Act, 1919, effected further improvements in the administration of Scheduled tracts. By section 7 of Government of India Act, 1919, the Secretary

58. Quoted in *Report of the Scheduled Areas and Scheduled Tribes Commission,* Vol. 1, p. 7.

of State was empowered to declare any part of India as backward and give instructions for the administration. Section 52-A (2) empowered the Governor General in Council to declare any territory to be a backward tract and, with the sanction of the Secretary of State, to direct that the Government of India Act shall apply to the territory with such exceptions and modifications as may be prescribed in his notification.

The backward areas were divided into two classes: (i) those wholly excluded tracts, and (ii) those in which the scheme should be introduced with modifications. In accordance with this formula, the following areas were declared Backward tracts.

1. Laccadive Islands and Minicoy
2. Chittagong hill tracts
3. Spiti
4. Angul district
5. Darjeeling district
6. Lahaul
7. Ganjam Agency
8. Godavari Agency
9. Chota-Nagpur Division
10. Sambalpur district
11. Santal Parganas district
12. Garo hills district
13. British portion of Khasi and Jaintia hills excluding Shillong Municipality and Cantonment
14. Mikir hills
15. North Cachar hills
16. Naga hills
17. Lushai hills
18. Sadiya Balipara and Lakhimpur Frontier and tracts.

From 1919 onward, the two familiar terms connoting tribal tracts were: "Wholly Excluded Areas" and "Areas of Modified Exclusion."

The Act of 1935 took special measures for the protection of tribal tracts. For the first time in the Constitutional history of India prior to Independence, interest was evinced in safeguarding the tribal population. The tribal areas were reclassified into "Total" and "Partially Excluded Areas" which were self-governed units. The two important considerations for classifying areas as "Excluded Areas" were the preponderance of tribal population and the inaccessibility of those regions for the introduction of any regular system of administration. It was taken for granted that the tribes were politically backward. Section 19 of Fifth Schedule defined the terms "Backward Areas" and "Backward Tribes" as follows: " 'Backward Areas' and 'Backward Tribes' mean respectively such areas and tribes as His Majesty in Council may from time to time declare to be areas and tribes to which a special system of representation is more appropriate."

The Sixth Schedule denoted Excluded Areas and Partially Excluded Areas as stated below:

Part I Excluded Areas

The North-East Frontier (Sadiya Balipara and Lakhimpur tracts)

The Naga hills district

The Lushai hills district

The Chittagong hill tracts

Part II Partially Excluded Areas

The North Cachar hills (in the Cachar district)

The Garo hills district

The Mikir hills (in Nowgong and Sibsagar districts)

The British portion of the Khasi and Jaintia hills district, other than the Shillong Municipality and Cantonment

The district of Angul

The Chota-Nagpur division

The district of Sambalpur

The Santal Parganas district

The Darjeeling district
The Laccadive Islands including Minicoy
The Ganjam, Vizagapatam and Godavari Agencies

The Sub-Committees of the Constituent Assembly pointed out some shortcomings of the Act of 1935. It stated that the "Excluded Areas" could not be regarded as covering the entire tribal population of the country. As tribes are scattered over different parts of the country, mostly in non-excluded areas, any future classification of Scheduled Tribes and Scheduled Areas should consider the case of tribes concentrated in non-excluded areas of the 1935 Act. The Sub-Committee also pointed out the futility of grouping tribal areas into Partial and Total Exclusion areas, as they produced no tangible results in improving the social, economic, and educational conditions of the aborigines. The recommendations made by the Sub-Committee found place in the Republican Constitution of India, 1950. From the above analysis we find that the terms "Scheduled tracts," "Backward tracts," "Backward areas," "Excluded and Partially Excluded areas" have culminated in the term "Scheduled Areas" under the Constitution of India today.

British tribal policy

The Scheduled Tribes were neglected and isolated from the rest of the population during the British regime. The tribes were studied for academic interest without any attempt to improve their conditions of life. It looked as if the tribes were preserved for purpose of display in the anthropological museum. They not only pursued the policy of isolating tribes from the purview of general administration, but encouraged the Zamindars (landowners) and moneylenders to exploit them. The encroachment on the tribal rights, particularly in the ownership of forest lands, often culminated in the rebellions. The most noted tribal rebellions were the Malpharia rising of 1772; the rebellion in Chota Nagpur, 1789-1808, which came to an end with armed intervention by the British; the mutiny of the Ho's of Singhbhum in 1831; the Khond uprising of 1846; the Santal rebellion of 1855; the Sardari agitation of 1887; the insurrection of the Andhra Agency; the Rampa rebellion in East Godavari; and the Bastar rising of 1911.

The uprisings and vociferous demands of certain domineering tribes aroused in British administrators the need for reforming them. The first step in this direction was the classification of tribal areas into Scheduled tracts, to safeguard the interests of the tribes from neighboring tracts. Thus, the tribes were given a voice in the administration of their tracts. From the administrative point of view, the policy of segregation and division followed by the British was healthy, insofar as it gave the tribals the right of self-determination. But on the social side such a policy was derogatory.

Yet another defect of British policy was the assumption that tribals were politically backward, incapable of exercising franchise. With this assumption, the tribals were kept away from the pale of political institutions and were deprived of their participation in the national life of the country. But the Franchise Committee realized the need for giving representation to the tribes. The Committee observed:

It is, in our opinion, of the greatest importance that the interests of these people, who live a life entirely apart from the rest of the population of India, should be protected by effective representation in the Councils, or, if this is not possible, by some other arrangement in the new Constitution.[59]

59. *Report of the Indian Franchise Committee,* Vol. 1, 1932, para. 339, p. 135.

The tribals were not elected to the legislatures but were nominated by the Governor for names sake. The Christian missionaries working in the tribal area enjoyed the opportunity of representing tribals in the legislatures of the country.

The problem concerning the inclusion or exclusion of Scheduled Tribes from the purview of Constitutional reforms did engage the attention of the British Government. Lord Eustace Percy remarked: "It is the most difficult problem in the world as to exactly how far you are to keep back in cold storage the aboriginal population, and as to how far you are to lead it on towards absorption into the wider community around it."[60] The disadvantage of safeguarding certain tracts of land and their population were widely discussed in the British Parliament. Even among the British, some bitterly criticized the British policy of isolating tribes. Earl Winterton commented:

> I believe far more in assimilation than in isolation. I do not think you want to turn areas into modern whipsnades where you have picturesque survivals and where Englishmen are able to go out and say, "This is a most interesting ethnological race of people divided by 500 or 1,000 years from the rest of India.[61]

A survey of the socio-economic and educational conditions of the tribes under British administration clearly reveals that nothing tangible was done toward the permanent rehabilitation of the tribes. In the economic field, by encouraging shifting cultivation, they introduced some complications in the land problem. In the social field, they fostered segregation. And in the political field, they kept them away from participation in the national life of the country. Independent India has inherited from the

---

60. Quoted in G. S. Ghurye, *The Scheduled Tribes,* 2nd edit., 1959, p. 117.
   61. *Ibid.,* p. 118.

British a complex tribal problem to be solved in the right perspective, in the larger interests of society.

The Scheduled Tribes and the Constitution

Coming to the Constitutional provisions for safeguarding the interests of Scheduled Tribes, it may be remarked that the birth of the Indian Constitution in 1950 marks a red-letter day in the history of equality of rights. A directive for the resurrection of backward Classes is given under Art. 46. It states:

> The State shall promote with special care the educational and economic interests of the weaker sections of the people, and, in particular, of the Scheduled Castes and the Scheduled Tribes, and shall protect them from social injustice and all forms of exploitation.

Further, concession is provided under Art. 164 (1) as follows: "Provided that in the States of Bihar, Madhya Pradesh and Orissa, there shall be a Minister in charge of tribal welfare who may in addition be in charge of the Welfare of the Scheduled Castes and backward classes or any other work."

The Fifth Schedule of the Constitution is related to the provisions concerning the administration and control of Scheduled Areas and Scheduled Tribes. The Sixth Schedule deals with the administration of Tribal Areas in Assam.

The Fifth Schedule, Part B, para. 4, provides for the setting up of Tribes Advisory Councils in certain States:

> 1) There shall be established in each State having Scheduled Areas therein and, if the President so directs, also in any State having Scheduled Tribes but not Scheduled Areas therein, a Tribes Advisory Council consisting of not more than twenty members of whom,

as nearly as may be, three-fourths shall be the representatives of the Scheduled Tribes in the Legislative Assembly of the State:

Provided that if the number of representatives of the Scheduled Tribes in the Legislative Assembly of the State is less than the number of seats in the Tribes Advisory Council to be filled by such representatives, the remaining seats shall be filled by other members of those tribes.

2) It shall be the duty of the Tribes Advisory Council to advise on such matters pertaining to the welfare and advancement of the Scheduled Tribes in the State as may be referred to them by the Governor.

3) The Governor may make rules prescribing or regulating, as the case may be,—

  a) the number of members of the Council, the mode of their appointment and the appointment of the Chairman of the Council and of the officers and servants thereof;

  b) the conduct of its meetings and its procedure in general; and

  c) all other incidental matters.

The introduction of the Tribes Advisory Councils forms a notable feature of the special provisions made for the welfare of Scheduled Tribes in the Constitution. The representatives of Scheduled Tribes are made to study the welfare schemes for their advancement, and make suggestions to the Government as regards their working. These Advisory Councils go a long way in the formulation of Welfare Schemes, in accordance with the needs of the tribal population of the area concerned. Another novel feature of these councils is the inclusion of nontribal members in the councils which makes them broad based.

Table 3-9 gives a detailed account of the formation of these councils in various States:[62]

62. *Report of the Scheduled Areas and Scheduled Tribes Commission,* Vol. 1, Table 5, pp. 53–54.

TABLE 3-9

State	Date of notification	Date of formation
Andhra Pradesh	1-5-1954	1-5-1954
Bihar	14-8-1951	26-3-1952
Bombay	30-8-1952	5-3-1953
Gujarat	19-8-1960	8-11-1960
Hyderabad	1953	1953
Madhya Bharat	1952	1952
Madhya Pradesh	4-12-1950	4-12-1950
Madras	1951	1951
Maharashtra	29-8-1960	14-11-1960
Orissa	24-6-1950	24-6-1950
Punjab	26-6-1952	1952
Rajasthan	12-9-1952	1952
West Bengal	25-8-1953	25-8-1953

The meetings held by the Tribes Councils are recorded in Table 3–10.[63]

Some of the suggestions made by the Commissioner for making Tribes Advisory Councils more effective are:[64]

i) The meetings of the councils may be held by rotation in different tribal areas of the State concerned so that the deliberations may take place in surroundings familiar to the tribal leaders, and the members who have not seen these areas can get a chance of seeing the areas and meeting the Scheduled Tribes residing therein. After such meetings, the tribal leaders of the area may be invited to meet the members of the Tribes Advisory Council and express their difficulties if any and their requirements.

ii) Seminars may be arranged from time to time by

63. *Ibid.*, Table 6, p. 56.
64. *Report of the Commissioner for Scheduled Castes and Scheduled Tribes*, 1961–62, Part I, para. 17.15, pp. 118–19.

TABLE 8-10

State	Number of meetings prescribed in a year	Number of meetings held										
		1951	1952	1953	1954	1955	1956	1957	1958	1959	1960	1961–62
Andhra Pradesh	4	—	—	1*	3*	2*	1	—	3	4	3	N.A.
Bihar	2	—	—	1	1	1	1	—	1	2	2	N.A.
Gujarat	—	—	—	—	—	—	—	—	—	—	1	2
Madhya Pradesh	2	1	2†	5†	7†	5†	4†	N.A.	2	2	2	2
Madras	2	1	1	1	1	2	1	1	2	2	2	1
Maharashtra	2	—	1	1	2	2	2	1	2	2	1	1
Orissa	2	1	1	1	1	1	1	1	2	1	1	1
Punjab	1‡	—	—	1	—	2	1	1	2	2	2	2
Rajasthan	4	—	—	1	2	4	1	—	2	1	1	N.A.
West Bengal	2	—	—	1	2	2	—	—	1	2	3	N.A.

* Includes figures for Hyderabad region.
† Includes figures for Madhya Bharat region.
‡ As often as necessary but not less than once a year.

the Research authorities with participation of the members of the Tribes Advisory Councils, to discuss practical issues of tribal welfare from different aspects. Through participation in these seminars the members will be able to develop informed opinion on various issues.

iii) The members should be associated with formulation of schemes and evaluation and implementations of schemes. For this purpose sub-committees may be formed to go round the State and make on the spot studies, and the Assistant Commissioners for Scheduled Castes and Scheduled Tribes of the regions concerned may also be included in those sub-committees.

These suggestions have been accepted by the States of Bihar, Maharashtra, Madhya Pradesh, and Rajasthan. The Governments of Orissa, Gujarat, and West Bengal have not yet taken any decision. The Government of Andhra Pradesh has not accepted this proposal on the ground that it would involve additional expenditure. The Madras Government has not felt the need for such a sub-committee.

Part C of the Fifth Schedule deals with Scheduled Areas. It states:

1) In this Constitution, the expression 'Scheduled Areas' means such areas as the President may by order declare to be Scheduled Areas.

2) The President may at any time by order—
   (a) direct that the whole or any specialized part of a Scheduled Area shall cease to be a Scheduled Area or a part of such an area;
   (b) alter, but only by way of rectification of boundaries, any Scheduled Area;
   (c) on any alteration of the boundaries of a State or on the admission into the union or the establishment of a new State, declare any territory not previously included in any State to be, or to form part of, a Scheduled Area;

and any such order may contain such incidental and consequential provisions as appear to the President to be necessary and proper, but save as aforesaid, the order made under sub-paragraph (1) of this paragraph shall not be varied by any subsequent order.[65]

Now the problem is, what should be the criteria for classifying Scheduled Areas. To study the problems of Scheduled Tribes, the Scheduled Areas and Scheduled Tribes Commission was appointed on April 28, 1960, in pursuance of Art. 339. This Commission was to report on:

(a) the administration of the Scheduled Areas under the Fifth Schedule to the Constitution, and, in particular as to

    (i) the functioning of the Tribes Advisory Councils;

    (ii) the laws applicable to the Scheduled Areas and the exercise by the Governors concerned of powers under paragraph 5 of the Fifth Schedule; and

    (iii) the principles to be followed in declaring any territory to be, or to form part of, a Scheduled Area, or directing that any territory shall cease to be, or cease to form part of, a Scheduled Area;

(b) the welfare of the Scheduled Tribes in the States, and in particular, whether the development plans in relation to matters connected with welfare of Scheduled Tribes require any alteration in respect of objectives, priorities or details of working; and

(c) any other matter connected with the administration of Scheduled Areas or the welfare of the Scheduled

---

65. See Scheduled Areas (Part A States) Order 1950, Ministry of Law Order No. C.O.9, dated January 26, 1950, Gazette of India Extraordinary, p. 670. (Part B States) Order 1950, Ministry of Law Order No. C.O.26, dated December 7, 1950, Gazette of India Extraordinary, Part II, Section 3, p. 975.

Tribes in the States which may hereafter be specifically referred to the Commission for investigation and report.

The Commission issued a questionnaire to the State Governments and Union Territories, to consider whether the following factors to be present for classifying an area as Scheduled Area:

- (i) Strict necessity;
- (ii) preponderance of tribal population;
- (iii) reasonableness of the size;
- (iv) susceptibility of the area to special administrative treatment;
- (v) compactness;
- (vi) inaccessibility;
- (vii) exclusiveness and distinctive way of life of the tribal population;
- (viii) marked disparity in economic standards in relation to the people of the surrounding area;
- (ix) disparity in the level of education; and
- (x) relative development of the area vis-à-vis the rest of the State.[66]

The State Governments were not unanimous in their views about the criteria suggested in the questionnaire. After a detailed study of the problem, the Commission suggested the following criteria for determining Scheduled Areas.

- (1) preponderance of tribals in the population,
- (2) compact and reasonable size,
- (3) underdeveloped nature and the area, and
- (4) Marked disparity in economic standards of the people.[67]

As regards the application of these criteria to the Union Territories which are directly controlled by the Centre,

---

66. *Report of the Scheduled Areas and Scheduled Tribes Commission,* 1961–62, para. 8.4, p. 60.
67. *Ibid.,* para. 8.13, p. 63.

the Commission recommended: "We are, therefore, of the view that for the purpose of scheduling areas, no distinction should be drawn between the States and the Union Territories."[68]

Two questions of importance which engaged the attention of the Commission were, first, the application of the criteria suggested by the Commission to the present Scheduled Areas, and secondly, what should be the criteria for descheduling areas? The Commission found that the application of the criteria already suggested would disqualify many areas since, they fall short of the requisites required for scheduling them. But with regard to the descheduling of Scheduled Areas, the commission pointed out:

> No area can be de-scheduled unless after examination of the relevant data Government are satisfied that in point of economic development, education, health, communications and other services it has reached a stage where it can no longer remain a Scheduled Area. In our view no Scheduled Area has yet reached the stage where de-scheduling can be considered.[69]

Additional areas suggested for scheduling and to be declared as Scheduled Areas by the State Governments are indicated in Table 3-11.[70]

For enhancing the pace of economic development in tribal areas par excellence, other than what has been ensured in the Fifth Schedule, the Commission suggested that:

> The State Government should undertake general legislation applicable throughout the Scheduled and

68. *Ibid.*, para. 8.14, p. 64.
69. *Ibid.*, para. 8.32, (b) , p. 69.
70. *Ibid.*, p. 65.

TABLE 3–11

State	Area in sq. miles	Total population	Tribal population	Percentage of tribal population to total population
Gujarat	2,833	918,991	562,493	61.2
Kerala	1,064	176,129	112,000	63.5
Madhya Pradesh	14,840	—	1,800,621	—
Maharashtra	10,194	1,157,722	678,517	58.6
Orissa	7,100	893,053	375,395	42.9
Punjab	112	5,514	—	—
Rajasthan	9,804	1,458,594	863,748	59.0
Andaman and Nicobar Islands	1,036	14,691*	N.A.	—
Himachal Pradesh	4,228	87,866	83,866	95.0
Manipur	7,686	246,148*	N.A.	—

* 1961 Census figures.

non-scheduled Areas for protection of the rights of tribals in land and forests and protection from exploitation by money-lenders and this legislation should be implemented within a period of ten years. Pending enactment of such general legislation the regulatory powers of the Governor under Para. 5 (2) of the Fifth Schedule may be utilised for the promulgation of corresponding regulations for the Scheduled Areas. Simultaneously all tribal areas should be grouped under Tribal development blocks so that the bulk of the tribal population is brought under intensive development schemes. The blocks should concentrate on the following four activities—economic development, education, health and communications and should have specific targets. With the fulfilment of the targets in all Tribal development blocks and the passing and implementation of protective legislation, the objects of the Fifth Schedule would have been achieved and it could conveniently be abrogated.[71]

Part B, para. 5 of the Fifth Schedule deals with the powers of the Governor over the Scheduled Areas. It states:

---

71. *Ibid.,* para. 8.32 (d) , p. 70.

1) Notwithstanding anything in this Constitution, the Governor, may by public notification direct that any particular Act of Parliament or of the Legislature of the State shall not apply to a Scheduled Area or any part thereof in the State or shall apply to a Scheduled Area or any part thereof in the State subject to such exceptions and modifications as he may specify in the notification and any direction given under this sub-paragraph may be given so as to have retrospective effect.

2) The Governor may make regulations for the peace and good Government of any area in a State which is for the time being a Scheduled Area.

In particular and without prejudice to the generality of the foregoing power, such regulations may—

(a) prohibit or restrict the transfer of land by or among members of the Scheduled Tribes in such areas;

(b) regulate the allotment of land to members of the Scheduled Tribes in such area;

(c) regulate the carrying on of business as money-lender by persons who lend money to members of the Scheduled Tribes in such area.

(3) In making any such regulation as is referred to in sub-paragraph (2) of this paragraph, the Governor may repeal or amend any Act of Parliament or of the Legislature of the State or any existing law which is for the time being applicable to the area in question.

(4) All regulations made under this paragraph shall be submitted forthwith to the President and, until assented to by him, shall have no effect.

(5) No regulation shall be made under this paragraph unless the Governor making regulation has, in the case where there is a Tribes Advisory Council for the State, consulted such council.

Part A, para. 3 further lays down:

The Governor of each State having Scheduled Areas therein shall annually, or whenever so required by the President, make a report to the President regarding the administration of the Scheduled Areas in that State and the Executive power of the Union shall extend to the giving of directions to the State as to the administration of the said areas.

The following table (3-12) shows the submission of those reports:[72]

TABLE 3–12

State	1951	1952	1953	1954	1955
Andra Pradesh	—	4-9-53	18-11-55	18-11-55	29-6-56) 31-7-56)
Bihar	9-1-52	7-10-53	25-8-54	5-9-55	24-5-57
Gujarat	—	—	—	—	—
Maharashtra	—	—	1955	12-4-56	1957
Madhya Pradesh	24-2-53	15-12-53	19-8-55	15-12-55) 28- 4-55)	7-1-57)
Madras	—	6-3-54	—	14-7-55	—
Orissa	15-3-52	20-3-53	26-6-54	23-11-55	14-12-56
Punjab	—	—	3-4-54	—	30-4-56
Rajasthan	—	—	—	29-2-56	20-12-56

State	1956	1957	1958	1959	1960
Andhra Pradesh	8-7-57	1-9-59	1-9-60	6-6-61	—
Bihar	6-8-58	21-6-60	25-1-61	—	—
Gujarat	—	—	—	—	—
Maharashtra	29-11-58	17-10-59	10-12-60	—	—
Madhya Pradesh	6-10-58	18-7-59	19-3-60	—	—
Madras	—	—	—	—	—
Orissa	20-1-58	24-1-59	24-1-60	23-1-61	—
Punjab	12-8-57	14-11-58	23-10-59	—	31-10-60
Rajasthan	4-4-59	20-2-59	12-6-59	24-9-60	—

From the aforesaid table it is clear that there is irregularity in the submission of Governors' reports. The reasons for such a state of affairs is, no instructions from the Union Government are binding on these reports. Hence, the States evince very little interest in the preparation of the reports. But the States are provided with ample material by way of the reports of field staff, Deputy Commis-

---

72. *Ibid.*, Table 4, pp. 45–46.

sioners, Commissioner for Scheduled Castes and Scheduled Tribes, and discussions in Tribes Advisory Councils. These sources furnish valuable information about the Scheduled Areas and tribal people which would be of great importance in the implementation of welfare schemes. In view of such importance, it is necessary to take steps to make Governors' reports more analytical and objective. For this purpose, it is felt that the reports should not only be discussed in Tribes Advisory Councils, but also be bound to accept the Councils' suggestions on vital matters.

These loopholes have made the regulatory powers of the Governors mere goodwill provisions. For the proper implementation of the Fifth Schedule and to safeguard tribal interests, the Commission has recommended: "The Union Government should take with the State Governments the necessity of having a definite and consistent policy of protection in relation to subjects mentioned in the Fifth Schedule."[73]

Article 275 deals with grants given to States for the implementation of welfare schemes to better the conditions of Scheduled Tribes. It provides:

1) Such sums as Parliament may by law provide shall be charged on the Consolidated Fund of India in each year as grants-in-aid of the revenues of such States as Parliament may determine to be in need of assistance, and different sums may be fixed for different States:

Provided that there shall be paid out of the Consolidated Fund of India as grants-in-aid of the revenues of a State such capital and recurring sums as may be necessary to enable that State to meet the costs of such schemes of development as may be undertaken by the State with the approval of the Government of India for the purpose of promoting the welfare of the Scheduled Tribes in that State or raising the level of administration

---

73. *Ibid.,* p. 52.

of the Scheduled Areas therein to that of the administration of the rest of the areas of that State:

Provided further that there shall be paid out of the Consolidated Fund of India as grants-in-aid of the revenue of the State of Assam sums, capital and recurring, equivalent to—

(a) the average excess of expenditure over the revenues during the two years immediately preceding the commencement of this Constitution in respect of the administration of the tribal areas specified in Part A of the table appended to para. 20 of the Sixth Schedule; and

(b) the costs of such schemes of development as may be undertaken by that State with the approval of the Government of India for the purpose of raising the level of administration of the said areas to that of the administration of the rest of the areas of that State.

2) Until provision is made by Parliament under clause (1), the powers conferred on Parliament under that clause shall be exercised by the President by order made by the President under this clause shall have effect subject to any provision so made by Parliament:

Provided that after a Finance Commission has been constituted no order shall be made under this clause by the President except after considering the recommendations of the Finance Commission.

The grants made under this article are of a discriminatory nature, but, since they are made for purposes of launching welfare schemes for the benefit of Scheduled Tribes and Scheduled Areas and aim at the correction of inter-State financial disparities, they cannot be considered unconstitutional. But these special provisions should be treated as supplementary benefits to amplify the general welfare schemes of the States, for the advancement of Scheduled Tribes and the development of Scheduled Areas.

The total amount of grants-in-aid given to the States
under Art. 275 is recorded in Table 3-13:[74]

TABLE 3–13

Year	State sector schemes (Rs.)	Centrally sponsored schemes (Rs.)	Total (Col. 2 & 3) (Rs.)
1	2	3	
1950–51	5,400,000	—	5,400,000
1951–52	15,975,000	—	15,975,000
1952–53	19,971,000	—	19,971,000
1953–54	26,273,000	—	26,273,000
1954–55	37,672,000	—	37,672,000
1955–56*	51,374,000	—	51,374,000
1956–57*	22,237,800	16,189,000	33,926,800
1957–58*	26,101,600	20,285,000	46,386,600
1958–59*	25,492,000	28,867,000	54,359,000
1959–60*	36,470,100	45,624,000	82,094,100
1960–61†	35,367,300	84,763,000	120,130,300
Grand Total (1950–61)	302,333,800	191,228,000	493,561,800

* Grant-in-aid actually utilized by the State Government.
† Grant-in-aid released to the State Government.

In view of the change in emphasis on the conditions
governing the grants made under Art. 275, particularly
during the third plan, which laid special emphasis on population, the Scheduled Areas Commission has suggested
the criteria for allocating grants as follows:

(a) Population;
(b) Level of development reached by the State in
welfare activity for the Scheduled Tribes and in raising
the level of administration in the Scheduled Areas at the
beginning of each plan period; and

74. *Ibid.,* Table 8, p. 75

(c) Financial position of the State along with its willingness to contribute its quota.[75]

Besides, the commission made a special reference to the problem of the border States. In view of frequent foreign aggression, the border States experience a severe dislocation of their economy. Hence, these border States should be given greater assistance to counterbalance the effects of dislocation.

After a detailed study of the problem of grants-in-aid, considering the views of the State Governments, the Commission commented on Art. 275 as follows:

> The Article thus does not contain sufficient safeguards for the proper expenditure of the funds given to the States, as provided in the Constitutions of the United States, United Kingdom, Canada, etc. Beyond allocating funds to the States, the Union Government have no adequate machinery for ensuring that the funds given have been properly spent and for the purposes intended. We recommend that the proposed Department to be set up at the centre in the Ministry of Home Affairs should contain an Accounts cell exclusively for the purpose of maintaining accounts of the funds disbursed to the State Governments, Union Territories and non-official organisations.[76]

Sixth Schedule of the Constitution is devoted to the provisions as to the administration of Tribal Areas in Assam. Tribal Areas within the State of Assam are specified in Parts A and B.

Part A
1. The United Khasi-Jaintia Hills District
2. The Garo Hills District

---

75. *Ibid.*, para. 9.18, p. 78.
76. *Ibid.*, para. 9.30, pp. 81–82.

3. **The Mizo District**
4. 'The Naga Hills district' omitted by the Naga Hills—Tuensang Area Act, 1957 (42 of 1957), S.3, w.e.f. 1-12-1957
5. The North Cachar Hills
6. The Mikir Hills

Part B

1. North East Frontier Tract including Balipur Frontier tract, Tirap frontier tract, Abor Hills District and Mismi Hills District
2. The Naga Hills—Tuensang Area (The Naga Tribal Area' shall be omitted by the State of Nagaland Act, 1962 (27 of 1962))

The Naga Hills-Tuensang Area is now known as Nagaland according to the Nagaland Regulation 1961. Its three constituent areas are: the Naga Hills District, Tuensang division, and the Naga Tribal Area. Originally the Naga Hills District was in the Part A, Tribal Areas, Tuensang division of N.E.F.A., and the Naga Tribal Area were in Part B of the Tribal Areas.

The Tribal Areas under Part A are autonomous districts. Para 2 of the Sixth Schedule of the Constitution provides:

1) There shall be a District Council for each autonomous district consisting of not more than twenty four members, of whom not less than three fourths shall be elected on the basis of adult suffrage.

2) There shall be a separate Regional Council for each area constituted an autonomous region under subparagraph (2) of para 1 of this schedule.

Sub-para (2) of para 1 reads:

"(2) If there are different Scheduled Tribes in an autonomous district, the Governor may, by public notification, divide the area or areas inhabited by them, into autonomous regions."

Consequently, District Councils have been constituted in the Districts of North Cachar Hills, Garo Hills, Mikir Hills, United Khasi and Jaintia Hills, and Mizo. There is also a Regional Council in Pawi Lakher Region of Mizo District.[77]

The tribals are governed in N.E.F.A. according to their own traditional institutions. However, efforts have been made to put down antisocial customs of the people through persuasive methods rather than by legal enactments.

Integration of Scheduled Tribes

With the dawn of Independence, the problem of Scheduled Tribes is engaging the attention of social scientists and administrators alike. Hitherto, the tribes were studied for academic interest as rare specimen of humanity in the anthropological museum. But now the time has come for applied research in the variegated color of the tribals, who differ so widely in their social and economic environments, culture, language, and customs. The social fabric of tribals calls for a cautious scrutiny and scientific investigation in the process of their transformation. Any scheme of ameliorative measures should cater, first and foremost, to the preservation of tribal culture. As the Scheduled Areas and Scheduled Tribes Commission pointed out: "The problem of problems is not to disturb the harmony of tribal life and simultaneously work for its advance; not to impose anything upon the tribals and simultaneously work for their integration as members and part of the Indian family."[78]

The Five Fundamental principles advocated by Nehru were:

---

77. *Report of the Commisioner for Scheduled Castes and Scheduled Tribes*, 1961–62, para. 17.18, p. 120.

78. *Report of the Scheduled Areas and Scheduled Tribes Commission*, 1961–62, para. 1.27, p. 6.

1) People should develop along the lines of their own genius and we should avoid imposing anything on them. We should try to encourage in every way their own traditional arts and culture;

2) Tribal rights in land and forests should be respected;

3) We should try to train and build up a team of their own people to do the work of administration and development. Some technical personnel from outside will, no doubt, be needed, especially in the beginning. But we should avoid introducing too many outsiders into the tribal territory;

4) We should not over-administer these areas or overwhelm them with a multiplicity of schemes. We should rather work through and not in rivalry to their own social and cultural institutions;

5) We should judge results not by statistics or the amount of money spent, but by the quality of human character that is evolved.[79]

The drawbacks of imposition have been described by Verrier Elwin as follows:

Imposition has many implications. It is not confined to giving orders and forcing people to do things. The imposition of example can be equally injurious. The presence of a large number of officials, in unfamiliar and comparatively expensive dress, staying in houses of a type unsuited to the rural scene and climate and not adaptable to the tribal family or way of life, may cause the tribes to adopt a way of living that is too costly for them and which they will discover later is unsuited to their economy. It may cause them to despise their own arts, social and political institutions, and kind of life in a pathetic belief that to imitate a Junior official is to be modern.[80]

79. Nehru's Foreword to the Second Edition of Dr. Verrier Elwin's, *"A Philosophy of NEFA,"* 1960.

80. *Report of the Committee on Special Multipurpose Tribal Blocks,* 1960, p. 14.

Now the question may be raised: Does not the introduction of a new economic pattern, a change over from Forest economy to modern methods of agriculture, infuse new culture into the tribal organizations? The possibilities of introducing new culture can be given benefit of doubt. As the Elwin Committee remarked:

> It must be admitted, of course, that in many places tribal culture is in a state of decay. Contact with the outside world has tended to shake the people's faith in themselves. New religions have competed for their allegiance, new taboos have been introduced. There are many things in the development programmes which cannot easily be adjusted to the old way of life. Some bad things have disappeared, but many good and vitalising things are disappearing as well.[81]

To illustrate, "Today some of the educated tribal leaders are trying to stop dancing among their own people, which is partly due to a quite mistaken notion that 'upper class' people do not dance."[82]

As the tribal people come more and more into contact with the outside world they tend to take from our society its bad rather than its good points and to adopt the very things which India as a whole is eliminating from its life. There is an increasing emphasis on caste distinctions. In Orissa, particularly, "whereas ten years ago you would never hear a tribal speak of himself as an Adivasi or of a Dom as a Harijan, today these expressions are all too often used."[83]

The Government of India have to be commended for the keen interest evinced in the problem of Scheduled Tribes. Experts on tribals are summoned to analyze the problems of tribals in the field of education, the role of

---

81. *Ibid.,* p. 138.
82. *Ibid.,* p. 140; see pp. 139–41 for more details on the decay of fine arts among the tribals.
83. *Ibid.,* p. 96.

Tribal Research Institutions, Voluntary Agencies, preservation of tribal institutions, etc. Particular mention has to be made of the valuable contribution of Verrier Elwin for his scientific study of the tribes. Not only the Constitution but also the Five Year Plans are ample testimony to this awareness of the overall development of Scheduled Tribes and their integration with the rest of the population of the country.

Then again, education as a means for integrating tribals presents complexities, partly because of the diversity of tribals in their racial groupings, and partly because of linguistic differences. These differences become confounded in devising the medium of instruction for tribal education. The problem of whether the tribals should be taught in their mother tongue or the language of the market in which they have contact needs careful tackling. Those who advocate introducing tribal dialects enumerate the advantages which would accrue to tribal children in learning the three R's in their own mother tongue. But a deeper probe leads to the conclusion that along with the mother tongue, the language of the market should be compulsorily taught to the tribals. Because, as the tribals come in contact with the rest of the population for trading purposes, it is of utmost importance that they should be conversant with the language of the market. As the Tamia Report pointed out: "From the point of view of the tribal people themselves as well as from the point of view of the larger interest of the nation, it is vital that the consequences of education should not take away the best element in the village to outside areas."[84]

So the problem of tribal education centers around the factors: the creation of a band of tribals who would govern their areas, the introduction of a correct method of education for the tribals who would turn out to be better agriculturists and profess varied arts of their latent capacity.

---

84. *Ibid.*, p. 85.

The tribals should not be exposed to the present-day educational system with the craze for degrees culminating in an unemployment problem. So the basic education with Ashram Schools is the best method suited to tribal needs. However, the tribals should be given the option in selecting the education of their choice—basic education or the Western type of education which is prevalent in the country. A carefully worked out program of education with special emphasis on crafts will produce better results. By the application of this method, in the words of the Elwin Committee:

> We will ultimately have well trained tribal officers to develop their own areas, a process which is bound to continue for many years to come, we will have on the other-hand a contented and enlightened peasantry who will not be ashamed to work with their hands and who will see in the farmer's life one of the ideal professions.[85]

To preserve the beauty of tribal culture, Tribal Research Institutes have been set up in States where there is preponderance of tribal population. These Institutes were set up on the recommendations of the Commissioner for Scheduled Castes and Scheduled Tribes. They play a very important part in counterbalancing the impact of industrialization on tribal population. Five Research Institutes are set up in the States of Bihar, Madhya Pradesh, Orissa, Rajasthan, and West Bengal. In the States of Assam, Bombay, and Madhya Pradesh the universities and other voluntary agencies are actively engaged in preserving the cultural heritage of the tribals. Besides, the Departments of Sociology and Anthropology of several universities are taking up "tribes" as research topics for advanced studies and specialization. The twin objectives of these Cultural Research Institutes appear to be:

85. *Ibid.,* p. 97.

1. the collecting of data about tribal life which would help in the formulation of the schemes and also equip the officers working in the tribal areas with necessary background knowledge and serve as a training centre; and

2. to study the schemes under execution and to report on their shortcomings, etc.[86]

The activities of the Tribal Research Institutes of Bihar and Madhya Pradesh are quite vigorous. Equally progressive is the work done by the Anthropological Survey of India, Research Department of North East Frontier Agency, and the universities of Bombay, Calcutta, Gauhati, Gorakhpur, Gujarat, Karnatak, Lucknow, Nagpur, Patna, Punjab, Rajasthan, Ranchi, and Saugar.

For the better functioning of the central and State Research Institutes, it has been suggested that there should be perfect coordination and collaboration between the State and Central Governments, both in the formulation and implementation of welfare programs for tribals. The recommendations made by the Study Team on Social Welfare and Welfare of Backward classes are:

a) A central Institute of Tribal Welfare should be established with the following functions:

i) to coordinate research on an all-India basis;

ii) to make studies of special problems which extend beyond the jurisdiction of any one State;

iii) to pool ideas and to disseminate them among the State Governments and other authorities charged with the implementation of tribal development and Welfare; and

iv) to provide expert advice and guidance.[87]

---

86. *Report of the Commissioner for Scheduled Castes and Scheduled Tribes,* 1958–59, Part I, para. 11, p. 189.

87. *Report of the Study Team on Social Welfare and Welfare of Backward Classes,* 1959, para. 65, p. 156.

TABLE 3–14

Type of Institute	Name of the State	Allocation made in the Second Five Year Plan	Amount utilized during the year 1956–57	Amount earmarked for the year 1957–58
(a) Cultural Research Institute	1. Bihar	850,000	63,776	53,615
	2. Madhya Pradesh	—	31,300	78,377
	3. Orissa	225,000	24,667	9,882
	4. Rajasthan	235,000	1,200	6,800
	5. West Bengal	164,800	23,400	22,400
(b) Other Organizations	1. Assam (i) Gauhati University	175,000	30,000	25,000
	2. Bombay (ii) University of Bombay ⎫ (ii) Gujarat Research Society ⎬ (iii) Anthropological Society of Bombay ⎭	Not fixed	6,201	Nil
	3. Madhya Pradesh (i) Bharatiya Lok Kala Mandal	Not fixed	6,500	6,500
	Total	1,449,800	187,044	202,574

Table 3-14 records the expenditure incurred on these cultural Research Institutes during the Second Plan period:[88]

The expenditure (in lakhs*) incurred on the Research Schemes in the Central Sector of the Third Plan are given in Table 3–15:[89]

TABLE 3–15

State	Plan Provision	Allocation made during 1961–62	Expenditure incurred during 1961–62
Andhra Pradesh	5.75	0.95	Nil
Assam	11.00	1.80	0.24
Bihar	10.10	1.64	Nil
Gujarat	5.75	0.95	Nil
Madhya Pradesh	15.00	2.48	0.09
Maharashtra	5.75	0.95	Nil
Orissa	7.50	1.27	0.75
Rajasthan	5.75	0.95	0.43
West Bengal	10.00	1.65	0.32
Total	76.60	12.64	1.83

*10 lakhs=1 Million

Constructive work has been done by non-official agencies in the implementation of welfare schemes among the tribals. The Christian Missionaries may be regarded as pioneers in evincing keen interest in the well being of tribals. They inspired in them the idea of progress. Some of the non-official agencies working for the well being of Scheduled Tribes are:

Bharatiya Adimjati Sevak Sangh
Servants of India Society
Sarva Seva Sangh
Gandhi Smarak Nidhi

88. *Report of the Commissioner for Scheduled Castes and Scheduled Tribes*, Part I, 1957–58, p. 136.
89. *Ibid.*, 1961–62, Part I, p. 105.

The Tata Institute of Social Sciences, Bombay
The Indian Council of child welfare, Chhindwara
Bharatiya Lok Kala Mandir, Udaipur
Bharatiya Adimjati Sevak Sangh is the biggest organization working for the welfare of Scheduled Tribes. The chief activities of the organization are confined to the starting of educational institutions and hostels for the benefit of Scheduled Tribes students, training of welfare personnel for implementing welfare programs, publicity on tribal problems by issuing a quarterly journal entitled *Vanyajati,* and the publication of books on Tribals, etc. Tribal conferences are frequently held in different parts of the country and problems relating to tribal welfare are discussed by eminent authorities.

The Ramakrishna Mission, Cherrapunji, is chiefly concerned with the educational development of the tribal students.

Tata Institute of Social Sciences, Bombay, concentrates on the training of tribal welfare personnel.

The Indian Council of Child Welfare is concerned with the running of Balwadis (Primary Schools), particularly in M.P.

Ramakrishna Mission, Shillong, is distinguished for its mobile dispensary of Scheduled Tribes.

The details of expenditure (in rupees) on various schemes by some of the non-official organizations are illustrated in Table 3–16:[90]

The second plan allocation for Voluntary Agencies was Rs. 7.5 millions. The Third Plan marked an increase in the expenditure, the sum allotted being Rs. 12.5 millions. The details of the grant-in-aid made for the year 1961–62 are given in Table 3–17:[91]

---

90. *Report of the Scheduled Areas and Scheduled Tribes Commission,* 1961–62, Table 52, p. 306.

91. Compiled from the *Report of the Commissioner for Scheduled Castes and Scheduled Tribes,* 1962–63, Part I, p. 45.

TABLE 3–16

Name of the non-official organization	Education	Health	Economic develop-ment	Other activities including adminis-tration	Total
Andhra Sramik Dharma Rajya Sabha, Kovvur, Andhra Pradesh	11,585	—	5,105	6,400	23,090
Assam Seva Samithi, Gauhati, Assam	—	116,760	3,890	135,955	256,605
Adimjati Seva Mandal, Ranchi, Bihar	570,225	—	12,000	37,035	619,260
Santal Pahadia Seva Mandal, Deoghar, Bihar	268,305	148,500	—	37,120	453,925
Dang Seva Mandal, Nasik, Maharashtra	288,920	—	—	13,567	302,487
West Khandesh Bhil Seva Mandal, Nandurbar, Maharashtra	180,645	—	5,700	18,025	204,370
Vanavasi Seva Mandal, Mandla, Madhya Pradesh	848,704	16,061	8,389	111,339	984,493
Bhil Seva Mandal, Dohad, Gujarat	369,070	3,715	60,000	27,784	460,569
Ashok Ashram, Kalsi, Dehradun, Uttar Pradesh	1,413	5,512	52	6,085	13,062
Adimjati Shiksha Ashram, Imphal, Manipur	351,060	1,211	12,028	—	364,299
Rajasthan Adimjati Sevak Sangh, Jaipur, Rajasthan	532,815	—	15,000	43,560	591,075

TABLE 3–17

Name of the organization	Amount of grant-in-aid	Expenditure incurred
Bharatiya Admjati Sevak Sangh, Delhi	121,900	130,663
Ramakrishan Mission, Chirapunji	341,190	223,257
Tata Institute of Social Sciences, Bombay	83,250	74,404
Andhra Pradesh, Adimjati Sevak Sangh, Hyderabad	48,720	43,051
Indian Council of Child Welfare, Delhi	38,780	N.A.
Ramakrishna Mission, Shillong	10,000	N.A.

One of the recommendations made by the Committee on Special Multipurpose Tribal Blocks with regard to the working of non-official agencies was:

Government should also ensure that the various non-official organisations should avoid duplication of activities not only as amongst themselves but also with those undertaken by Government in the same area. To achieve this, the scope of work of each non-official organisation and its field of activity should be clearly defined in an integrated and phased program carefully planned in advance.[92]

Lastly, it is necessary to make a reference to the traditional tribal institutions in furthering the process of tribal transformation. Traditional tribal institutions are mostly found in tribal areas where there is exclusive tribal population. These institutions are very active even to this day in Nagaland, NEFA, Assam and Manipur. But the Sched-

92. *Report of the Committee on Special Multipurpose Tribal Blocks,* 1960, p. 175.

uled Areas with mixed population do not encourage full-fledged operation of traditional tribal councils. It is lauda-ble to note that these tribal councils are not hindered from functioning even today, as they constitute the keynote of tribal administration. The remnant of tribal adminis-tration is personified in the functioning of tribal councils. So it is largely felt that they should not be disturbed.

In the words of the Scheduled Areas and Scheduled Tribes Commission:

> If the traditional Tribal Councils are weakened, the fabric of tribal life will also be weakened. We do not, therefore, contemplate the submerging of these tradi-tional councils under the impact of the new Panchayats. It is essential that the tribal people should decide how they well manage their own lives in social and religious matters.[93]

But the issue is complicated by the emergence of the Panchayat Raj Institution. Article 40 emphatically states: "The State shall take steps to organise village Panchayats and endow them with such powers and authority as may be necessary to enable them to function as units of self-government." The solution offered by the Elwin Com-mittee for the juxtaposition of Tribal Councils and Statu-tory Panchayats was: "One is to keep in being, strengthen and, where necessary, revive the existing tribal machinery; the other is by the introduction of Statutory Panchayats."

But the dangers of introducing Statutory Panchayats were summarized by the Committee as follows: "The in-troduction of the new Panchayats may defeat the very object of having them, for they may come to be looked upon as alien institutions, something superimposed on tribal culture and not evolving naturally out of it."[94]

93. *Report of the Scheduled Areas and Scheduled Tribes Commission,* 1961–62, para. 28.28, p. 347.
94. *Report of the Committee on Special Multipurpose Tribal Blocks,* 1960, p. 169.

Moreover, in view of the fact that the tribal people have many customary laws which differ to some extent from those of other people, and they have always liked to settle their own affairs within the borders of their own community, "it will not be easy for mixed Panchayats to give proper consideration to the tribal point of view."[95]

Statutory Panchayats have failed to impress tribal people and very little progress has been made by these Panchayats wherever they are introduced. So under the existing situation, the Elwin Committee was of the firm conviction that:

> The Tribal Councils have great potentialities. Established in history and tradition, supported by social and religious sanctions, expression of a genuine democracy representing the cooperative and communal temperament of the people, they can be used not only to support law and order but also to further the progress of development throughout the tribal areas.[96]

To sum up, much has been done to safeguard tribal culture and social organisation, to gradually integrate them with the rest of the population. It is gratifying to note that the Government of India have made a cautious approach to the tribal problem. As Nehru remarked: "There are two extreme approaches. One is the museum approach, keeping them as interesting specimens for anthropologists to discuss. The other may be called the 'open door' approach. Both are equally bad."[97] Luckily, a via media of these two extremes has been struck, to enhance the process of assimilation of Scheduled Tribes.

The general attitude and approach to the tribes has improved throughout the country. Thirty years ago they were generally regarded either as picturesque "museum

---

95. *Ibid.*, p. 170.
96. *Ibid.*, p. 171.
97. Extract of Nehru's speech entitled "Approach to the Tribes," *Nehru's speeches,* Vol. 3, 1953–57, p. 458.

specimens" to be collected or as ferocious savages to be avoided. Today there is a very wide measure of respect for the tribal civilization and a recognition that these fine people have a real contribution to make to the rest of India and that, as they get opportunity, they will play an important part in her life.[98]

The integration of Scheduled Tribes should be well timed, properly planned and cautiously executed. Freedom from fear, want and imposition would civilize them. They should be allowed to forge ahead by natural evolution rather than imposition.

Enumeration of Other Backward Classes

The problem of "Other Backward Classes" is one of determining who the Other Backward Classes are. The framers of the Constitution have left vague the definition of the term. As a result, it has become one of the most controversial topics of discussion among legal experts, administrators, and social scientists. The issue is complicated because "the Scheduled Castes," and "the Scheduled Tribes" who constitute sections of Backward Classes are defined in the Constitution, under Art. 366 (24) and (25), with the omission of Other Backward Classes. It is of considerable interest to note why the term "Other Backward Classes" is not defined in the Constitution. Perhaps it was left to the Commission contemplated in the Constitution under Art. 340 to determine who the Other Backward Classes are. In the absence of a precise definition, it is also reasonable to expect legal experts to interpret this vague term of the Constitution. In the process of interpretation, the Judiciary has played an important role in classifying the meaning of the term "Other Backward Classes." But

---

98. *Report of the Committee on Special Multipurpose Tribal Blocks,* 1960, p. 20.

there are instances in our Constitutional history where the judicial pronouncements are invalidated by amending the Constitution and incorporating suitable clauses to defend Governmental policies. To illustrate, the Constitution (First Amendment) Act, 1951, by virtue of which Art. 29 (2) was amended. This amendment was necessitated by *Champakam Dorairajan* v *State of Madras,* when the Madras G.O. was invalidated by the Judiciary, as it violated Art. 29 (2). The result was the amendment of the Constitution by incorporating clause (4) in Art. 15, which empowered the State to make reservations for Backward Classes, who in the State are considered to be socially and educationally backward.

The term "Backward Classes" occurs in Articles 15 (4), 16 (4) and 29 (2), respectively. Art. 15 (4) states:

Nothing in this article or in clause (2) of Article 29 shall prevent the State from making any special provision for the advancement of any socially and educationally backward classes of citizens or for the Scheduled Castes and the Scheduled Tribes.

Art. 16 (4) provides:

Nothing in this article shall prevent the State from making any provision for the reservation of appointments or posts in favour of any backward class of citizens which, in the opinion of the State, is not adequately represented in the Services under the State.

Art. 29 (2) a corollary of Art. 15 (4) reads:

Nothing in clause (2) of Art. 29 shall prevent the State from making any special provision for the advancement of any socially and educationally backward classes of citizens or for the Scheduled Castes and the Scheduled Tribes.

That the advancement of Backward Classes has been made a State responsibility by the Constitution is clear from the aforesaid articles. The State is empowered to give these classes of citizens special concessions in the field of employment, education, etc. But it does not point out precisely who are backward. It is not proper to make special provisions for a certain section of society without defining who constitute that particular section, qualified for special concessions. In the First Five Year Plan an attempt was made to explain the term "Other Backward Classes." It pointed out:

> The term "backward Class" is difficult to define. Backwardness is expressed in lack of adequate opportunity for group and individual self-development, especially in economic life and in matters of health, housing and education. It is measured in terms of low levels of income, the extent of illiteracy, and the low standards of life demonstrated by living conditions.[99]

This, however, did not provide a satisfactory definition.

Article 15 (4) refers to what are called "socially and educationally backward classes." It would have been helpful if this expression had been precisely defined in the Constitution itself since it is capable of different interpretations. The word "social" means "living in communities"; "relating to society." So it could be inferred that those communities which occupy lower rungs of the ladder in society and which are poor in educational attainments are backward. Thus viewed, the word "social" could be used in the same sense as "economic."

Another interpretation attributes the definition of the term "Other Backward Classes" to Art. 338 (3). The argument is:

---

99. *First Five Year Plan,* p. 634.

the authors of the Constitution felt no need to define the term "Backward Classes." This article is in the nature of an explanation to the definition of the terms "Scheduled Castes" and "Scheduled Tribes." This is based on the maxim that *inclusio unius est exclusio alterius* (the inclusion of one is the exclusion of another). It means the exclusion of any other basis of determination of the Backward Classes.[100]

Article 338 (3) reads:

In this article, references to the Scheduled Castes and Scheduled Tribes shall be construed as including references to such other backward classes as the President may, on receipt of the report of a Commission appointed under clause (1) of article 340, by order specify and also to the Anglo-Indian community.

According to the aforesaid interpretation, the reason for not defining the term "Other Backward Classes" in the Constitution is attributed to the fact that the terms "Scheduled Castes" and "Scheduled Tribes" are defined in the Constitution which are equivalent to "Other Backward Classes." Any further definition of the term "Other Backward Classes" would have amounted to tautology and hence the definition of the term was avoided by the framers of the Constitution.

But this interpretation does not give a satisfactory explanation for the failure to define the term "Other Backward Classes" in the Constitution. A cautious study of Art. 338 (3) hints that the Constitution makers entrusted the responsibility of defining the term "Other Backward Classes" to the Commission to be appointed under Art. 340 (1). Perhaps the framers of the Constitution might have felt that the circumstances contributing to the back-

---

100. L. G. Havanur, *Mysore Law Journal,* Vol. 41, November 10, 1963, No. 21, p. 18.

wardness of citizens varies from State to State. It is gratifying to note that even though the framers of the Constitution failed to define the term "Other Backward Classes," they left it for the administration to decide this question according to changed conditions. But much to the discernment of the framers, the Backward Classes Commission gave neither a precise definition of this term nor evolved workable criteria for classification. The result is, the term "Other Backward Classes" still remains vague and ambiguous, exercising the minds of legal experts, administrators, and researchers at large.

Explaining the necessity for using the word "Backward" in clause (3) of Art. 10 in the Draft Constitution, B. R. Ambedkar remarked:

> We have to safeguard two things, namely, the principle of equality of opportunity and at the same time satisfy the demand of communities which have not had so far representation in the State, then, I am sure they will agree that unless you see some such qualifying phrase as "backward," the exception made in favour of reservation will ultimately eat up the rule altogether. Nothing of the rule will remain. That I think, if I may say so, is the justification why the Drafting Committee undertook on its own shoulders the responsibility of introducing the word "backward," which I admit, did not originally find place in the fundamental right in the way in which it was passed by this Assembly.[101]

Ambedkar defined the term "Backward" as follows: "A Backward Community is a community which is backward in the opinion of the Government." Answering the question whether such a definition is apt and whether it is justifiable to place responsibility in the hands of local or State Governments, he observed:

---

101. *Constituent Assembly Debates,* November 1948, p. 702.

Personally I think it would be a justiciable matter. If the local Government included in this category of reservations such a large number of seats, I think one could very well go to the Federal Court and the Supreme Court and say that the reservation is of such a magnitude that the rule regarding equality of opportunity has been destroyed and the Court will then come to the conclusion whether the local Government or the State Government has acted in a reasonable and prudent manner.[102]

So the task of defining the term "Other Backward Classes" was left entirely to the States' discretion, subject, however, to Judicial review in the event of discriminatory classification detrimental to the Fundamental Rights and the "equality of opportunity" of the citizens.

It would not be out of place to mention a few observations made by the Backward Classes Commission, appointed by the President, to probe into the problem of Backward Classes. The Commission came into being on January 29, 1953, with the following terms of reference:

a) to determine the criteria to be adopted in considering whether any sections of the people in the territory of India (in addition to the Scheduled Castes and Scheduled Tribes specified by notifications issued under Article 341 and 342 of the Constitution) should be treated as socially and educationally backward classes; and in accordance with such criteria, prepare a list of such classes setting out also their approximate numbers and their territorial distribution;
b) to investigate the conditions of all such socially and educationally backward classes and the difficulties under which they labour;

and make recommendations—

---

102. *Ibid.*

    i) as to the steps that should be taken by the Union or any State to remove such difficulties or to improve their condition; and

    ii) as to the grants that should be made for the purpose by the Union or State and the conditions subject to which such grants should be made;

    c) to investigate such other matters as the President may therefore refer to them; and

    d) to present to the president a report setting out the facts as found by them and making such recommendations as they think proper.

Likewise, the Backward Classes Commission prepared a questionnaire for the determination of backwardness dealing with the social, economic, educational, and caste aspect of the problem. On the basis of this questionnaire, the criteria adopted by the Commission for general guidance were:

    1) Low social position in the traditional hierarchy of Hindu society;

    2) Lack of general educational advancement among the major section of a caste or community;

    3) Inadequate or no representation in Government service;

    4) Inadequate representation in the field of trade, commerce and industry.[103]

The task entrusted to the Backward Classes Commission was no doubt complex, demanding objective tests for classifying "Other Backward Classes." But the majority of the members of the Commission overemphasized the importance of "caste" in any classification of "Other Backward Classes." Making caste the primary criterion, the Commission prepared a list of Backward Classes for the country as a whole, comprising as many as 2,399 commu-

---

103. *Report of the Backward Classes Commission,* 1956, para. 25, p. 46.

nities. In this way, millions were included within the
category of Backward Classes and no useful purpose was
served by an inquiry conducted by a special Commission
of this nature. It was observed in the Memorandum on
the Report of the Backward Classes Commission that:

> It has become necessary that some positive and work-
> able criteria should be devised for the specification of
> the socially and educationally backward classes of peo-
> ple, so that they may be given adequate assistance and
> relief in all suitable ways to make up for the leeway of
> the past and to acquire the normal standards of life
> prevalent in the country.[104]

The failure of the Backward Classes Commission to find
out a workable criteria for classifying Other Backward
Classes necessitated the Government of India to summon
the Deputy Registrar General of India to conduct a pilot
survey, with the basis of occupation as the test for determining the social and educational backwardness of the
people. Accordingly, a survey was conducted at West Bengal, Bombay, and Madras to express the new scheme. The
tests formulated for the determination of backwardness
were:

> a) any non-agricultural occupation in any State in
> India in which 50 percent or more of the persons belong
> to the Scheduled Castes or the Scheduled Tribes;
> b) any non-agricultural occupation in which literacy
> or percentage of the persons depending thereon is less
> than 50 percent of the general literacy in the State.[105]

But all the State Governments were not prepared to
accept the preceding criteria.

---

104. *Memorandum on the Report of the Backward Classes Commission*,
1956, p. 4.
105. Quoted in *Report of the Commissioner for Scheduled Castes and
Scheduled Tribes*, 1958–59, Part I, p. 12.

Yet another Committee to go through the problem of Other Backward Classes was "the Study Team on social welfare and welfare of Backward Classes," 1959, constituted by the Committee on Plan Projects. This Committee was of the following view:

We feel that in the absence of an objective and workable definition of "backwardness," the list of backward communities tends to expand converting backwardness into, as it were, a privilege conferred by birth. A landless labourer requires relief regardless of the community to which he belongs. The same principle holds good for those who are homeless or jobless, in ignorance or in disease. We are therefore in favour of abolishing the entire category of the so-called "Other Backward Classes."[106]

The Commissioner for Scheduled Castes and Scheduled Tribes, 1956-57 made a similar observation, and remarked that it was advisable to do away with the term "Backward Classes," for:

1) our aim is to have a classless and casteless society and we cannot continue for ever classifying people according to castes and classes appelations.

2) Backwardness has a tendency to perpetuate itself and those who are listed as backward try to remain as such, due to various concessions and benefits they derive, and thus backwardness itself becomes a vested interest.[107]

In view of the difficulties involved in evolving positive and workable criteria for determining backwardness, there is a feeling that "Other Backward Classes" should be done

---

106. *Report of the Study Team on Social Welfare and Welfare of Backward Classes*, 1959, para. 22, p. 7.

107. *Report of the Commissioner for Scheduled Castes and Scheduled Tribes*, 1956–57, Part I, p. 120.

away with. But such a drastic step could not be taken at a short notice. The Constitutional safeguards for Backward Classes would appear to be a decorative piece, if the entire category of "Other Backward Classes" is abolished, without defining who are backward. The criteria suggested by various Committees and pursued by the State Governments may be better termed as the trial-and-error method.

The criteria put under trial were:

    i) Caste criterion;
    ii) Criterion of Social Backwardness;
    iii) Criterion of Educational Backwardness; and
    iv) Economic criterion;
    v) Toward a satisfactory criteria.

The validity of each of these criteria is discussed in the forthcoming section to see how far it proves to be a satisfactory one in practical application.

Caste Criterion

Caste, the most distinguishing trait of Hinduism, constitutes the very basis of our social system. It plays an important role in the structure of Indian society and hence the relevance of caste criterion for classifying Other Backward Classes. A historical study of the caste system marked by Brahmanical supremacy emphasizes the relevance of caste for determining backwardness. It is crystal clear that the entire social structure of Indian society was based upon caste. Caste and caste alone was the lever of social stratification of society. It regulated not only the social life of the people but also the economic set-up, religion, and even the conjugal life of the individual. Moreover, the social fabric of Indian society is such that it is not possible to exclude any sections of society from the clutches of the caste system. As Ambedkar remarked:

> The fundamental principle of Hindu Law as enunciated in Mulla's Law Edition was that there was no Hindu who did not have a caste. If, therefore, reserva-

tions were made in favour of the backward classes which were nothing but a collection of certain castes, those who were excluded would belong to certain other castes. In the circumstances of the country it was impossible to have reservations without excluding some people who have a caste.[108]

The arguments put forward in favor of the caste criterion center around historical factors, where caste was chiefly responsible for social hierarchy. Then again, caste is intimately related to the social, educational, and economic backwardness of the people. Social exclusiveness and the sense of high and low were fostered by the caste elements. The economic stratification of society was also responsible for the caste system. Superior jobs were performed by high castes and menial and unclean jobs were thrust upon low castes under Brahmanical supremacy. Such a correlation between the economic status of the people and their caste may be a debatable one. Yet it has some justification in our society, insofar as the Functional Theory constitutes one of the origins for the genesis of the caste system. The fact that caste was chiefly responsible for giving unequal educational opportunities to the people is an accepted conviction. Hence, it is felt that since caste was responsible for the creation of "social misfits" and Backward Classes in the country, it is justifiable that castes neglected and downtrodden in the past should be given Constitutional privileges in the new set-up of our social system. The Backward Classes Commission also stated that backwardness of the people should be gauged by the factor of social hierarchy based on caste. It observed: "Following the analogy of the proverb, viz., 'using the thorn to remove a thorn,' we held that the evils of caste could be removed by measures which could be considered in terms of caste alone."[109]

---

108. *The Hindu*, May 19, 1951.
109. *Report of the Backward Classes Commission*, 1956, para. 57, p. XIII. (Extract of the Forwarding letter of the Chairman.)

At this juncture, it is necessary to examine the decisions of the Judiciary as regards the relevance of "caste criterion" from the point of view of "equality clause" and "non-discrimination" ensured in the Constitution. In the judicial pronouncements it has been made clear that the backwardness referred to in Art. 15 (4) is social and educational. If we look back to the evolution of the caste system, we find that caste was responsible for the social and educational backwardness of certain caste groups of the lower rungs of the caste hierarchy. Hence, the judiciary had to admit the relevance of the caste criterion in the determination of Backward Classes. But to ensure the "equality clause" and "non-discriminatory clause" of the Constitution, it introduced a limitation in the caste criterion by suggesting that the importance of the caste factor should not be overemphasized or exaggerated. In *M. R. Balaji* v *State of Mysore,* Gajendragadkar J. remarked:

> In dealing with the question as to whether any class of citizens is socially backward or not, it may not be irrelevant to consider the caste of the said group of citizens. In this connection it is, however, necessary to bear in mind that the special provision is contemplated for classes of citizens and not for individual citizens as such, and so, though the caste of the group of citizens may be relevant, its importance should not be exaggerated.[110]

Further, the fact that caste cannot be the basis for determining backwardness is nowhere specified in the Constitution. Backward Classes are nothing but groupings from specific castes. It may be presumed that the term "class" might have been substituted for the term "caste" for the formulation of secular ideas and democratic principles. Hence, "Backward Classes" may be presumed to mean "Backward Castes." In *Ramakrishna Singh* v *State of Mysore,* S.R. Das Gupta, C.J. has observed:

---

110. *A.I.R.* Vol. 50, 1963, para. 22, p. 659.

. . . the competence of the Government to treat certain castes as Backward Classes cannot be ruled out. It would certainly be open to the Government to determine the classes on any other basis, e.g., geographical, or occupational.

He further remarked:

I am inclined to accept the contention of the learned Government pleader that the basis on which classification of Backward Classes may be made would vary from State to State. In some States people residing in a particular geographical area may be grouped together as Backward Classes and in another certain castes may be determined as such Backward Classes.[111]

Caste as the criterion for classifying Backward Classes was not ruled out by the Mysore High Court as well. In *Partha* vs. *State of Mysore,* Narayana Pai J. and Mir Iqual Hussain J. observed:

What the Constitution really prohibits is a discrimination based on grounds only of caste. If, however, a group of persons clearly identifiable by their caste is really backward socially and educationally and is on that basis given the benefit of certain reservations, the ineligibility of a person belonging to another caste to secure those reservations is clearly not based on the ground of caste but is a consequence of the reservation properly in favour of a backward class.

They further interpreted that:

Such a classification will be open to challenge only if it can be shown that the criterion adopted for determining their backwardness is useless as a test of back-

---

111. *Mysore Law Journal,* Vol. 38, 1960, pp. 663–64.

wardness, so that the preference given to them will virtually amount to a preference on the ground of caste alone, the description as backward being illusory or fictitious.[112]

Backwardness is a relative term, an inevitable result of poverty, rigidity of custom and tradition imposed by the caste barrier. As a result of this, the specification of "Other Backward Classes" on a uniform basis throughout India is confronted with many difficulties. It is reasonable to infer that these difficulties might have deterred the framers from defining the term. So the discretion of classifying them was given to the States. If caste groups constitute Backward Classes in particular States, the State has every reason to consider caste as a criterion for determining backwardness. In certain cases, States are bound to accept castes as backward and even the Judiciary has justified the standpoint of the States in this direction. For instance, in the *State of Kerala* v R. Jacob Mathew, M. S. Menon J. accepted:

> We have no hesitation in holding that the Ezhavas, Muslims and the Latin Catholics inclusive of Anglo-Indians constituted "the socially and educationally Backward Classes of citizens," within the meaning of Art. 15 (4) of the Constitution.[113]

The validity of caste as one of the factors for ascertaining backwardness has been widely accepted. The Judiciary has interpreted, time and again, that mere consideration of the caste factor would not amount to discrimination in classifying Backward Classes. But when it is made the sole factor, an all-in-all determinant of backwardness, it amounts to gross injustice, anathema to the spirit of the Constitution. In *R. Chitralekha* v *State of Mysore,* Subba

---

112. *Ibid.,* Vol. 39, 1961, pp. 175–76.
113. *A.I.R.,* Vol. 51, 1964, para. 9, p. 318.

Rao J. stressed: ". . . the authority concerned may take caste into consideration in ascertaining the backwardness of a group of persons; but, if it does not, its order will not be bad on that account."[114] It has been realized that the caste system had been a hindrance to the establishment of egalitarian society in the past. So for creating equality some have emphasized the caste criterion for determining backwardness. In his minute of dissent, S. D. S. Chaurasia emphatically stated: "My only criterion was and still is that all the so-called shudras amongst Hindus, excepting Kayasthas in the North and a few castes like Commas and Reddis in the South, are backward."[115] Caste has not disappeared from the social plane altogether. In the words of K. M. Panikkar: "The time has not come when we can say that it is merely a survival without an active hold on peoples minds."[116]

Besides, "our society was not built essentially on an economic structure but on the medieval ideas of 'varna, caste and a social hierarchy.' "[117] The colossal extent of backwardness of a large number of communities in the country is the result of the defective social organization supported by an equally defective social ideal which had been accepted for generations.

But the caste criterion has certain drawbacks. In view of justice and equality, enshrined in the Constitution, any reference to "caste" would amount to injustice and would be sure to fan the flame of discontent among different religious groups. This fact was stated by the chairman of the Backward Classes commission: "My eyes were however opened to the dangers of suggesting remedies on caste basis when I discovered that it is going to have a most unhealthy effect on the Muslim and Christian sections of

114. *Ibid.*, para. 15, p. 1833.
115. *Report of the Backward Classes Commission*, 1956, Vol. 3, p. 22.
116. K. M. Panikkar, *The Foundations of New India*, 1963, p. 54.
117. *Report of the Backward Classes Commission*, 1956, Vol. 1, para. 2, p. 39.

the nation."[118] Besides, it creates another problem: what should be the criterion for classifying Backward Classes among the Christians and Muslims. It is a well-known fact that there was mass conversion of Hindus to other religious beliefs in the past. So caste-wise enumeration of "Other Backward Classes" would definitely affect these converts. But this problem has been solved by suggesting that converts from non-Backward Classes should be presumed to belong to advanced sections among Christians, Muslims, and Sikhs, respectively.

Moreover, the strict adherence to secularism would be vitiated by identifying backwardness with caste. The problem before us is to find out who are backward in the country socially and educationally, and the States owe an obligation to these weaker sections of society for their overall progress. Hence, special concessions guaranteed to Backward Classes under Article 15 (4), 16 (4) and 29 (2) cannot be declined to deserving poorer sections of society on the sole consideration of caste. It is not reasonable to assume that persons belonging to specific caste groups are "well off" or "ill off," as the case may be. This does not appear to be an objective approach to the problem. Poverty, ignorance, and squalor are not the monopoly of any single caste. They are found in all castes, as for that matter everywhere. But the only difference is the degree of backwardness may vary among different caste groups. Hence any emphasis on caste would be contradictory to the spirit of the Constitution. In the Minutes of Dissent of the Backward Classes Commission Report, a number of scholars have brought out the cross purposes that would be served by the caste criterion. Anup Singh, M.P., remarked: "If we continue to stick to the narrow, stereotyped caste and group loyalties of the past, we as a nation would not be at a standstill only but we would be leisurely speeding

---

118. *Ibid.*, para. 19, p. VI. (Extract of the Forwarding letter of the Chairman.)

backward."[119] Similarly, Arunangshu De stated that only harm would result by laying emphasis on the caste criterion for specifying Other Backward Classes. He observed:

> By making caste the basis of ameliorative measures we create vested interests in an institution against which we profess to be battling and thus unwillingly give it a new lease of life. It would defeat the very object of creating a casteless society.[120]

Besides, there are innumerable difficulties in making caste the criterion for measuring backwardness. Synonymous caste names are found both among the high and the low castes. The change of caste names creates lot of trouble in the classification of Other Backward Classes. This shortcoming of caste-wise classification of Backward Classes has been amply illustrated by the Backward Classes Commission. "The surname 'Valmiki' is used by Brahmans fishermen, ex-criminal tribes, and also by scavenging castes."[121]

English spelling and typographical errors also have created a number of castes, which also have led to strange confusion. Dasa is a community among the Shudra. Dasa means a servant or a slave. Pious people use the suffix Dasa when they accept some name of the deity as their own. Even men of the upper castes thus call themselves Dasa. Purushottamdas, Purandaradas, Prabhudas are instances in point. And, as irony would have it, some of the Jains were divided into two groups of ten families and twenty families, popularly known as Dasa and Visa, meaning ten and twenty, respectively. Now, Dasa meaning ten was also spelt Dasa. So, the Dasa among the Jains, a flourishing mercantile community, were confused with the

---

119. *Ibid.*, Vol. 3, p. 4.
120. *Ibid.*, p. 5.
121. *Ibid.*, para. 75, p. XIX.

Shudra community, Dasa. Such difficulties could of course be obviated by using the Nagri spelling of words, but it is not easy for the next Census to secure detailed and accurate figures and information about castes.[122]

Yet another difficulty arises from inter-caste marriages, where progeny have the option of selecting any caste or religion of their parents. There is likely to be a temptation among people to change over to the caste specified as Backward for purposes of enjoying special concessions. In the absence of a frank declaration of their social status, the caste-wise classification of Backward Classes would defeat the very purpose of the Constitutional guarantee for the betterment of weaker sections of society. The clamor for getting included in the list of Backward Classes would be intensified.

Then comes the problem of the well-organized and fairly advanced groups of Backward Classes, who have hitherto enjoyed Governmental concessions at the expense of the inarticulate sections. Northern India has given us the formula of "Ajgar," a word formed by taking the initial letters of the four communities: Ahir, Jat, Gujjar, and Rajput. Ajgar means the boa constrictor that quietly swallows and leisurely digests all sort of animals. Such Ajgar communities are to be found in both the upper and the lower castes. In Sind, the Amils dominated all the rest, whether Hindus or Muslims. In Gujarat, it was the Nagar, the Patidar, and the Anavil who are said to have dominated all the rest; and sometimes the Patanwadias or Padhiars have retaliated in desperation. In Maharashtra, besides the Brahman it is the Maratha who claimed to be the ruling community in the villages, and the Prabhu that dominated all other communities. In Karnataka the Lingayat and the Vokkaliga; in Andhra, the Kamma and the Reddy; in Tamilnad, the Mudaliar and the Naidu; in Kerala, the Nayar and the Ezhava; in Bengal, the Kayastha

---

122. *Ibid.*, para. 76, p. XIX.

and the Baidya; in Assam, the Ahom; in Bihar, the Rajput and the Bhumihar; in Orissa, the Khandayat and Karnam; and so on, are declared to be dominant.[123]

Thus, it has been argued that the most vocal and powerful castes would not only represent their case for being included in the list of Other Backward Classes, but also grab the lion's share of opportunities in enjoying special concessions. The less vocal castes either fail to represent their case for getting included in the list of Other Backward Classes, or fail to compete with the more pushful castes. Such being the case, many critics believe that the caste criterion would not serve the purpose of catering to the needs of the weaker sections of society. There is some truth in this hypothesis.

The fact that no reference should be made to caste has been voiced since 1901, particularly in the Census Reports. At every Census it was felt that any record on caste or undue emphasis on caste would accentuate caste-consciousness and would be injurious to national solidarity. But J. H. Hutton observed:

> It is, however, difficult to see why the record of a fact that actually exists should tend to stabilise that existence. It is just as easy to argue and with at least as much truth, that it is impossible to get rid of any institution by ignoring its existence, like the proverbial ostrich, and indeed facts themselves demonstrate that in spite of the recognition of caste in previous decades the institution is of itself undergoing considerable modification.[124]

Whatever the arguments for the retention of caste in Census Reports, "caste" is deleted from Census records since 1951. Instead, the term "special groups" occurs in Census Reports for purposes of classifying Backward Classes. In every Census before 1951, a record was made of the "race,"

---

123. *Ibid.,* para. 94, p. XXII.
124. *Census Report 1931,* para. 182, p. 430.

"tribe," or "caste" of the person enumerated. Prior to 1931, castes and tribes were tabulated separately and so the data on caste was more precise. In the 1932 Census, tabulation was confined primarily to the enumeration of:

i) Exterior castes;

ii) Primitive tribes; and

iii) All other castes with the exception of

    (a) those whose numbers fell short of four per thousand of the total population; and

    (b) those for which separate figures were deemed to be unnecessary by the Local Government.

But in the 1941 Census, tabulation was restricted to "Scheduled Castes," Tribes, and Anglo-Indians.

The essential feature of the 1951 Census was that the Government of India discouraged the official encouragement of castes in the Census Reports. With a view to provide facilities for "Scheduled Castes" and "Scheduled Tribes," a relaxation was, however, made to that effect. The relaxation was:

. . . that no general "race," "caste" or "tribe" enquiries should be made but that an enquiry should be regarding race, caste or tribe only to the extent necessary for providing information relating to certain special groups of the people who are referred to in the Constitution of India.[125]

The problem of caste enumeration in the Census Reports was summarized by Sardar Vallabhbhai Patel, in his address to the Census Conference in February, 1950, as follows:

Formerly there used to be elaborate caste tables which were required in India partly to satisfy the theory that it was a caste-ridden country, and partly to meet the needs of administrative measures dependent upon caste

---

125. *Census of India, 1953, Special Groups*—1951 Census, para. 2, p. 1.

division. In the forthcoming Census this will no longer be a prominent feature.[126]

In the light of these facts, it may be argued that caste-wise enumeration of Other Backward Classes would be far from precise, in the absence of precise data on castes in the Census Reports since 1951. Further, it may be presumed that the Governmental decision to delete caste from Census enumeration as an official discouragement of caste-consciousness invalidates the caste criterion.

Then again, caste has already entered politics. Caste has been exploited by the politicians for election propaganda. As K. M. Panikkar noted: "Casteism is a new factor of importance which is misshaping Indian democracy."[127] So, if caste is accepted as the criterion, it would be strengthened as the basis for political conflict. It induces people to bank on caste loyalties for enjoying Constitutional privileges. In a country like ours where we have an economy of scarcity rather than plenty, the caste element introduces frustration instead of harmony. Caste cliques would be profitably exploited by political parties and hence undermine national solidarity. The caste criterion does not appear to be an objective or rational approach to the problem of classifying Other Backward Classes, particularly at a time when "casteism survives even in political elections in spite of its official death."[128]

Yet another presumption is that the term "Backward Classes" refers chiefly to such sections of society that are socially and educationally backward. Social, economic, and educational set-up of society is primarily a dynamic factor. It changes with the passage of time. But caste, on the contrary, is static, insofar as an individual's membership to a specific caste is determined by his birth rather than intel-

---

126. Extract *Quoted in Report of the Backward Classes Commission*, 1956, para. 4 (a) pp. 9–10.
127. K. M. Panikkar, *Hindu Society at Cross Roads*, 1961, p. 18.
128. *Report of the Backward Classes Commission*, 1956, para. 4 (b), p. 10.

lectual or material attainments. Hence it may be questioned as to how a static factor (caste), may serve as the basis for determining dynamic process (backwardness). Particular castes incorporated in the list of Other Backward Classes may not remain the same always. There is every likelihood of change in the social, educational, and economic position of the individual families grouped under caste. Caste therefore does not help us to redress the grievances of the extremely poorer sections of society, in view of the limited resources at the disposal of the Government. Caste being the basis of backwardness, rich and poor alike belonging to a specific caste apply for the concessions. There is no guarantee that the poorer sections of a specific caste would benefit always. It is only a matter of chance and influence. So the caste criterion cannot be given undue importance.

Constitutionally speaking, any discrimination on the grounds of caste, race, sex, religion, etc., is repugnant to the spirit of the Constitution. It contradicts the equality clause of Articles 14, 15, and 16. The Judicial pronouncements on various G.O.'s throw sufficient light on this fact. The Madras G.O., which refused admission to a candidate on the sole ground of belonging to the Brahman community, was subject to judicial review. According to the Madras G.O., out of every 14 seats, 6 were to be filled by non-Brahmin Hindus, 2 by Harijans, 1 by Anglo-Indians and Indian Christians, and 1 by Muslims. But the Supreme Court invalidated the Madras G.O. as a violation of Art. 29 (2).[129]

Similarly, the Mysore G.O. of July 31, 1962, reserving 50 percent of the total number of seats in technical institutions for Backward Classes, was declared a fraud on the Constitution, quite inconsistent with Art. 15 (4).[130] Caste

---

129. See *Champakam Dorairajan* v *State of Madras, A.I.R.,* 1964, pp. 226–28.

130. *M. R. Balaji* v *State of Mysore, A.I.R.* 1963; Vol. 50, para. 36, p. 664.

criterion was emphasized as the sole determinant of Backward Classes by the Mysore Government, on the recommendations of "the Mysore Backward Classes Committee," constituted under the chairmanship of Nagan Gowda, on January 8, 1960. Commenting on this criterion, Gajendragadkar J. observed: "The Executive action taken by the State must be based on an objective approach free from all extraneous pressures. The said action is intended to do social and economic justice and must be taken in a manner that justice is and should be done."[131] A similar view was expressed in *R. Chitralekha* v *State of Mysore*. Pointing out the invalidity of making caste the sole criterion for determining backwardness, Subba Rao, J. observed:

> It may be that for ascertaining whether a particular citizen or a group of citizens belong to a backward class or not, his or their caste may have some relevance, but it cannot be either the sole or the dominant criterion for ascertaining the class to which he or they belong.[132]

From the above judicial pronouncements we could infer that caste criterion does not appear to be objective or rational. In the first place, it has been clearly stated by judges that caste cannot be equated with class, nor is the term "caste" anywhere found in the Articles specified for purposes of giving special concessions to Backward Classes. This situation was lucidly explained by Subba Rao, J.:

> The important factor to be noticed in Art. 15 (4) is that it does not speak of castes, but only speaks of classes. If the makers of the Constitution intended to take castes also as units of social and educational backwardness, they would have said so as they have said in the case of the Scheduled Castes and the Scheduled Tribes. Though it may be suggested that the wider expression "classes"

---

131. *Ibid.*, para. 36, p. 664.
132. *R. Chitralekha* v *State of Mysore, A.I.R.*, 1964, Vol. 51, para. 19, p. 1833.

is used in clause (4) of Art. 15 as there are communities without castes, if the intention was to equate classes with castes, nothing prevented the makers of the Constitution to use the expression "Backward Classes or Castes." The juxtaposition of the expression "Backward Classes" and "Scheduled Castes" in Art. 15 (4) also leads to a reasonable inference that the expression "classes" is not synonymous with castes.[133]

The caste criterion is not supported on the ground that it brings about more caste antagonisms in society. C. Rajagopalachari commented: "We seek to do away with all caste divisions; but all statutory and other concessions, given for the uplift of the backward elements, are prescribed on the basis of caste, although castes and sub-castes are branded as wicked and stand abolished in the national ideology."[134] In a democracy, it is the individual who constitutes the unit rather than castes or communal groups. Unless we cater to the well-being of the individual, democracy does not thrive. The futility of reviving caste has been further remarked by S. Radhakrishnan: "Caste is a source of discord and mischief, and if it persists in its present form, it will affect with weakness and falsehood the people that cling to it."[135] The chairman of the Backward Classes Commission himself admitted: "It is only when the Report was being finalized that I started thinking anew and found that backwardness could be tackled on a basis or a number of bases other than that of caste."[136]

Backwardness is not confined to lower castes alone, nor intelligence to higher castes. Even if we suppose caste to be the lever for measuring social rankings, the difficulty props up in practical application of the hypothesis. In actual practice we find that, even though the members be-

---

133. *Ibid.*
134. *Satyam Eva Jayate*, Vol. 2, p. 643.
135. S. Radhakrishnan, *Eastern Religions and Western Thought*, 1940, p. 378.
136. *Report of the Backward Classes Commission*, 1956, para. 22, p. VI.

long to a particular caste, there is no guarantee that all the members of that particular caste occupy the same social status or intelligence. There is no doubt that the ritual status of a particular caste group would be the same with all the individuals. But the same may not be the case with social, cultural and economic status of the members constituting the caste.

So, it is largely felt, that special concessions given on caste basis to Backward Classes have resulted in creating a vested interest in casteism. People who are victimized on caste grounds feel that backwardness is not associated with particular caste groups. Mrs. Hansa Mehta, while presiding over the ninth session of the Indian conference on social work held at Jaipur on December 28, 1956, urged the need for substituting caste by some other criteria. She remarked:

> Special reservations for castes needed to be substituted by general provisions for different categories of needs, with priorities allotted to those who were particularly handicapped or underprivileged. This would eliminate those people who nominally belong to backward classes but virtually have attained social and economic statue that would not entitle them to additional safeguards and privileges.[137]

The advantages of introducing a criterion other than caste was also felt by Kaka Kalelkar, even though caste was emphasized in the Report of the Backward Classes Commission. He admitted:

> . . . once we eschew the principle of caste, it will be possible to help the extremely poor and deserving from all communities. Care of course must be taken to give pref-

---

137. Extract of a speech appeared in *Vanyajati* Quarterly Magazine published by Adimjati Sevak Sangh, Vol. 5, January 1957, No. 1, p. 52.

erence to those who come from the traditionally neglected social classes.[138]

Caste criterion was in vogue particularly in the southern States of Andhra Pradesh, Kerala, Madras, and Mysore. But in the light of judicial pronouncements, which have ruled out the G.O.'s of the States as ultra vires of the Constitution, it was necessitated to rule out the validity of caste criterion. The Government of India has suggested to all the State Governments/Union Territories to do away with the lists of "Other Backward Classes" based on castes and to apply economic tests in the determination of Other Backward Classes. Most of the States have accepted the Union decision. The Governments of Gujarat and Maharashtra are following the "Income test" for determining backwardness. The Mysore Government has made a drastic change by switching over to economic and occupational test. But Kerala has retained the caste criterion. Caste criterion is therefore not favored by the Government of India for classifying "Other Backward Classes." But how far this suggestion would be put in to practice remains to be seen.

Criterion of Social Backwardness

The Constitution does not contain any definition of the term "Social Backwardness," even though a specific reference of it is made in Art. 15 (4). Hence there is lot of controversy as regards its interpretation. A number of factors contribute to social backwardness. It not only varies from State to State but also between the divisions of the same State. As a result, its determination is a complex problem which demands careful scrutiny and objective approach. The word "social" means "concerned with the mutual relations of men or classes"; "relating to society."

---

138. *Report of the Backward Classes Commission*, 1956, para. 22, p. VII.

In this context it could be analyzed as the result of caste, illiteracy, poverty and occupation in the main. The judicial interpretation has also emphasized the aforesaid factors.

Generally in India, social backwardness is attributed to the defective social organization of the country, fostered by the caste system. The Backward Classes Commission pointed out: "We wish it were easy to dissociate caste from social backwardness at the present juncture."[139] Backwardness has greater affinity to caste than any other factors. Explaining the inevitability of emphasizing caste, the Commission further observed:

> The Brahman, taking to tailoring, does not become a tailor by caste, nor is his social status lowered as a Brahman. A Brahman may be a seller of boots and shoes, and yet his social status is not lowered thereby. Social backwardness, therefore is not today due to the particular profession of a person, but we cannot escape caste in considering the social backwardness in India.[140]

This aspect was discussed earlier in the section on caste criterion in this chapter.

Another determinant of social backwardness is illiteracy. Denial of educational opportunities to lower orders of society is held to be chiefly responsible for this state of affairs. This aspect is discussed under the next heading, "Criterion of Educational Backwardness."

The third test is poverty which is discussed in the section on "Economic Criterion." The Judiciary has placed special emphasis on this factor in ascertaining backwardness. The observation made by Gajendragadkar J. in M. R. Balaji *v* the State of Mysore was:

> Social backwardness is on the ultimate analysis the result of poverty to a very large extent. The classes of citi-

---

139. *Ibid.,* para. 10, p. 41.
140. *Ibid.*

zens who are deplorably poor automatically become socially backward. They do not enjoy a status in society and have, therefore, to be content to take a backward seat.[141]

Hence the "Poverty test" has been assumed to be one of the requisites of social backwardness.

The three constituents of social backwardness—caste, illiteracy, and poverty—are discussed in detail in different sections of this chapter. So in view of the fact that a re-examination of these factors would amount to tautology, they are briefly discussed here.

Yet another factor constituting social backwardness is "Occupational test," which we shall examine at length now. It has been stated by Gajendragadkar J. that:

. . . the occupations of citizens may also contribute to make classes of citizens socially backward. There are some occupations which are treated as inferior according to conventional beliefs and classes of citizens who follow these occupations are apt to become socially backward.[142]

This idea of grouping communities with poor representation in Public Service, under the category of Backward Classes, was expressed by the Miller Committee also.[143]

In India, Government service has been esteemed very high compared to any other profession. No other country in the world attaches so much importance to Government service as the people in India. As the Census Superintendent, 1931, has commented:

Matriculation has in fact assumed much the same importance in the social sphere as a Public School Education has done in England. The ambition to "make a gentleman" of their son is not confined to the parents of the lower classes of any one country and in Assam

141. *A.I.R.*, 1963, Vol. 50, para. 23, p. 659.
142. *Ibid.*
143. *Miller Committee Report 1918.*

this takes the form of matriculation; and a job which does not involve manual labour. The respectability of a community in Assam, can, in fact, be generally measured by the number of persons belonging to that community who are in Government Service.[144]

It is very interesting to observe that a detailed study of the "Occupation test" points us to the fact that it revolves around the social status in caste hierarchy. It has been emphatically stated by Sir Denzil Ibbetson and J. C. Nesfield that "caste is mainly occupational in origin, i.e., occupations which were organised into guilds slowly became exclusive and stratified into caste."[145] The hereditary association of a caste with an occupation has been so striking, it has been argued that caste is nothing more than the systematization of occupational differentiation.

The fact that caste has great affinity to the occupations pursued has been pointed out by the Mysore Population Study, conducted by the Government of India, jointly in cooperation with the United Nations. The statistical data on the occupational test of particular caste groups in Bangalore city is given in Table 3-18:[146]

TABLE 3–18

Percentage of Males with Principal Activity Working

Hindus	Professional technical managerial and sales occupations	Manual workers, craftsmen, process production, and service workers	Others
Scheduled Castes	6.9	86.2	6.8
Backward Castes	18.0	68.7	13.4
Non-Backward Castes	42.3	51.9	5.8
Muslims	44.8	43.8	11.6
Indian Christians	21.2	71.8	7.1

144. *Census Report of India*, 1931, para. 146, p. 338.
145. Quoted in "The Ethnic Theory of Caste" by G. S. Ghurye, *Man in India*, Vol. 4, 1924, p. 209.
146. *The Mysore Population Study*, United Nations Publication, New York, 1961, para. 59, p. 209.

In the light of the statistical data, the Study Team assessed that the "white-collar jobs" and high percentage of literacy are commanded by the non-Backward Castes and the Muslims in rural and urban areas as well. The preponderance of other castes in the field of manual workers is distinct.

Similar information has been recorded by the Mysore Backward Classes Commission. The percentage of Backward Classes and Brahmans engaged in Public Service as recorded in the Table 3-19 speaks for itself the close relationship of caste to the occupational structure of society.[147]

TABLE 3–19

Caste	Population	Percentage of employment to total posts excluding class IV
Brahmans	905,657	23.213
Kshatriyas	78,187	1.243
Mudali	112,208	0.609
Vaisya	144,750	0.922
Kodaga	56,164	1.402
Other Non-Scheduled Hindus	703,551	16.964
Muslims	2,119,899	13.221
Christians	453,441	4.613
Buddhists	1,860	
Sikhs	4,271	
Zorastrians	1,000	0.199
Jews	201	
Others (whose religion is not known)	1,092	
Total	4,582,281	62.386

In contrast, the percentage of Backward Classes in Government service shows a very poor record as indicated in Table 3-20:

147. *Mysore Backward Classes Committee Interim Report*, 1960, pp. 15–16.

TABLE 3–20

Caste	Population	Percentage of employment in total posts excluding class IV
Agasa	248,777	0.307
Banajiga	332,427	1.089
Bedaru	1,002,074	0.157
Parsi	64,992	0.024
Devanga	221,049	0.871
Gangakula	460,813	0.146
Ganiga	90,695	0.363
Idiga	528,613	0.183
Kumbara	109,103	0.166
Kuruba	1,455,754	2.054
Maratha	861,724	0.200
Meda	28,318	0.004
Nayinda	120,763	—
Neygi	141,989	0.077
Rajput	43,822	0.098
Satani	36,604	0.166
Thigala	152,668	0.161
Uppara	220,743	0.295
Vokkaliga	2,744,346	7.580
Viswakarma	482,366	1.231
Yadava	310,681	0.363
Voddar	359,843	—
Lamani	178,417	—
Jains	147,548	0.433
Lingayats	3,293,042	14.160
Nayar	24,609	0.087

There are scholars who refute the association of occupation with caste. G. S. Ghurye does not believe in the occupational structure based on caste. He has stated emphatically: "We cannot grant the hereditary nature of occupation as a sound test of caste."[148] His argument runs on the line that there was mobility in people's choice of profession and the Epics and the Vedic literature throw

148. *Man in India*, Vol. 4, 1964, p. 220.

light on this factor. The lower classes had ample choice in selecting their profession from a medley of professions. So hereditary occupations, particularly manual labor, cannot be identified with lower castes. Explaining the circumstances under which people pursued hereditary occupations, he remarked: "The son of a carpenter may take to the profession of his father not because society prevents him from following other occupations but because, under the circumstances, he finds it easier to serve his apprenticeship to his father."[149] He attributed hereditary occupations to the influence of family rather than to social restrictions. The problem as to how far occupation is related to caste and vice versa is a much debatable one. But our object is mainly to examine the propriety of "Occupation test" as one of the criteria for classifying Other Backward Classes.

But it is a matter of observation at the present day, as the statistical data recorded in Tables 3-18, 3-19, and 3-20 clearly illustrate, that occupations have some affinity to caste. The traditional occupational structure has no doubt undergone some radical changes. Still castes involved in traditional occupations are not lacking completely. Even today it is possible to identify castes occupation-wise. Because, even though there was mobility in the choice of occupation, the adoption of an occupation contrary to the hereditary one depended on the social esteem of the occupation. The desire to pursue occupations, rated high in social esteem, was striking. On the contrary, people's option for occupations rated low under the stigma of pollution was very faint. Social status therefore was dependent on the occupations pursued. In short, unlike Western countries, our society is not guided by the principle of dignity of labor. Manual labor was always accorded low social status. The reconciliation between learning and labor is not effected. The entire position

---

149. *Ibid.*

might be summed up in a triangle, with social status at the base and caste and occupation as two angles.

Thus "Occupation test" seems to be an objective criterion for determining backwardness. An important reason for emphasizing this test is that grievances are already reported from Backward Classes as regards the evasion of the social factor in preference to the economic criterion for classifying Backward Classes. The All India Federation of Scheduled Castes, Scheduled Tribes, and Other Backward Classes, in their Memorandum to the President, have urged for the emphasis on the social and educational standards of the people in any classification of Backward Classes. The Memorandum reads: "The persons who traditionally earned their livelihood through manual labor were backward classes and the issue of socially and educationally backward classes should not be mixed up with that of the economically backward people."[150] Even the Backward Classes Commission urged the necessity for considering social backwardness. It remarked: "Care of course must be taken to give preference to those who come from the traditionally neglected social classes!"[151] Besides, social backwardness is particularly emphasized in Art. 15 (4), as one of the conditions for giving special concessions to Backward Classes. Hence the "Occupation test" as a criterion for measuring the backwardness of the people is justifiable and workable.

It is gratifying to note that the Mysore Government has taken into account the "Occupation test" as one of the criteria for determining Other Backward Classes. These are: " (1) Economic conditions and (2) occupation." The Government order concludes:

Hence classes of people whose annual income is Rs. 1200/- per annum or less and who are pursuing occu-

---

150. *Deccan Herald,* November 17, 1964.
151. *Report of the Backward Classes Commission,* 1956, para. 22, p. VII.

pations set out in Para 3 above, i.e., (1) actual cultivator; (2) artisan; (3) petty businessman; (4) inferior service (class IV Government servants and corresponding class or service in private employment) including casual labour; and (5) any other occupation involving manual labour are hereby classified as socially and educationally backward.[152]

But social backwardness determined by the "Occupation test" as a criterion has certain inadequacies. In the first place, the bona fide declaration of the occupations pursued is doubtful, in the absence of licensed artisans in the country. The desire for enjoying special concessions, particularly by way of reservation to high education (technical and professional) and reservation in public service, might induce a large number of dishonest persons to profess to belong to one of the occupations set out in the list of Backward Classes. Apart from Government servants, others who are employed in private enterprises also seize the opportunity to get themselves included in one of the categories specified as backward according to "Occupation test," although they do not belong in any. But comparatively speaking, these drawbacks appear to be negligible. In an underdeveloped country like ours with scarce economy and appalling poverty, we cannot expect a frank declaration of one's social position. Social position is likely to be artificially boosted up. Whatever the criteria suggested, there would be some drawbacks. So in view of the complexity of the problem, the "Occupation test" holds good as one of the criteria for determining Other Backward Classes. It would not only be in conformity with the spirit of the Constitution, but also appears to be an objective and workable criterion. But it could not be taken as the sole determinant.

---

152. *Mysore Government Order* No. ED 75, TGL 63, dated 26–7–1963.

Criterion of Educational Backwardness

Educational backwardness is another criterion which deserves a thorough consideration in our study. A reference to this is made in Art. 15 (4), which states:

> Nothing in this article or in clause (2) of article 29 shall prevent the State from making any special provision for the advancement of any socially and educationally backward classes of citizens or for the Scheduled Castes and the Scheduled Tribes.

From this article we could infer that backwardness is also attributed to the educational factor. Educational backwardness could primarily be measured by the percentage of literacy.

Generally speaking, the percentage of literacy in the country is very low compared to the other advanced countries of the world. The overall progress of literacy in the country from 1911 to 1961 has been worked out as follows:

Year	Percentage
1911	5.9
1921	7.2
1931	8.0
1941	N.A.
1951	16.6
1961	24.0

Caste-wise, literacy percentage in select South and North Indian States for the years 1921 and 1931 shows the preponderance of Brahmans over the other castes in the educational field.

The literacy percentage caste-wise for North Indian States is given in Table 3–21.[153] From the foregoing data it could be stated that lower castes with traditional occupations were educationally backward in Northern India, with the exception of a few trading communities. In the majority of cases, the Brahmans outnumbered the rest of

---

153. Compiled from *Census Report of India*, 1931, Table V, pp. 342–45.

TABLE 3–21

Caste	Number per 1,000 who are literate				Number per 10,000 literate in English			
	1931		1921		1931		1921	
	Males	Femalels	Males	Females	Males	Females	Males	Females
Bengal								
Baidya	777	476	714	431	5,295	1,402	4,458	618
Brahman	645	216	654	169	2,888	332	2,504	103
Kayastha	571	209	559	154	2,740	354	2,285	123
Barui	284	56	356	38	721	58	716	13
Kamar	150	37	322	24	450	42	413	9
Jogi (Jugi)	240	33	290	14	396	32	288	7
Napit	198	25	245	16	333	28	308	7
Baishnab	284	37	259	18	417	35	224	7
Kaibartta (Chari)	324	39	218	11	472	19	241	3
Goala	165	24	181	12	293	19	227	5
Dhoba	137	19	142	8	150	12	148	3
Namasudra	145	15	142	6	224	9	134	2
Kaibartta (Jalia)	120	22	110	6	133	22	102	3
Jolaha	133	40	81	4	209	65	39	1
Bagadi	34	4	40	2	20	3	30	—
Hari	36	5	36	1	18	4	14	—
Bauri	14	5	11	1	9	—	7	—
Santal	14	4	8	—	7	—	2	—
Bombay								
Brahman	788	231	652	144	2,507	221	1,612	72
Lohana	470	74	343	77	790	25	443	61
Lingayat	293	20	231	15	136	1	69	1
Maratha	223	28	58	3	148	2	20	1
Agri	98	3	41	3	14	1	9	—
Mahar (Dhed)	63	5	23	1	28	1	13	1
Bhaswad	25	2	10	1	3	—	2	—
Bhil	10	—	4	—	1	—	—	—
Punjab								
Khatri	438	114	397	61	1,277	85	1,006	39

Baniya (Agarwal)	490	34	386	20	468	17	324	10
Arora	364	64	294	30	435	29	255	10
Brahman	268	34	214	19	453	20	342	8
Saiyid	216	33	172	26	483	26	341	11
Sheikh	198	43	141	24	545	43	351	7
Pathan	140	26	100	13	356	21	226	7
Kashmiri	140	32	64	11	409	33	167	7
Rajput	89	11	58	6	169	9	85	6
Tarkhan	70	9	38	5	95	3	30	1
Jat	55	7	32	3	76	3	36	1
Kanet	49	1	36	1	29	—	24	—
Awan	60	6	36	1	96	3	43	—
Arain	56	8	28	3	112	9	52	1
Nai	48	4	28	2	50	1	24	1
Mirasi	41	3	28	1	28	1	17	1
Lohar	51	5	26	2	55	3	36	1
Ahir	30	2	22	1	49	1	27	1
Jhinwar	42	4	22	2	39	2	22	—
Julaha	32	3	20	1	28	1	10	—
Biloch	24	2	18	1	23	1	12	9
Teli	24	2	13	1	24	1	9	—
Mochi	20	2	10	1	16	—	4	—
Kumhar	21	2	9	1	21	1	7	—
Chamar	14	1	9	—	7	—	2	—
Macchi	17	2	7	1	19	1	5	—
Chuhra	13	3	4	—	14	4	4	—

the communities in education. It is only in Punjab that
the Baniyas surpassed the Brahmans in literacy. In this
connection it is necessary to make a reference to the Census Commissioner's observation. J. H. Hutton remarked:

> Those with a high social status are not by any means
> always so high in order of literacy, though of necessity
> the trading classes are always high in male literacy,
> while the figures of feminine literacy do not necessarily
> correspond at all to those of masculine.[154]

154. *Ibid.,* para. 141, pp. 330–31.

But this is only an exceptional case. The literacy percentage of petty artisans like Namasudra, Jolaha, Bagdi,
Hari, Bauri, Goala, and Jogi in Bengal; Agri, Mahar
(Dhed) Bharwar, and Bhil in Bombay; Jat, Kanet, Arain,
Nai, Lohar, Ahir, Jhinwar, Teli, Mochi, Chamar, Macchi,
and Chuhra in Punjab, is positive proof that educational
backwardness is closely associated with the lower castes
with inferior social status. This is because they were forced
to pursue traditional occupations which did not demand
education. The position of these classes remains very much
the same, for we find that in spite of the failure of the
1951 Census to provide caste-wise figures regarding literacy
percentage, the Backward Classes Commission classified as
backward most of the castes with poor educational standards of the 1931 Census, under the category of "Other
Backward Classes" in their report.

Coming to the situation in the South, we may point out
that the domination of Brahmans over the rest of society
in literacy is more distinct in the South than in the North,
as Table 3–22 records:[155]

TABLE 3–22

| Caste | Number per 1,000 who are literate | | | | Number per 10,000 literate in English | | | |
| | 1931 | | 1921 | | 1931 | | 1921 | |
	Males	Females	Males	Females	Males	Females	Males	Females
Madras (including Cochin and Travancore)								
Brahman	800	286	608	152	3,271	183	1,895	83
Nayar	604	276	491	215	694	137	483	49
Komati	615	68	521	54	354	13	288	9
Chetti	447	97	387	25	248	15	235	5
Vaniyan	152	8	298	21	78	—	109	6
Kammalan	462	95	277	26	73	8	69	3
Labbai	438	27	300	15	240	6	92	4
Kaikolan	186	10	261	18	172	6	79	2
Kshatriya	764	625	264	38	3,329	723	263	17

155. *Ibid.*, Table V, pp. 342–45.

Kallan	235	8	163	5	98	3	38	1
Telaga	149	25	119	17	220	8	182	6
Mappilla	265	45	117	8	96	4	19	—
Idaiyan	472	264	112	9	1,288	135	90	4
Pallan	56	1	46	2	10	—	7	—
Paraiyan	56	6	37	3	25	3	16	1
Golla	45	3	29	3	40	1	26	1
Mala	16	1	16	1	70	—	7	—
Madiga	9	1	9	1	4	—	5	—
Cheruman	13	3	8	1	—	—	1	—
Hyderabad								
Brahman	701	79	437	63	708	67	338	36
Komati	258	17	270	10	78	14	36	2
Lingayat	88	8	76	3	60	4	26	1
Kapu	64	8	47	2	50	7	12	—
Telaga	42	4	26	3	76	3	36	1
Maratha	30	4	23	2	24	2	9	—
Madiga	10	1	2	1	7	1	1	—
Mysore								
Brahman	783	344	707	203	3,386	345	2,399	112
Sheikh	302	102	206	50	350	34	187	7
Lingayat	301	22	203	11	140	5	63	1
Vokkaliga	122	5	75	3	53	3	25	1
Kuruba	68	3	40	1	34	1	13	—
Beda	58	4	36	3	21	1	8	—

From this table we find that the educational standards among Vaniyan, Kammalan, Kallan, Telaga, Golla, Kaikelan, Labbai, Pallan, Pariyan, Madiga, Kuruba, Beda, Kapu are very low. These castes were confined to menial jobs like oil pressing, petty traders, agricultural laborers, smiths, hunters, shepherds, cattle rearers, etc. These very castes are classified by the Backward Classes Commission for respective States under the category of "Other Backward Classes."

The literacy percentage, caste-wise, in select North Indian and South Indian States clearly illustrates that in India educational backwardness is dependent not only on the caste factor but also on the occupational factor. This is mainly due to the fact that occupations were merged with castes in Hindu society. There are castes of carpenters, tailors, goldsmiths, blacksmiths, weavers, oil pressers, meat sellers, shepherds, herdsmen, barbers, agriculturists, planters, gardeners, fishermen, potters, vegetable sellers, bards, musicians, etc. Thus people not only specialized in their traditional professions but passed on professional skill from generation to generation. The result was that education in ancient India was vocational. Only the privileged classes—Brahmans—took to education seriously as a means of livelihood. This fact was precisely stated by the Census Commissioner of India in 1931:

> As a result of the caste system there is an insistent demand for education on the part of those castes who have been accustomed to look to literacy to provide them with a livelihood, and their tendency under competition is to demand higher education. On the other hand there is no widespread demand among other castes for education at all.[156]

A comparative study of a handful of lower castes with that of Brahmans illustrates, that lower castes compare very poorly with Brahmans in education.

To illustrate the close affinity of caste to illiteracy, it is necessary to record the percentage of literacy in English, because of the popular notion in India that English education is a necessity for securing white-collar jobs. The assumption is that English education means high social status and a handsome profession. Hence, caste-wise enumeration of literates in English has been specially mentioned. The literates in English on caste basis among the selected few castes are given in Table 3-23:[157]

156. *Ibid.*, para. 145, p. 335.
157. *Ibid.*, para. 143, p. 332.

TABLE 3-23

Literates per 10,000 population

Caste	Males	Females
Baidya	5,279	1,373
Kayastha	2,418	293
Khatri	1,320	109
Brahman	1,073	86
Nayar	693	137
Lushei	160	9
Rajput	135	5
Vishurabrahman	86	4
Jat	70	3
Kumbi	69	2
Mali	53	2
Oraon	46	9
Teli	48	0.5
Momin	43	6
Parayan	25	3
Yadava	23	1
Mahar	15	0.8
Kumbar	16	0.5
Baloch	17	0.4
Dom	9	2
Bhangi	6	2
Gond	4	0.4
Chamar	3	0.3
Bhil	1	—

Here again we find Brahmans, Baidya, Kayastha, Khatri, and Nayars having the highest percentage of literacy among men and women. But one interesting feature notable in the preceding table is that few communities other than Brahmans have shown remarkable progress. We may mention Khatri, that is silk weavers (Rajput) ; Kayastha, that is Shudras; Baidya, who come under the category of both Rajputs and Brahmans; and Nayars moved high and even surpassed the Brahmans in literacy. So poor literacy was mainly due to the fact that education was denied to the lower castes under Brahmanical supremacy. It was for this reason that lower castes constituted the educationally Backward Classes in Independent India. With the emergence of British administration, the portals of educational institutions were opened for all, irrespective of caste distinctions. The introduction of mass literacy in the country by the British put an end to Brahmanical monopoly of education. Since then we find that the other castes have evinced interest in education, as is clearly illustrated in the above tables. Hence it could be presumed that social status in caste hierarchy for pursuing education sounds vague. Given the facilities and equal opportunities, all castes could acquire education. It would be no glaring blunder to remark that the caste system was chiefly responsible for the educational backwardness of the lower castes. There is ample testimony to this fact. For, with the introduction of mass literacy, we find certain trading communities of the North, Baidya, Khatri, and Kayasthas outnumber Brahmans in education.

The causes for educational backwardness among the Backward Classes were summed up by the Backward Classes Commission as:[158]

1. Traditional apathy for education on account of social and environmental conditions or occupational handicaps.

2. Poverty and lack of means of a large number of communities to educate their children.

3. Lack of educational institutions in the rural areas.

4. Living in inaccessible areas and lack of proper communication.

5. Lack of adequate educational aids in the form of freeships, scholarships, and monetary grants for the purchase of books and clothing.

6. Lack of residential hostel facilities in places where educational institutions are situated.

7. Unemployment among the educated acting as a

---

158. *Report of the Backward Classes Commission*, 1956, para. 186, pp. 107–8.

TABLE 3-24

Caste Composition of the Hindu Population in the Sample for Zones and Strata

Zone and stratum	Number in sample					Percent		
	Total Hindus	Scheduled Castes	Scheduled Tribes	Backward Castes	Non-Backward Castes	Scheduled Castes	Backward Castes	Non-Backward Castes.
Zone I (Rural Hills)	4,557	674	—	893	990	14.8	19.6	65.6
Zone II (Rural Hills)	6,608	1,276	32	1,084	4,216	19.3	16.4	63.8
Zone III (Rural Plains)	10,730	2,724	17	2,691	5,298	25.4	25.1	49.4
Towns	4,395	609	10	880	2,896	13.9	20.0	65.9
Bangalore city	16,491	3,914	—	1,782	10,795	19.2	10.8	70.0
Total stratum I (Over 35 percent Muslims)	1,818	433	—	217	1,168	23.8	11.9	64.2
Stratum 2 (Over 35 percent Christians)	2,660	918	—	289	1,453	34.5	10.9	54.6
Stratum 3 (Over 35 percent Scheduled Castes)	4,067	2,030	—	541	1,496	49.9	13.3	36.8
Stratum 4 (Other Hindu, male literacy over 60 percent)	4,291	48	—	343	3,900	1.1	8.0	90.9
Stratum 5 (Other Hindu, male literacy below 60 percent)	3,655	485	—	392	2,778	13.3	10.7	76.0

damper on the desire of some of the communities to educate their children.

8. Defective educational system which does not train students for appropriate occupations and professions.

Hence the problem of education in most of the States is chiefly the problem of the Backward Classes, for it is they who are extremely backward in education.

The Mysore population study, 1961, further testifies to the low literacy percentage of Backward Classes, as indicated in Table 3-24.[159]

So the fact that Backward Classes are educationally poor in comparison with the Brahmans, or non-Backward Classes, is amply illustrated in the Census Reports dating back to 1921. The position remains unaltered in the State of Mysore even up to 1961, as recorded by the Mysore population study, sponsored by the United Nations.

Estimated percentage of literacy caste-wise in 1951 as gathered by the Mysore Backward Classes Committee is shown in Table 3–25.[160]

Educational backwardness as a criterion for classifying Other Backward Classes appears objective and satisfactory for two reasons. Firstly, it refers to the traditional social classes who were deprived of education under Brahmanical supremacy. Secondly, Art. 15 (4) makes a special reference to the educational aspect of the Backward Classes. But these arguments hold good for theoretical discussion and academic interest. In practical administration this criterion is beset with many difficulties.

At the outset, doubt arises as to the unit for measuring literacy. Should it be "family" or "caste" is the problem. If "family" is taken as the unit, statistical enumeration regarding literacy position becomes not only cumbersome but practically an impossibility, considering the huge num-

---

159. *The Mysore Population Study*, para. 9, Table 7.2, p. 56.
160. *Mysore Backward Classes Committee Interim Report,* Statement IV, p. 14.

TABLE 3–25

Above the State Average		Below the State Average	
Caste	Estimated percentage of literacy	Caste	Estimated percentage of literacy
1. Brahman	93.8	Ganiga	19.5
2. Vaisya	70.7	Kunchatiga	17.3
3. Christian	65.9	Nayinda	17.3
4. Mudali	58.8	Hallikar	14.7
5. Nagartha	58.0	Vokkaliga	13.3
6. Jains	47.9	Idiga	10.9
7. Rajput	47.9	Kumbara	10.6
8. Darzi	47.2	Meda	9.5
9. Kshatriya	42.0	Tigala	8.4
10. Satani	39.3	Kuruba	8.2
11. Muslims	37.2	Agasa	8.1
12. Devanga	31.9	Gangakula	7.4
13. Viswakarma	30.6	Beda	7.3
14. Neygi	30.4	Yadava	7.3
15. Lingayat	29.8	Uppara	7.3
16. Banajiga	29.6	Jogi	4.0
17. Maratha	29.3	Scheduled Castes	4.6
All communities	20.6 (Actual)	Scheduled Tribes	0.2

bers involved in an overpopulated country like ours. If "caste" is made the unit, statistical enumeration no doubt is rendered easy. In fact, Census Reports up to 1951 have already recorded caste-wise literacy percentage. The Backward Classes Commission Report, 1956, Mysore Backward Classes Committee Report, 1960, and the Mysore Population Study, 1961, have made contributions to this fact. But the unit of "caste" raises lot of controversy from the point of view of justice and equality. The Constitution emphatically states that no discrimination should be made on grounds of caste, etc. Any emphasis on caste would be repugnant to the spirit of the Constitution. It is a well-known fact that preferential treatment given to Backward

Classes on the basis of caste is invalidated by the Judiciary, as communal G.O.'s were declared ultra vires of the Constitution.[161]

Yet another difficulty is that since the general level of education in the country is low, it is reasonable to assume that educational backwardness would swell the list of Other Backward Classes. This doubt was echoed in the Constituent Assembly by T. T. Krishnamachari:

> I say the basis of any future division as between "backward" and "forward" or "non-backward" might be in the basis of literacy. If the basis of division is literacy, 80 percent of our people fall into the backward class of citizens. Who is going to give the ultimate award? Perhaps the Supreme Court.[162]

But if occupational groups are taken as the unit, it would be more appropriate to record educational backwardness of the people. In such a case, it would serve the dual purpose of dealing with social backwardness, for occupations set out in the list of Other Backward Classes refer mostly to the traditionally neglected classes, and meanwhile it would indicate the literacy position of these classes. Thus, the criterion of educational backwardness with "occupational groups" as the unit of measurement would be in consonance with Art. 15 (4) of the Constitution. For the social backwardness of any class of people would be reflected in their percentage of literacy with reference to the State percentage of literacy.

Economic Criterion

The economic criterion to determine backward classes has been necessitated by the fact that the Judiciary has not

---

161. See *Champakam Dorairajan* v *State of Madras, A.I.R.,* 1951, Vol. 38, *M. R. Balaji* v *State of Mysore, A.I.R.,* 1963, Vol. 50, *R. Chitralekha* v *State of Mysore, A.I.R.,* 1964, Vol. 51.

162. *Constituent Assembly Debates,* 1948, p. 699.

only invalidated the caste criterion but has also declared ultra vires the communal G.O.'s of the State Governments. As a consequence of this, the Government of India has suggested to all the State Governments/Union Territories to do away with the lists of Other Backward Classes based on castes, and to apply economic tests in the determination of Other Backward Classes. This suggestion of the Government is not, however, novel, for the economic criterion was suggested by the Study Team on Social Welfare and Welfare of Backward Classes even earlier. The recommendations made by this Committee were:

(a) An economic rationale should be introduced in the scheme of assistance concentrating on aid to those individuals who are economically less advanced among the other backward classes.

(b) These norms should be objectively determined and should be applied in no ungenerous or rigid manner. They may be periodically reviewed in the light of the changing position.[163]

The Committee was of the opinion that economic criterion should be applied even in the classification of Scheduled Castes and Scheduled Tribes. It further observed:

. . . the ultimate objective would be to entirely eliminate criteria other than economic, so that backwardness would be judged only on the basis of economic considerations. It is envisaged that the economic basis of need would then constitute the nucleus of a system of social security which can be extended in proportion to the expanding national resources.[164]

It has been further pointed out that "for the larger part inequalities arise from long-established features of a tra-

163. *Report of the Study Team on Social Welfare and Welfare of Backward Classes,* para. 14, p. 127.
164. *Ibid.,* para. 12, p. 126.

ditional society, such as feudal rights and tenures, or privileges and handicaps associated with the social structure."[165] It is greatly felt that economic disparities among the different castes are largely attributable to the rigid caste structure. So economic disparities should be got rid of by placing emphasis on economic conditions alone, in any determination of Other Backward Classes. Besides, it is also felt that the economic criterion is in consonance with the spirit of the Constitution, as it does not create any discrimination on the basis of caste, race, creed, etc. In a welfare state it is justified that those who are economically underprivileged should enjoy preferential treatment.

The economic welfare of the community can best be measured by the income. In an underdeveloped country like ours, there is no doubt that the "Economic test" for determining backwardness would bring difficulties in practical administration. A look into the statistical data on rural population with agricultural occupations and their subsequent per capita incomes would clearly illustrate the gravity of the situation. Out of a total population of 439,235,082, the rural population accounts for 359,772,165. People engaged in agricultural occupation in 567,169 villages come up to 307,464,557. The per capita monthly expenditure of a rural laborer is Rs. 19.7 only. Annual per capita income of an agricultural laborer is Rs. 99.4.[166] This constitutes the economic set-up of only the agricultural laborers. The expectation of better standards for the people engaged in menial jobs, in fields other than agriculture, is none too bright. So it would not be surprising, even if the whole country (with the exclusion of a fraction of a minority) comes under the category of Other Backward Classes by virtue of economic test. However low the "means test" may be, we could expect large num-

---

165. *Third Five Year Plan*, p. 16.
166. *Census of India*, 1961, figures for 1962–63.

bers to constitute Backward Classes by the application of the economic criterion. These arguments cannot be ruled out as mere figments of fancy. They could very well be supported by the practical difficulties experienced in administration. The Education officer, Sangli, reported: "The office of the Education officer, Zilla Parishad, Sangli, has received about four cartloads of applications for economically backward class free studentships from School and College Students."[167] Well, here the problem arises as to how to scrutinize the applications and how to do justice when such large numbers are involved. Critics may very well point to the ineffectiveness of the economic criterion on this score.

Besides, the All India Federation of Scheduled Castes, Scheduled Tribes, and Other Backward Classes has ruled out the propriety of the economic criterion in the determination of Backward Classes. They believe that "backwardness of a community should be judged by social and educational conditions and not on economic grounds alone.[168] Further, "the persons who traditionally earned their livelihood through manual labor were Backward Classes and the issue of socially and educationally Backward Classes should not be mixed up with that of the economically backward."[169]

Yet another loophole is that the economic criterion does not come under the purview of Art. 15 (4), because it is specifically mentioned in that article that special concessions are to be given to those who are "socially and educationally backward." We might argue as well that the economic criterion is not referred to in this article, hence it is ultra vires. If the makers of the Constitution intended to include the economic factor as a determinant of backwardness, they would have included it with social

---

167. *Indian Express*, July 20, 1966.
168. *Deccan Herald*, November 17, 1964.
169. *Ibid.*

and educational backwardness, referred to in Art. 15 (4).
The exclusion of the economic factor drives us to the
inference that the term "socially and educationally backward" could not be interpreted as referring to the economic factor. It is true that backwardness is a relative term,
an interaction of various factors. But constitutionally
speaking, the term "economic" is not referred to in Art.
15 (4). Hence, any emphasis on the economic criterion
would be outside the purview of Art. 15 (4). If the importance of the economic criterion is felt under present circumstances, then a constitutional amendment to this effect
is inevitable. Unfortunately, we find that without any
such amendment the "Economic criterion" has been suggested as the sole criterion for determining backwardness
by the Government of India, to the omission of "social
and educational backwardness," which are referred to in
Art. 15 (4). It is reasonable to presume from the foregoing arguments that the Government has evaded solving
the problem of social and educational backwardness of the
people by emphasizing the economic criterion as a determinant for classifying Other Backward Classes.

Thus, though the philosophy behind the economic criterion that those who are poor should enjoy preferential
treatment irrespective of caste, creed, etc., holds good, it
is not in conformity with Art. 15 (4) of the Constitution.
It would have been more apt and workable if the economic factor was emphasized along with the social and
educational backwardness referred to in the Constitution.
Economic criterion alone would not serve the purpose of
classifying Other Backward Classes. Conditions being different in different States, a sole uniform criterion could
not be advocated for the entire country, as the Government of India has done at present by suggesting the "Economic test." Kerala stands as a solid example in showing
that uniform criterion is inapplicable throughout India.
The Government of Kerala has not only defied the sugges-

tion of the Union Government, but has emphatically stated that "in the present circumstances of the State, a wholesale classification of all persons below a certain economic level as socially backward is not justified."[170] Besides, it ignores the historical context which testifies to the fact that economic backwardness itself is the result of the defective social organization. Hence the economic criterion as the sole determinant of backwardness does not appear to be objective and workable.

Toward A Satisfactory Criterion

Knowledge quails to suggest a workable and satisfactory criterion for the complicated problem of classifying Other Backward Classes. The nature of the problem is such that we could only provide a working hypothesis. This problem necessitated the constitution of many competent committees of All India nature, and these committees have evolved criteria after a thorough investigation of the problem. But in spite of this, the problem is still without solution. One such commission was the Backward Classes Commission, appointed by the President under Art. 340 of the Constitution, on January 29, 1953. The criteria suggested by this Commission were:

1) Low social position in the traditional caste hierarchy of Hindu society.
2) Lack of general educational advancement among the major section of a caste or community.
3) Inadequate representation in Government service.
4) Inadequate representation in the field of trade, commerce and industry.[171]

By the application of these criteria, the Commission

---

170. *Report of the Commission for Reservation of Seats in Educational Institutions, Kerala,* 1965, p. 36.
171. *Report of the Backward Classes Commission,* 1956, para. 25, p. 46.

listed as many as 2,399 communities as backward for different States. Hence it was felt that since the bulk of the country's millions were grouped under the category of Other Backward Classes, it would serve no purpose. The criteria suggested by the Commission failed to be objective and workable, so it was dispensed with on the ground that caste was made the sole identity for conferring special concessions.

Similarly, the Study Team on Social Welfare and Welfare of Backward Classes recommended: "The ultimate objective would be to entirely eliminate criteria other than economic, so that backwardness would be judged only on the basis of economic considerations."[172] The Union Government has also suggested to State Governments/Union Territories to apply the economic test for the determination of Other Backward Classes. But the economic criterion is not unanimously accepted. Because, according to this criterion, there is an assumption that backwardness is mainly economic, though social and educational factors might be taken into consideration. It is also interpreted that social backwardness referred in Art. 15 (4) applies to economic backwardness. But Constitutionally speaking, the economic criterion is nowhere mentioned, either in Art. 15 (4) or in the terms of reference of the Backward Classes Commission, appointed under Art. 340 of the Constitution. If the Constitution makers thought that backwardness was mainly economic, they would have said so by specifying "socially and economically backward" or "economically and educationally backward." Hence, assumption cannot override specific terms referred to in the Constitution. If the terms are not specifically stated, then they give scope for various interpretations. But no purpose would be served by interpreting the specific terms of the Constitution by way of assumption. What is needed in

---

172. *Report of the Study Team on Social Welfare and Welfare of Backward Classes,* 1959, para. 12, p. 126.

the present circumstances is an elaborate investigation and a scientific approach to the problem.

Various criteria have been discussed—caste, social backwardness, educational backwardness, and economic backwardness. It appears from a detailed examination of the problem that backwardness could be measured by no single criterion. Backwardness is relative and it could be attributed to a number of factors which are interrelated. Chain action and reaction of social, educational, economic, environmental, and habitual factors have contributed to backwardness. Efforts should therefore be made to investigate the problem with objective tests.

Then again, it appears that a uniform criterion cannot be suggested for the whole of India. The conditions being different in different States, it is of utmost importance that diversities should not only be considered but also respected. The fact that there cannot be a uniform criterion throughout India has been demonstrated by Kerala. In spite of the Union Government's suggestion to apply the "Economic test" for the determination of Other Backward Classes, Kerala has emphasized the caste criterion. The argument for emphasizing the caste factor is that: "Social backwardness, though to a considerable extent dependent on economic factors, depends also to a large extent in this State upon popular conceptions of the status of a caste or community."[173]

Another factor to be taken into consideration is that any criteria suggested should be in consonance with Art. 15 (4). It should refer to "socially and educationally backward classes."

From the foregoing analysis it could be inferred that the three important requisites to make any criteria more objective and workable are:

1. A sole criterion is ineffective and insufficient to determine backwardness;

---

173. *Report of the Commission for Reservation of Seats in Educational Institutions, Kerala,* 1965, p. 36.

2. There cannot be a uniform criterion for the whole of India; and

3. Any criteria suggested should be within the purview of Art. 15 (4).

In the light of the lapses of criteria suggested by various committees and the difficulties involved in practical administration, it could be suggested that each State should make an elaborate investigation of the problem of backwardness and devise expert opinion on it. The facts of social, educational, and economic changes are difficult to measure periodically on an All India basis, owing to the size and diversity of the country. What is true of one State at a specific period may not be true of others. The statistical data available pertain only to those aspects for which inquiries have been made. Hence they would be incomplete and inadequate. In such circumstances, the conclusions arrived at by All India Committees would be based on generalizations from inadequate statistical data and circumstantial evidence rather than from basic realities. Owing to these difficulties, the States are placed in a more favorable position than the Union to tackle the problem of classifying Other Backward Classes, State-wise.

The States should undertake fact-finding inquiries and frame the criteria on the report of such inquiries. As the Pillai Commission pointed out: "It is for the State to consider the matter and decide it in a manner which is consistent with the requirements of Art. 15 (4) ."[174] Any workable and satisfactory criteria should be examined in the light of justice and objectivity. The States should review the position of Other Backward Classes at least once in five years, and those who have attained normal standards should be excluded from the list. Besides, a rigid single criterion would serve no purpose. Social evolution is a gradual process governed by many factors. So it could not be measured by a single criterion. The criteria framed by the States should be such that they should not tend toward

---

174. *Ibid.,* p. 23.

the creation of a new class of underprivileged. The working hypothesis for a thorough investigation of the problem by the States for evolving a satisfactory criteria should take the following factors into consideration:

(a) Traditionally neglected social classes;
(b) Poor education;
(c) Inadequate political power;
(d) Economic backwardness (poverty) ; and
(e) Lack of white-collar jobs.

Now the problem is what should be the unit for measuring backwardness on the above-mentioned score. Here the problem revolves around the assessment of "traditionally neglected social classes." As regards education, percentage of literacy serves the purpose. Political power is ascertained by the number of representatives in the country's Parliament, State Legislatures, and local Governments. Poverty determines economic backwardness, which could be measured by income. Representation in white-collar jobs could be recorded by the percentage of people in key positions in public service. But for sorting out traditionally neglected classes, the States should investigate cautiously which groups constitute low social classes. If caste constitutes the cause for inferior social position, it could very well be made the unit for measuring backwardness. Here the consolation that emphasis on caste would not amount to injustice lies in the fact that caste would be diluted by various other associated tests—literacy, poverty, political power, and public service. By way of illustration, we might mention the recommendations of the Pillai Commission, Kerala. It is gratifying to note that, though the Commission has emphasized caste as the chief determinant of backwardness, it has diluted the caste factor by two checks. First is the "poverty test" and second the "merit test." It is specifically said, that the benefit would accrue to the members of the favored communities whose family income does not exceed Rs. 4,200 per annum.

Secondly, no concession would be given to the members of the favored communities as regards the minimum marks for eligibility. These are welcome features, for preferential treatment is intended to cater to the poorer and the intelligent sections of the caste groups.

Yet another unit measuring low social classes could be the "occupation test." But the States should specify clearly the occupations rated low, in accordance with the conditions prevailing in the State. There should not be any ambiguity in the statement of occupations rated low in the States.

Thus educational advancement, political power, positions in public service, and economic progress account for social status in society. Backwardness is after all not static. Given the opportunity to advance on these lines, backwardness could be transformed into forwardness. There are instances in our own country where Commas and Reddis in Andhra Pradesh, and Kayasthas of North India, who once constituted the "traditionally low social classes," are more advanced, chiefly by their wielding of political power, educational advancement, white-collar jobs, and financial stability. So as Ambedkar remarked: "If you produce big people from amongst them, the backwardness would go. The backwardness is only a sort of inferiority complex."[175]

The complexity of the problem of Other Backward Classes is chiefly due to scarce economy. The disparity between the scarce resources at the disposal of the States and the vast majority of Other Backward Classes relying on Government concessions is responsible for the present malaise. The result is, whatever the criteria suggested, it fails to satisfy some sections of Backward Classes, who fail to enjoy preferential treatment in spite of being eligible for it, for want of resources. Similar is the case of advanced sections who feel victimized for not being eligible for

---

175. *Report of the Backward Classes Commission*, 1956, Vol. 3, p. 75.

special concessions. Then again, lack of private enterprises and organizations coming forward to meet the educational expenses of the youth of the country and opening employment opportunities induce the entire population to look to the State for all facilities. So to achieve better results with scarce economy, a remolding of the social institutions to bequeathe in the people a better sense of social values is necessary.

A Brief Note on Denotified Communities

Denotified Communities constitute a section of Backward Classes deserving special attention. The "criminal tribes," as they were formerly termed, pose a problem perhaps peculiar to India alone. As regards the origin of these tribes, several theories are advanced. The most accepted theory is that they belong to non-Aryan races of the country. Crime is supposed to be the inherited avocation of these tribes.

Prior to Independence, certain castes and tribes were liable to be classified as criminal tribes, according to the Criminal Tribes Act, 1924. The result was, the members of such castes and tribes, irrespective of their personal commitments, were branded as criminals. The Government of Bombay took a pioneering lead in rehabilitating the so-called criminal tribes. A Committee was constituted in January, 1947, under the membership of B. G. Kher; the then Chief Minister, Morarji Desai; Gulzarilal Nanda, and the Backward Class officer as secretary, to probe into the problem of criminal tribes. The deliberations of this Committee urged the necessity for treating the criminal tribes on par with other sections of the society. The irrational treatment of criminal tribes, dubbing of the entire community as criminal, called for a rethinking of the issue on rational lines. Accordingly, the Criminal Tribes Act, 1924, was repealed in August, 1949. Since then, the members of the criminal tribes are treated as Backward Classes and measures are taken for their uplift.

With the dawn of Independence, the Union Government realized the futility of treating the whole community as criminals. Such a treatment would be repugnant to the principle of justice enshrined in the Constitution. A Criminal Tribes Enquiry Committee was appointed in 1949 to review the act. It was felt that the policy of treating all members of the criminal tribes as criminals on attaining majority, and getting them registered as habitual offenders, was unjust. So the Criminal Tribes Act was repealed throughout India, effective from August 31, 1952, by the enactment of Criminal Tribes Laws (Repeal) Act, 1952. From then on the term "Criminal Tribes" was dispensed with. Instead we have the term "Denotified communities."

The population of ex-criminal tribes is about 3,500,000, consisting of 250 groups. These groups could be further divided as nomadic and settled. The nomadic groups lead an adventurous life. Some of the important gypsy groups are Sansias, Sonarias, Doms, Nats, Bhatus, Bedyars, Budu-budukulas, and Kepumaries.

The Backward Classes Commission deserves to be applauded for suggesting that they should not be called tribes. Nor should the terms "criminal" or "Ex-criminal" be attached to them. They should be simply called "denotified communities."[176] A similar view was taken by the Planning Commission which stated that the term "Denotified Communities" is more appropriate, as it includes both the tribals and other communities. So the term "Denotified Communities" has come to stay for all practical purposes.

As Denotified Communities were mainly criminal by occupation, it is of utmost importance that their cultural pattern be changed. They should be convinced of their futile antisocial habits by means of education.

---

176. *Ibid.,* Vol. 1, para. 48, p. 36.

The recommendations made by the Committee on Plan Projects for the Social and economic betterment of Denotified Communities were:

a) A correctional and welfare approach as against a penal one should be adopted in practice towards the rehabilitation of the Denotified Communities.

b) The habitual criminals among them should be isolated and treated under the ordinary law of the land.

c) The economic programme should go hand in hand with a dynamic and suitably oriented programme of social education so as to wean them away from socially undesirable tendencies.

d) The substantive economic content should be provided in the welfare programme for Denotified Communities keeping the adventurous spirit and traditional skills that prevail among them.[177]

The First Plan allocation for the overall development of Denotified Communities was to the tune of Rs. 35 millions inclusive of Other Backward Classes. About 17 settlements and 30 colonies were set up to rehabilitate these communities. Nearly 36,000 families were benefited by the First Plan Welfare Schemes. The allocation of the Second Plan was Rs. 31.2 millions, out of which Rs. 20.2 millions was earmarked under State Sector and Rs. 11.0 millions under the centrally sponsored schemes.

Statewise details of the Third Plan allocation under centrally sponsored schemes are recorded in Table 3-26.[178]

The Third Plan provision for the welfare projects of the Backward Classes including the Denotified Communities, nomadic and semi-nomadic tribes, was Rs. 67.8 millions under the State Sector. While this provision is quite

177. *Report of the Study Team on Social Welfare and Welfare of Backward Classes,* 1959, para. 16, pp. 205–6.

178. *Report of the Commissioner for Scheduled Castes and Scheduled Tribes, 1961–62,* Part I, Chap. 20, p. 143.

TABLE 3–26

(Rs. in lakhs)

State	Provision made in Third Plan (Physical Program)	Allocation made for 1961–62	Estimated expenditures incurred during 1961–62
Andhra Pradesh	25.70	3.60	2.69
Gujarat	24.25	4.73	1.25
Madhya Pradesh	34.91	5.92	2.22
Madras	79.85	13.18	12.76
Mysore	21.05	3.45	N.A.
Orissa	9.70	0.65	0.65
Punjab	14.14	2.34	2.53
Rajasthan	21.05	3.44	2.60
Uttar Pradesh	140.00	23.15	21.32
West Bengal	4.35	0.72	0.32
Total	375.00	61.19	46.34

encouraging, the implementation of the Welfare Schemes in States does not seem to be satisfactory. The States of Andhra Pradesh, Gujarat, Jammu and Kashmir, Madhya Pradesh, Maharashtra, Mysore, Rajasthan, Uttar Pradesh, West Bengal, and Delhi have shown very poor progress.

The scheme-wise distribution of the expenditure is indicated in Table 3-27.[179]

The educational program for Denotified Communities calls for special treatment. As criminality is considered to be a sort of revered profession by these communities, residential schools should be advocated for them. By sending the younger generations to residential schools, the community as a whole would be weaned away from hereditary criminality in the future. If children remain with their parents and are brought up in a traditional environment,

179. *Ibid.,* p. 147.

TABLE 3–27

(Rs. in lakhs)

Name of scheme	Third Plan provision	Allocation made for 1961–62	Expenditure incurred during 1961–62
Education	377.32	61.21	69.79
Agriculture	60.59	2.20	1.95
Cottage Industries	54.11	4.92	4.18
Cooperation	60.95	4.21	9.34
Animal Husbandry	1.50	—	—
Medical & Public Health	10.78	0.73	0.70
Housing	34.47	4.01	2.87
Communications	2.05	0.51	0.51
Rehabilitation	64.30	0.94	—
Miscellaneous	12.34	0.46	0.36
Total	678.41	79.19	89.70

they are likely to be influenced by the plague of criminality. It has been suggested by social reformers that such residential schools should be located away from the colonies inhabited by these communities. Denotified Communities are not given special reservation benefits in educational institutions on a par with Scheduled Castes and Scheduled Tribes. They are included along with the category of Other Backward Classes. It is doubted whether the students belonging to these communities would be capable of competing with Other Backward Classes in enjoying the reservation benefits guaranteed under Articles 15 (4), 16 (4) and 46, respectively. Fixation of a certain quota of seats to be alloted to Denotified Communities from the quota fixed for Other Backward Classes should be considered by the State Governments, for purposes of admission to educational institutions. Besides, a comparative study of the educational standards of all Backward Classes proves beyond doubt the lower literacy level of the Denotified Communities. Hence, it has been urged by some States to admit the students of Denotified Communities to Pre-Examination Training Centers for All India Services.

A comprehensive survey of the Denotified Communities has not yet been made. But it is gratifying to note that some suggestions have been made by the Police Department of Delhi. The Report reads:

> The problem is twofold: the first and the immediate problem is that the grown-up members of the erstwhile criminal tribes have to be provided with employment facilities for starting petty trades and thus afford them the opportunity to lead an honourable life; the second but probably more important problem is to segregate, temporarily or for a considerable period, young boys and girls of impressionable and tender age groups from the pernicious environments surrounding them. Therefore, the problem will have to be attacked simultaneously and on both the fronts.[180]

The All India Punar Vasit (Denotified Tribes) Jatis Federation is taking a lively interest in accelerating the progress of Denotified Communities, by arranging seminars to focus the problems of these Communities, and to recommend measures for their progress in education, economic field, social customs, etc.

Social uplift of the Denotified Communities constitutes a major problem. The process of emancipation is slow. The Commissioner for Scheduled Castes and Scheduled Tribes has remarked that "the progress achieved both with regard to the Central Sector and the State Sector Schemes, for the welfare of the Denotified Communities, is indeed very poor."[181]

---

180. Quoted in *Report of the Commissioner for Scheduled Castes and Scheduled Tribes, 1962–63*, Part II, Appendix XLI, p. 162.
181. *Ibid.*, Part I, para. 21.3, p. 169.

The program of rehabilitation of Denotified Communities is not only important but urgent. It is different from the general problem of raising the standard of living of the people, for this particular section of Backward Classes has certain handicaps and maladjustments of a special nature. The neglect of this problem may even endanger the peace of other sections, if the historic avocation of criminality is to assert itself. Hence, measures should be taken for the social and economic rehabilitation of Denotified Communities. Before starting any welfare schemes, a comprehensive survey of their present conditions at regional levels is necessary. The liberation of Denotified Communities from the stigma of criminality and their rehabilitation is an essential human problem to be meticulously handled.

4

EDUCATIONAL ADVANCEMENT
OF BACKWARD CLASSES

Constitutional Provisions Governing Education

THE IMPORTANCE OF EDUCATION IN THE TRANSFORMATION of Backward Classes in a welfare state is well known. Eradication of illiteracy by teaching the three R's to the rural masses constitutes the keynote of the problem of educational advancement of the Backward Classes. Education is the birthright of every citizen. But a mere literacy drive would not serve the purpose. Education is not mere literacy; it should aim at the development of individual personality of the Backward Classes. It is only through education that the Backward Classes could be made to realize their rights and privileges and the role they have to play in the national life of the country. The future of these sections depends on their progress in the field of education. Education is the only means to place them along a clearcut path to realize their aspiration of life. It has become increasingly important for the Government to rescue these sections from the plight of backwardness. The object is to make them intelligent citizens of the nation, conscious of their responsibilities and to shoulder the burden of the State. Adult suffrage should be followed by universal education, if democracy is to survive its trial in India. As the children of today are going to be the citizens of tomorrow, it is the first and foremost duty of the State to pay great attention to the educational advancement of these under-privileged classes. A man, apart from being an individual, is greater still as a member of society. He is a social being with some responsibilities to society. Without education he cannot project his social self and come closer to his fellow beings. If he is to be useful to society as a member, he should be educated. Thus, education plays an important part in transforming individuals as cultured members of society. Just as food is essential for physical survival of the people, education is essential for mental survival.

In view of the importance of education, it has been made a Constitutional guarantee. The Constitutional provisions relating to cultural and educational rights of the citizens are contained in Articles 29, 30, 45, and 46. Article 29 explicitly states:

1) Any section of the citizens residing in the territory of India or any part thereof having a distinct language, script or culture of its own shall have the right to conserve the same.

2) No citizen shall be denied admission into any educational institution maintained by the State or receiving aid out of State funds on grounds only of religion, race, caste, language or any of them.

Similarly Art. 30 provides that:

1) All minorities, whether based on religion or language, shall have the right to establish and administer educational institutions of their choice.

2) The State shall not, in granting aid to educational institution, discriminate against any educational institution, on the ground that it is under the management of a ministry, whether based on religion or language.

Under Directive Principles of State Policy, Art. 45 states:

> The State shall endeavour to provide, within a period of ten years from the commencement of this Constitution, for free and compulsory education for all children until they complete the age of fourteen years.

In conformity with this Article, legislation has been enacted in the States of Andhra Pradesh, Assam, Gujarat, Madhya Pradesh, Mysore, Punjab, West Bengal, and Delhi for the introduction of Compulsory Primary Education. The progress made in this direction is recorded in Table 4-1:[1]

TABLE 4–1

Year	Number of schools	Number of students on rolls	Number of teachers	Direct expenditure in millions
1950–51	209,671	18,293,967	537,918	364.9
1955–56	278,135	22,919,734	691,249	537.3
1960–61	330,397	26,642,253	741,695	734.4
1961–62	351,799	29,344,795	795,324	824.2

The implementation of Art. 45 has great significance in the field of education. In 1947, only 35 percent of the children in the age group 6-11 were in schools. This percentage rose to 40 at the beginning of the First Plan; to 50 at end of the First Plan and 61.3 at the end of the Second Plan. The Third Plan proposes to raise it still further to 80 percent. The total enrollment in this age group has increased from about 14 millions in 1947–48 to 18.5 millions in 1950–51; to 25.1 millions in 1955–56; and 34.9 millions in 1960–61. By the end of the Third Plan this enrollment

1. *India 1964*, Reference Annual, p. 67.

is likely to rise by 16.3 millions and reach the figure of 51.2 millions. The outlay on primary education is Rs. 2,090 millions during the Third Plan. The number of primary schools is likely to increase from 210,000 in 1950–51 to 415,000 in 1965–66.[2]

Article 46 supplements further:

The State shall promote with special care the educational and economic interests of the weaker sections of the people, and, in particular, of the Scheduled Castes and the Scheduled Tribes, and shall protect them from social injustice and all forms of exploitation.

These Articles compare favorably with Art. 26 of the Universal Declaration of Human Rights with some limitations. It reads:

Everyone has the right to education. Education shall be free, at least in the elementary and fundamental stages. Elementary education shall be compulsory. Technical and Professional education shall be made generally available and higher education shall be equally accessible to all on the basis of merit.

Literacy of Backward Classes

The general level of literacy is very low and is lower still in the case of Backward Classes. For a clear exposition of this situation, a brief outline of the general literacy at various stages of education since 1901 to 1961 is attempted.

The position of literacy between 1901 to 1931 is stated in Table 4-2.[3]

There was steady progress in the percentage of literacy since 1931 which is indicated in Table 4-3.[4]

---

2. Further details in the *Times of India Directory and Year Book 1965–66.*

3. *Census Report of India,* 1931. Vol. 1, Table VII, p. 347.

4. *Report of the Backward Classes Commission,* Vol. 1, 1956, Appendix IV, p. 251.

TABLE 4-2

Class of Institution	Number of Institutions					Scholars				
	1931	1921	1911	1901	1931	1921	1911	1901		
Universities and colleges	333	233	193	186	92,028	59,595	31,447	20,447		
Secondary schools	13,581	8,816	6,442	5,416	2,286,411	1,239,524	890,061	582,551		
Primary schools	204,384	158,792	118,413	97,116	9,362,748	6,310,451	4,575,465	3,150,678		
Special schools	8,891	3,946	5,783	956	315,650	132,706	164,544	33,950		
Unrecognized schools	34,879	33,929	39,491	43,292	632,249	639,125	630,438	617,818		
Total	262,068	206,016	179,322	146,966	12,689,086	8,381,401	6,281,955	4,405,988		

TABLE 4–3

State	Literacy percentage		
	1951	1941	1931
Uttar Pradesh	10.8	8.4	4.7
Bihar	12.2	9.3	4.3
Orissa	15.8	8.5	5.2
West Bengal	24.5	19.9	11.6
Chandernagore	42.3	—	—
Assam	18.1	11.4	6.8
Manipur	11.4	—	3.3
Tripura	15.5	—	1.1
Sikkim	7.3	—	3.0
Madras	19.3	14.4	9.3
Mysore	20.3	—	9.1
Travancore-Cochin	46.4	—	24.7
Coorg	27.2	—	15.5
Bombay	24.6	18.9	8.6
Saurashtra	18.5	—	N.A.
Kutch	17.1	—	N.A.
Madhya Pradesh	13.5	9.9	5.1
Madhya Bharat	10.8	—	5.1
Hyderabad	9.2	—	4.1
Bhopal	8.2	—	3.1
Vindhya Pradesh	6.1	—	3.5
Rajasthan	8.4	—	3.6
Punjab	16.1	12.0	5.2
Pepsu	12.0	—	4.0
Ajmer	20.1	—	10.6
Delhi	38.4	—	14.1
Bilaspur & Himachal Pradesh	7.7	—	3.5
Andaman & Nicobar Islands	25.8	—	N.A.

All India literacy percentage in 1961 excluding NEFA, Goa, Daman, and Diu is stated in Table 4-4.[5]

"The progress of general literacy has been sluggish throughout the country. It has increased at an average of 0.7 percent per year for the general population, 0.9 for

5. *The Gazetteer of India*, Vol. 1, 1965, Table VIII, p. 346.

TABLE 4–4

Description	Rate (percent)		
	P	M	F
Literacy rates in:			
Cities over 1 million	56.40	63.85	46.36
Cities of 0.5 to 1 million	49.60	58.38	38.43
Cities of 0.1 to 0.5 million	48.52	58.51	36.78
Cities above 100,000	51.81	60.74	40.65
Non-city urban population	42.99*	54.69*	29.73*
Urban India	46.94*	57.46*	34.48*
ALL INDIA	24.02	34.44	12.95

* Excludes Union Territories except Delhi.

males and 0.5 for females."[6] Besides, the increase in percentage of literacy is not uniform throughout the country. A few States have shown marked progress, while the others are lagging behind. A comparative study of the general literacy level in 1951 and 1961 shows clearly the preponderance of some States over the others in literacy figures. Table 4-5 illustrates this fact.[7]

When the general education in the country is so poor it goes without saying that education among the Backward Classes is extremely low. As the Backward Classes Commission pointed out: "The problem of education in most of the States is chiefly the problem of the backward classes, for it is they who are the extremely backward in education."[8]

The percentage of literacy among the Backward Classes in relation to post-matriculation stages of education for the year 1955-56 was worked out at:[9]

6. *Census of India,* 1961.
7. *Indian Population Bulletin,* Number II, 1961, Table 12, p. 83.
8. *Report of the Backward Classes Commission,* 1956, para. 193, p. 109.
9. *Report of the Commissioner for Scheduled Castes and Scheduled Tribes,* 1956–57, p. 29.

TABLE 4–5

General literacy rates in 1961 and 1951

Rank 1961	State	Rate per 1,000 1961	Rate per 1,000 1951	Rank 1951
1.	Delhi	510	384	2
2.	Kerala	462	407	1
3.	Andaman & Nicobar Islands	336	258	3
4.	Gujarat	303	231	5
5.	Madras	302	208	7
6.	Maharashtra	297	209	6
7.	West Bengal	291	240	4
8.	Assam	258	183	9
9.	Mysore	253	193	8
10.	Punjab	237	152	12
11.	Laccadive, Minicoy & Amindivi Islands	233	152	13
12.	Tripura	222	155	11
13.	Orissa	215	158	10
14.	Andhra Pradesh	208	131	14
15.	Bihar	182	122	15
16.	Uttar Pradesh	175	108	16
17.	Madhya Pradesh	169	98	17
18.	Rajasthan	147	89	18
19.	Himachal Pradesh	146	77	19
20.	Jammu & Kashmir	107	—	—

(a) All Communities, including Scheduled Castes, Scheduled Tribes and Other Backward Classes . . . 0.158

(b) Other Backward Classes . . . 0.053

(c) Scheduled Castes . . . 0.033

(d) Scheduled Tribes . . . 0.015

The literacy percentage of Backward Classes, however, showed an upward curve for the year 1956-57, as recorded in Table 4-6:[10]

10. *Ibid.*, 1958–59, p. 53.

TABLE 4-6

Stage of Education	Percentage of increase in enrollment during:			
	1955–56 as compared to 1951–52		1956–57 as compared to 1955–56	
	Backward Classes	All (including Backward Classes)	Backward Classes	All (including Backward Classes)
Pre-matric	50.15	27.60	3.28	6.54
Post-matric	145.11	55.33	20.40	9.37

The progress of education among the Backward Classes is very essential for the realization of Constitutional safeguards guaranteed to them. Comparatively speaking, among the Backward Classes, the percentage of literacy of the Scheduled Tribes is very low. The Other Backward Classes top the list of literacy percentage and next to them are Scheduled Castes. From the Reports of the Commissioner for Scheduled Castes and Scheduled Tribes, we could state that the percentage of literacy of Backward Classes at pre-matric stage is going high in comparison with collegiate and higher education. To raise the level of education at college level, the Government of India has to spend large amounts of money.

Besides, among Backward Classes, the category of Other Backward Classes enjoys the least Government concessions by way of scholarships. The percentage of scholarships awarded to these classes is very low, and this is in accordance with the high percentage of literacy prevailing among them. However, the State Governments are compensating them by giving free studentships and scholarships from their own schemes, in the absence of liberal Central Government grants. Moreover, unlike the Scheduled Castes and Scheduled Tribes, the Other Backward Classes are not exempted from the payment of tuition fees in all the universities. The exemption of tuition fees for Scheduled Castes and Scheduled Tribes in most of the States enables the Central Government to spend lavishly on scholarships for these sections. The number of applications received and the number of scholarships awarded to Backward Classes shows the great disparity in awarding scholarships to the different categories of Backward Classes.

Scholarships Scheme: Inland and Overseas

The scheme of granting scholarships to Backward Classes was instituted in the year 1944-45. The benefit of granting scholarships was confined solely to the Scheduled Castes up to 1948. But in 1948-49 this benefit was extended to Scheduled Tribes and the following year (1949-50) to Other Backward Classes. Table 4-7 shows the expenditure incurred on post-matric scholarships from 1944 to 1959.[11]

The scholarships awarded to the Scheduled Castes and Scheduled Tribes during 1960-61 and 1961-62 are given in Table 4-8:[12]

TABLE 4-8

Category	1960–61		1961–62	
	Expenditure incurred in rupees	Number of scholarships actually paid	Expenditure incurred in rupees	Number of scholarships actually paid
Scheduled Castes	16,782,412	42,007	21,027,032	47,844
Scheduled Tribes	3,085,814	6,861	3,508,960	8,132
Total	19,868,226	48,868	24,535,982	55,976

11. *Ibid.,* Part II, p. 180.
12. *Ibid.,* 1961–62, Part I, p. 37.

TABLE 4-7

Year	Number of Scholarships awarded				Expenditure incurred (in rupees)			
	Scheduled Castes	Scheduled Tribes	Other Backward Classes	Total	Scheduled Castes	Scheduled Tribes	Other Backward Classes	Total
1944–45	144	—	—	114	47,697	—	—	47,697
1945–46	292	—	—	292	211,962	—	—	211,962
1946–47	527	—	—	527	470,397	—	—	470,397
1947–48	655	—	—	655	539,307	—	—	539,307
1948–49	647	84	—	731	452,317	45,986	—	498,303
1949–50	879	186	349	1,414	515,512	94,965	246,327	856,804
1950–51	1,316	348	517	2,181	726,651	185,301	357,504	1,269,456
1951–52	1,604	575	655	2,834	817,976	281,780	441,186	1,540,942
1952–53	3,404	1,093	1,947	6,444	1,435,551	522,452	1,094,264	3,052,267
1953–54	5,954	1,587	4,393	11,934	2,636,316	818,538	2,651,100	6,155,954
1954–55	10,034	2,356	8,268	20,658	4,580,498	1,237,733	4,970,769	10,789,000
1955–56	16,081	2,883	12,487	31,451	6,378,432	1,305,238	7,370,266	15,053,936
1956–57	21,744	3,482	14,259	39,485	8,798,891	1,577,850	8,351,641	18,728,382
1957–58	26,447	4,300	13,668	44,415	10,037,379	1,897,538	8,218,575	20,153,492
1958–59	32,551	4,821	12,590	49,962	12,586,131	2,076,206	7,649,338	22,311,675

From the table it can be observed that the Government's scholarships scheme marked an increase by 14 percent and 19 percent respectively, in awarding scholarships to Scheduled Castes and Scheduled Tribes during 1961-62 as compared with the previous year's record. The Government's scholarships scheme for Backward Class students is working out very successfully.

Expenditure incurred on scholarships during 1962-63 is recorded in Table 4-9:[13]

TABLE 4–9

Category	No. of scholarships awarded and paid	1962–63 Expenditure incurred			No. of scholarships awarded and paid
		Home* Ministry	Education† Ministry	State† Government	
Scheduled Castes	48,706	127.68	124.83	9.21	55,568
Scheduled Tribes	8,440	25.75	19.92	—	10,247
Total	57,146	153.43	144.75	9.21	65,815

* Figures based on progress reports.
† As reported by the Ministry of Education.

By the percentage of scholarships awarded to Backward Classes, it is clear that the Government is giving first preference to technical and professional courses at the university level of education, as Table 4-10 indicates.[14]

To avoid hardships to Scheduled Caste and Scheduled Tribe students by the late payment of scholarships, the Ministry of Home Affairs decided in 1956-57 to make ad hoc payment to the students. This concession was extended to the Other Backward Classes in the year 1957-58,

13. *Ibid.*, 1962–63, p. 57.
14. *Ibid.*, 1958–59, Part II, Appendix XXII, pp. 170–71.

TABLE 4–10

Course of study	Pecentage of Scholarships Awarded			
	1955–56	1956–57	1957–58	1958–59
Professional	18.8	18.3	18.9	19.9
Post-graduate stage	2.6	2.6	2.4	2.5
Graduate stage	16.8	18.1	17.6	18.1
Under Graduate	61.6	60.8	61.0	59.2
Trade course	0.2	0.2	0.1	0.3

particularly to the scholarship holders who continued their studies at the same stage of education, that is, promotion from junior to senior class in the faculties of Arts and Science.

Besides this concession, the Ministry of Education has delegated the powers of sanctioning post-matric scholarships to State Governments/Union Territories, since July 11, 1959, to avoid delay in the disbursement of scholarships.[15] But even then, the scholarships scheme suffers at the State level due to administrative delay. The Study Team on Social Welfare and Welfare of Backward Classes made the following obeservations as regards this fact:

> The Scholarships Scheme at the State level also suffers from complicated and protracted procedure, insistence on too many formalities and subsequent delays in sanction and payment. Our field study shows that in a sample of 212 scholars interviewed in 9 different States, 60.9 percent in Madras, 24 percent in Bihar and 12.5 percent in Assam encountered difficulties in securing scholarships.[16]

In view of the difficulties experienced by students in securing the scholarship amount in time to meet their aca-

15. Circular letter No. F.28-1/59. S–4, dated July 11, 1959.
16. *Report of the Study Team on Social Welfare and Welfare of Backward Classes,* para. 48, p. 175.

demic needs, it could be suggested that there should be
further decentralization in the administration. The universities should be authorized to award the scholarships
directly with regard to post-graduate students, and prin-
cipals should be in charge of awarding scholarships as regards the undergraduates. This would not only prevent administrative delay but would be beneficial as regards the
fixation of the amount of scholarships covering the expenses at respective stages of education.

The criterion for granting scholarships is income-cum-
merit. This method is justifiable from all points of view.
It is also termed as "poverty cum means test." The field
study conducted by the research unit of the Study Team
clearly shows the application of this test in the granting of
scholarships. Table 4-11 records the study of 212 scholars
spread over different parts of India.[17]

TABLE 4–11

Income Group (annual)	Number	Percentage
Rs. 0 to 500	96	45.3
Rs. 501 to 1,000	64	30.2
Rs. 1,001 to 1,500	25	11.8
Rs. 1,501 to 2,000	12	5.7
Rs. 2,001 to 2,500	9	4.2
Rs. 2,501 and above	6	2.8

The performance of the scholarship holders in examinations is reported satisfactory. It was found by the Study
Team that the incidence of failure of scholarship holders
for the year 1957-58 was very small. Forty-eight percent of
the students in Madhya Pradesh, 80 percent in Orissa, and
45 percent in Rajasthan secured Third Division. In the
overall sample, the incidence of failure is, however, only
3.8 percent. The majority of cases (61.4 percent) have

17. *Ibid.*, para. 51, p. 177.

recorded average performance or above; 10.3 percent can be classed as meritorious; 31.1 percent have secured 1st Division; 38 percent 2nd Division; and 34 percent have secured 3rd Division.[18]

States having highest and lowest percentage of respondents according to different classifications of results are stated in Table 4-12:[19]

TABLE 4–12
Results

States with	Meritorious	1st Division	2nd Division	3rd Division	Failed
Highest percentage	Assam (85%)	Bombay Gujarat (30%)	Uttar Pradesh (64%)	Orissa (80%)	Madhya Pradesh (16%)
Lowest percentage	Madras (nil)	Rajasthan (nil)	Orissa (16%)	Bombay Gujarat (5%)	Madras Orissa Assam Bombay Bihar (nil)

Recently, the Ministry of Education prompted the State Government/Union Territory Administrations to carry out a sample survey confining to the year 1959-60, in respect of 1 percent cases of successful and 5 percent cases of failed students, at various stages of post-matric education, in order to ascertain how far students belonging to Scheduled Castes and Scheduled Tribes have benefited from the scheme. The information was not furnished by all the States. But with the available information the result was analyzed by the Ministry of Education as follows:[20]

18. *Ibid.*, para. 52, p. 177.
19. *Ibid.*, p. 178.
20. *Report of the Commissioner for Scheduled Castes and Scheduled Tribes*, 1962–63, Part I, para. 8.28, pp. 58–59.

(i) Failures are due mostly to weak foundation at pre-matric stage.

(ii) Students do not have enough facilities at home.

(iii) Students do not utilize scholarship money for the intended purposes, i.e., purchase of books and equipments, etc.

(iv) Health and diet of students is generally poor.

(v) Students do not take active part in extra-curricular activities.

(vi) There is inadequacy of hostel facilities.

(vii) Distracted by financial difficulties, students are not in a position to purchase costly books of engineering and medical courses.

(viii) Inadequacy of good teaching staff.

Attention has been drawn to the condonation of scholarships to Scheduled Caste and Scheduled Tribe students failing in the examination, even first time in courses other than technical. Concession of first failure is, however, given to the students pursuing engineering and medicine. But it is felt that such a scheme would be detrimental to the career of Scheduled Caste and Scheduled Tribe failed students. So to overcome this shortcoming, it has been recommended by the Commissioner for Scheduled Castes and Scheduled Tribes that this rule should be suitably modified in order to allow condonation of one failure in the case of students pursuing general and academic courses and two failures in the case of those pursuing technical and professional courses.[21]

It is further suggested that the value of scholarships should be raised in conformity with the high cost of living. Besides, relaxation is made as regards the awarding of scholarships to employed students. Hitherto, Scheduled Caste and Scheduled Tribe students employed on monthly emoluments exceeding Rs. 175.00 were not eligible for the award of scholarships. But now, according to the new rules of the Ministry of Education, those students whose

---

21. *Ibid.*, para. 8.34, p. 61.

family income does not exceed Rs. 360.00 per month are eligible for scholarships. This is highly beneficial to students of Scheduled Castes and Scheduled Tribes doing part-time jobs.

Scheduled Castes, Scheduled Tribes, and Other Backward Classes are given the benefit of overseas scholarships since 1949-50. In addition to this privilege, the Government of India has instituted the scheme of granting Tourist class/II class passage to Backward Classes who have secured merit scholarships in foreign universities not covering the cost of passage. The number of overseas scholarships granted to Backward Class students from 1949/50 to 1958-59 is indicated in Table 4-13:[22]

TABLE 4–13

Year	Name of the scheme	Number of Scholarships awarded to		
		Scheduled Castes	Scheduled Tribes	Other Backward Classes
1949–50	Central overseas scholarships scheme	—	—	1
1953–54	Central overseas scholarship scheme	—	—	1
	Indo-German industrial cooperation scheme	—	—	1
1954–55	Central overseas scholarships scheme	—	—	1
	Indo-German industrial Cooperation scheme	—	—	2
	Colombo Plan food technology	—	—	1
1955–56	Central overseas scholarship scheme	—	—	2 (one returned without completing studies)

22. *Ibid.*, 1958–59, Part II, Appendix XXIV, p. 186.

	Sisterhood relationship program of technical cooperation mission	—	—	1
1956–57	Colombo Plan	1	—	—
	Indo-German industrial cooperation scheme	—	—	1
1957–58	Central overseas scholarships scheme	1	—	3
1958–59	Central overseas scholarships scheme	—	—	1
	University of Philippines scholarships scheme	—	—	1
	Scholarships offered by the Hamburg Chamber of Commerce (West Germany) for practical training in West Germany	—	—	7
	TOTAL	2	—	23

The overseas scholarships offered by the State Governments and the expenditure incurred for the purpose for the year 1958 is given in Table 4-14:[23]

TABLE 4–14

State	Number of Scholarships awarded			Expenditure incurred on the scholarships awarded
	Scheduled Castes	Scheduled Tribes	Other Backward Classes	
				Rs.
Bombay	4	1	1	1,465,555
Orissa	1	—	—	—
Total	5	1	1	1,465,555

According to the information reported by the Ministry of Education, out of 57 Scheduled Caste and 13 Scheduled

23. *Ibid.*, p. 187.

Tribe candidates who applied for the Government of India overseas scholarships for the year 1961-62, five candidates from each category were awarded scholarships for higher studies abroad. The Ministry of Scientific Research and Cultural Affairs has also reported that one Scheduled Caste candidate was awarded a French Government scholarship for higher studies during the year. Since sufficient number of duly qualified candidates from these communities are forthcoming for higher studies abroad, it is considered desirable to encourage them for such studies by gradually increasing their number every year, as far as possible.

During the year 1962-63, five candidates from each category were awarded overseas scholarships. Apart from this, one Scheduled Caste candidate was awarded a scholarship under the Federation of British Industries overseas scholarship scheme.

Hostels have been established for the benefit of Backward Class students to promote social and community life among the students. Since 1958, mixed hostels are encouraged, offering concessions to non-Backward students living among Backward Classes. Mixed hostels are favored by the students throughout India with the exception of Uttar Pradesh, where exclusive hostels are demanded. The concessions offered to the students by various States in 1959 were analyzed by the Study Team as recorded in the following table:[24]

TABLE 4–15

| | Percentage of respondents getting concessions | | |
	Scheduled Castes	Scheduled Tribes	Other Backward Classes
Fully free	57.7	45	10
Partially free	24.8	8.8	—
Paying	17.5	46.2	90

24. *Report of the Study Team on Social Welfare and Welfare of Backward Classes*, para. 43, p. 173.

It has been proposed that the percentage of reservations in the general hostels for Scheduled Castes and Scheduled Tribes should be increased, with a corresponding increase in the rate of stipends offered to these classes. Madras has decided to offer residential scholarships to students of these communities securing admission in general hostels. The decision of the other States is not yet reported.

The expenditure incurred on hostels during 1961-63 is indicated in Table 4-16.[25]

Reservation in Educational Institutions

In pursuance of Article 15 (4), the States are authorized to reserve seats for Backward Classes in educational institutions. Article 15 (4) provides:

> Nothing in this Article or in clause (2) of Article 29 shall prevent the State from making any special provision for the advancement of any socially and educationally backward classes of citizens or for the Scheduled Castes and the Scheduled Tribes.

This clause was incorporated by the Constitution (First Amendment) Act, 1951, because, in the absence of this clause, reservation of seats for Backward Classes under Article 15 was a contradiction in terms.

Reservation of seats in professional and technical institutions poses a problem. The imbalance between the number of students wanting to join professional and technical courses and the intake of students by these colleges has necessitated the problem of reserving certain quota of seats to Backward Classes, as a sort of Constitutional guarantee for the educational advancement of these classes.

The Reservation Policy advocated by the Backward Classes Commission was that in all the science, engineer-

---

25. *Report of the Commissioner for Scheduled Castes and Scheduled Tribes,* 1962–63, para. 8.39, p. 62.

TABLE 4-16

Rs. in millions

Name of category	Third Plan allocation	1961–62		1962–63	
		Provision made	Expenditure incurred	Provision made	Expenditure incurred
Scheduled Castes	37,908	5,712	4,521	7,474	3,773
Scheduled Tribes	27,250	4,256	2,249	4,470	3,145
TOTAL	65,158	9,968	6,770	11,944	10,518

ing, medicine, agriculture, veterinary, and other technical and technological institutions a reservation of 70 percent of the seats should be made for qualified students of Backward Classes till such time as accommodation can be provided for all students eligible for admission. In making selection to the reserved quota of seats, qualified candidates from the extremely Backward Classes should be taken into consideration first. The remaining 30 percent, as also all seats unavailed of by Backward Classes, should go to the rest of the students.

States differ in the fixation of reserved seats for Backward Classes. But whatever the quota fixed, it should not exceed 50 percent of the total number of seats available, for all practical purposes. The Ministry of Education has requested all the Ministers of the Government of India, the State Governments, and the Union Territory Administrations, and also the universities throughout India, to give concessions to Backward Class students in technical institutions in particular. The concessions made were:[26]

a) 20 percent of the seats should be reserved for them;

b) Where admissions are restricted to candidates who obtain a certain minimum percentage of marks, and not merely the passing of a certain examination, there may be a 5 percent reduction for them, provided that the lower percentage prescribed does not fall below the minimum required to pass the qualifying examinations; and

c) the minimum age limit for the admission of students belonging to these communities should be raised by three years.

Expressing his distrust as regards the success of the Reservation policy, the Commissioner for Scheduled Castes and Scheduled Tribes made the following observations:

---

26. *Ibid.*, 1961–62, para. 7.34, p. 45.

On the whole, the pace of progress in giving the three-fold educational concessions to the Scheduled Castes and the Scheduled Tribes is not very encouraging and greater coordination and concerted efforts are needed to achieve the desired results. In order to have a constant watch on the progress in the implementation of the suggestions made by the Ministry of Education, it is considered desirable to prescribe a suitable proforma for observing at least annual progress reports from the implementing authorities. It is hoped that the Ministry of Education will take suitable action in this regard, in cooperation with the Ministries concerned of the Government of India, State Governments, Union Territory Administrations and the Universities.[27]

The Ministries of Information and Broadcasting, and Food and Agriculture, are giving special concessions by way of reservation to Scheduled Castes and the Scheduled Tribe persons in all the educational and technical institutions controlled by them.

The Ministry of Scientific Research and Cultural Affairs gives concessions to the Scheduled Caste and Scheduled Tribe students, only on condition that their percentage at the qualifying examination is not more than 10 percent below the marks obtained by others in the open competition.

The Ministries of Irrigation and Power, and Labor and Employment, have made 12½ percent and 5 percent reservations, respectively, for Scheduled Caste and Scheduled Tribe students. But the Ministry of Irrigation and Power does not give any concession as regards the relaxation of age limit for admission to technical institutions under their control. However, the Ministry of Labor and Employment has not prescribed the upper age limit for admission.

The Ministry of Mines and Fuel has made a reservation

27. *Ibid.,* para. 7.35, p. 45.

of 12½ percent for the Scheduled Caste, Scheduled Tribe and the Other Backward Classes, all combined. The relaxation of three years in age limit is also allowed for the Backward Classes. These concessions are admissible only in five Mining Training Institutions, whereas in the remaining thirteen institutions under their control there is no reservation.

The Ministry of Railways abides by the recommendations made by the Ministry of Education as regards reservation in all Railway Schools.

The universities of Visva Bharathi, Roorkee, and the Indra Kala Sangeet Viswavidyalaya, Khairgarh have made a reservation of 20 percent for the Scheduled Caste and Scheduled Tribe students. The University of Gujarat also makes a reservation of 20 percent for these classes with some changes in the percentage of reservation in some of the institutions affiliated to the university. Annamalai, Sri. Veenkateshwara, Nagpur and Mysore, have made a reservation of less than 20 percent for Scheduled Caste and Scheduled Tribe students. The universities of Poona, Punjab, and Bombay have also made a reservation of less than 20 percent. In the new universities of Gorakhpur, Kurukshetra, and Vikram there is no reservation in both professional and non-vocational institutions. The Banaras Hindu University gives the concession of reservation only in non-vocational institutions. The University of Delhi gives a concession of 5 percent marks to the Scheduled Caste and Scheduled Tribe students for admission to postgraduate courses in both science and social sciences.

The Commissioner for Scheduled Castes and Scheduled Tribes, while expressing his dissatisfaction at the poor implementation of the recommendations made by the Ministry of Education, has made the following suggestion for better implementation:

It is, therefore, considered desirable that a minimum

qualifying standard should be prescribed for admission to all technical and educational courses and the Scheduled Caste and the Scheduled Tribe students, securing 5 percent marks less than the prescribed minimum marks, should be admitted to the reserved seats, without any reference to the marks obtained by the last candidate admitted to the general seat.[28]

Let alone the question of diversity as regards reservation in the universities and ministries, the Government's reservation policy for Backward Classes is greatly debated. How far reservations lower the standard of technical education in the country is the problem of the day. On the other hand, how far the Backward Classes would be able to compete with the advanced sections, in the absence of reservation, is equally an important problem to be tackled. The Reservation Policy, like the concept of "equality" and "special preference," has become a contradiction in terms, a paradoxical question exercising the minds of educationists, academicians, administrators, and social scientists.

The recommendations made by the Backward Classes Commission were:

In the field of education, the Backward Classes must be made to feel that here at least they will have everything in their favour and that the nation is determined to give them the best chance of educating themselves and coming to the top. I have, therefore wholeheartedly supported the recommendations that up to 70 percent of the seats ought to be reserved for the best amongst the Backward Classes. The remaining 30 percent seats, and any seats not absorbed by candidates from "reserved" communities should go to the "unreserved" communities.[29]

---

28. *Ibid.*, para. 7.45, p. 47.
29. *Report of the Backward Classes Commission*, para. 45, p. XI.

In support of this suggestion, Kaka Kalelkar further remarked:

> If I have lent my full support to the demand for 70 percent of reservations in higher technical institutes of learning for the Backward Classes, it is not because I want to turn the upper classes into a new underprivileged class, but because I want opportunities for higher training to be multiplied with breakneck speed. It is only when the traditionally more promising sections of society are kept out of higher learning that those in authority and power will shed their traditional lethargy.[30]

Thus reservation, although it contravenes the principle of equality enshrined in Art. 15, is necessitated by circumstances prevailing in the country. Reservation is found inevitable for enhancing the importance of education among the Backward Classes. The only way to make them education-minded is by giving special concessions by way of reservation in general educational and technical institutions. Even Pandit Nehru, who was not in favor of reserving seats for Backward Classes, realized that the only way to stabilize the position of Backward Classes was through education. He remarked: "Not only must equal opportunities be given to all, but special opportunities for educational, economic and cultural growth must be given to backward groups, so as to enable them to cater up to those who are ahead of them."[31]

Besides, the principle of reservation holds good even from the point of view of social justice, provided it is kept within limits. The Report of the University Education Commission, upholding the principle of reservation, remarked: "The percentage of reservation shall not, however, exceed a third of the total number of seats. The

---

30. *Ibid.*, para. 49, p. XII.
31. *The Discovery of India,* 1948, p. 553.

principle of reservation may be adopted for a period of ten years."[32]

It is felt that reservation should not hamper the national good by depriving the intelligent students of the opportunities of higher education, just for the reason of accommodating Backward Class students. As the report of the University Commission observed:

To deny to the most talented members of the nation, Brahman or non-Brahman, Christian or Muslim, opportunities for self-development is not only unjust to them but is unfair to the nation which is deprived of high-class professional ability and social competence. Besides, we live in a competitive world in which mind yields itself only to an ascendancy of mind.[33]

Basic Education

Basic education befitting rural conditions is the only panacea for the liquidation of backwardness. A thorough change in the system of education to suit the country's needs is of prime importance. Basic education policy caters well to Indian conditions, for it not only teaches the three R's to the masses, but also inculcates in them basic social values by reviving past traditions of the country. It prepares them for vocations of their choice. Besides, basic education is the only way to put an end to the modern craze for degrees among the students. Gandhiji was a pioneer in devising the new pattern of basic education to reconstruct our society on sound lines. The expert educationists of the country are unanimous in the introduction of basic education as the best system for our country. As the Backward Classes are mostly functional, the system of basic education goes a long way toward training them in

---

32. *The Report of the University Education Commission,* Vol. 1, 1949, para. 37, p. 53.
33. *Ibid.,* p. 52.

traditional crafts. The basic objective of Ashram schools is to provide vocational training and guidance. An experiment has been made by starting vocational schools both residential and non-residential in Orissa, Bombay, and Bihar. The courses provided in these schools are of three to six years duration, with special emphasis on agriculture, carpentry, spinning, weaving, smithy, etc.

A distinctive feature of Ashram schools in Bombay State was that the voluntary agencies were given a free hand in the administration of Ashram schools. Valuable work has been done by these voluntary agencies and mention may be made of the Bhil Seva Mandal, Dohad. Likewise, the Bihar residential schools are of immense help to Paharias, who are trained in spinning. Adimjati Sevak Mandal and Santhal Paharia Seva Mandal are rendering valuable service in the diffusion of basic education to tribals in this area.

Through these basic schools, efforts have been made to revive the tribal culture. One notable feature of the Government's policy is that the tribals are not burdened with the task of learning alien languages. They are taught in their own language and so the language problem does not exist.

However, the success of basic education depends upon trained personnel to turn out best students. Teachers proficient in crafts and sympathetic to the difficulties of tribals in picking up crafts are to be recruited for imparting training in crafts to these classes. Handsome salaries and better service conditions are the only way of attracting experienced and talented staff to the Ashram Schools.

Well, doubts may be expressed at this stage about the perpetuation of the caste system by fostering traditional crafts among the Backward Classes. Does it not create misgivings among the Backward Classes that they are made to learn handicrafts and are given differential treatment? But these doubts have been cleared by the Backward Classes Commission by suggesting:

Basic education being the better kind of education, more virile and all round, should receive the highest patronage at the hands of the Government and of all communities. As regards perpetuation of caste, there is no fear of caste being perpetuated so long as all professions are thrown open to all persons, irrespective of caste or class.[34]

The recommendations made by the Backward Classes Commission, as regards the basic education, center around the establishment of basic schools (Panchkoshi basic schools) with trained artisan teachers. The standards and medium of instruction suggested are:

The education should be intensive, and the young men or women finishing the Basic course of Panchkoshi Village Schools should acquire as much knowledge as a student of the present-day intermediate standard possesses; only we should not burden those taking this course with the necessity of learning English. We would be content with teaching the students the regional language and Hindi. Those whose mother tongue is Hindi or any dialect thereof will do well to learn one more language, preferably of the South.[35]

The introduction of free and compulsory education would accommodate the Panchkoshi schools with students of all communities residing in the villages. This orientation in education should be followed by a network of hostels to encourage community life among the students.

The Commission also recommended the starting of Samata Ashram, an institution akin to ancient Gurukulas where teachers with their families live with students. Such a system of education fosters not only progressive education, but also collective living by encouraging cordial relations between teachers and students. "It is expected that

34. *Report of the Backward Classes Commission*, para. 205, p. 112.
35. *Ibid.*, para. 210, p. 114.

these Samata Ashrams will be the centers of a new Indian culture and they may become a pattern for any countries to follow."[36]

Panchkoshi schools and Samata Ashrams would automatically culminate in rural universities. The curriculum of these universities ought to be decided by the changing needs of society. The sole motive behind the new orientation in education by introducing Panchkoshi schools, Samata Ashrams, and rural universities is to replace competition by compassion and exploitation by integration.

Now the problem is, would the Backward Classes agree to the basic-education system? Are they not suspicious of the Advanced Classes in recommending the ideal form of education to them, while they confine themselves to the Western system of education. These are serious questions which complicate matters. But the Backward Classes Commission has solved this problem by suggesting the following remedy:

> In order to make basic education popular with the masses, and to carry conviction with them, it is necessary that Government should categorically declare that in selecting candidates for Government Service, especially of the upper grades, students trained in basic education will be given a decided preference.[37]

The need for basic schools in villages arises from the fact that schools are usually concentrated in towns and cities. The villages are deprived of the advantages of higher education because of lack of schools. This is one of the handicaps for poor literacy among the Backward Classes, who are mostly populated in villages. So the establishment of Panchkoshi and Samata Ashrams goes a long way in meeting the requirements of rural areas. These schools with special emphasis on vocational training would

36. *Ibid.*, para. 216, p. 116.
37. *Ibid.*, para. 222, p. 117.

not only curtail the mad rush to universities but also prove economical to the rural masses. As the Backward Classes Commission pointed out: "They will be the training ground for a casteless and classless society."[38]

Yet another factor which favors Ashram schools for Scheduled Tribes is, these sections of society present complex social structure, incapable of being treated on the same footing as the advanced sections, in the sphere of education. For instance, some tribes—like the Todas of Nilgiris, Santals in Bihar and West Bengal, Bhils in Madhya Pradesh and Rajasthan, Onges in Andaman—not only present a unique social structure but live in inaccessible areas. The environmental conditions of the tribals call for special education. The Scheduled Castes are, comparatively speaking, a little aware of the benefits of education, and they are making use of the concessions guaranteed under the Constitution. But the tribes are not yet aware of the value of education, and some of the tribes still remain beyond the pale of civilization. Ashram schools with craft education as the basis is the only way to convince the Scheduled Tribes that education would assist them in earning their livelihood, without injuring their cultural heritage. This type of education is conducive to the development of Tribes, as it does not imply regimentation or any imitation of Western type of education. Boarding schools of this type have already been tried at Bombay, Orissa, Bihar, and Madhya Pradesh, and they have shown bright prospects. These schools provide ample opportunities to study tribal culture along with the factors contributing to their integration in society. But the only asset for such schools is the recruitment of trained and efficient personnel, capable of shouldering the responsibility of the tribals.

Hence, the problem of Backward Classes is the problem of education. Any scheme for the liquidation of educa-

---

38. *Ibid.*, para. 243, p. 122.

tional backwardness should be followed by special educational concessions to these sections of society. A glance at the Government's expenditure under the First Three Five Year Plans clearly shows the interest evinced for the educational betterment of Backward Classes. The Constitution has made the educational advancement of Backward Classes a special responsibility of the Government. Among the welfare schemes for the all-round development of Backward Classes in the Five Year Plans, Education has been given the highest priority. During the First Plan Rs. 89.4 millions were spent on Scheduled Castes and Scheduled Tribes. In the Second Plan, a sum of Rs. 200.5 millions was spent on their education. The Third Plan allocation for Backward Classes was to the tune of Rs. 341.4 millions.

The working group on the welfare of Backward Classes has made the following recommendations for the further progress of these Classes.

The group has favored the abolition of cash incentives to parents to send their children to schools. It is said that educational aids and concessions, supply of clothing and midday meals are, however, important.

There is a great need for imparting vocational guidance to these students and to inform them of all the available employment opportunities.

Considering the fact that a majority of the Scheduled Caste and Scheduled Tribe students are still going in for general or academic education, the group has emphasised the need for dissemination of training and employment information more widely among the Backward Classes.[39]

Education thus plays a very important part in the development of rural society consisting mostly of Backward

39. *Deccan Herald*, May 28, 1965.

Classes. Social education superficially may mean mere literacy or abandonment of illiteracy. But this is not the meaning which is needed for the constructive program of educational advancement. The real meaning of the term "social education" should be the inducement of Backward Classes to a consciousness of their rights and privileges. Social education should be such that it should rouse them to know civic principles, village administration, covering all aspects of social life, economic betterment and political representation necessary for their amelioration. Education should aim at the development of society as a whole, not merely for a few individuals belonging to particular castes or tribes or classes or whatever. Education being the vital aspect of all development schemes for the advancement of Backward Classes, the Government has very rightly given it top priority.

5

ECONOMIC UPLIFT OF BACKWARD CLASSES

BACKWARDNESS IS GENERALLY ATTRIBUTED TO THE ECONOMIC conditions of the people. Apart from other causes like social, educational, environmental, and occupational, economic conditions play a great part in the assessment of the poverty of the masses. There can be no gainsaying the fact that Indian society, unlike Western societies, is not built on the economic framework. But still, economic conditions have constituted the keynote of backwardness in India too. Social evils and economic backwardness are so interrelated that they cannot be treated in isolation. Because of this interrelation, economic amelioration of the Backward Classes deserves special mention in any plan for the welfare of Backward Classes. To illustrate, the institution of caste in India by dividing society into several layers of social strata, culminated in the immobility of the labor force in the economic field because of the rigid functional grouping.

The reasons for economic backwardness in the country may be attributed to four factors:

(i) Dwindling of cottage industries which deprived the rural agriculturists of their supplementary income in slack season;

(ii) Growth of population;

(iii) The destruction of village autonomy; and

(iv) The pressure on land in the absence of cottage industries and its related drawbacks.

With the dawn of Independence, efforts have been made to rectify the defective economic policy pursued under foreign rule. The Five Year Plans have been launched in succession, to revive the indigenous handicrafts and make villages not only the unit of self-sufficiency but also the unit of administration. Decentralization and village autonomy are in the forefront in any scheme of rural reconstruction.

As the First Plan emphasized:

> Maximum production, full employment, the attainment of economic equality and social justice which constitute the accepted objectives of planning under present-day conditions are not really so many different ideas, but a series of related aims which the country must work for. None of these objectives can be pursued to the exclusion of others; a plan of development must place balanced emphasis on all of these.[1]

The economic schemes launched for the welfare of Backward Classes are comprehensive. But to incorporate all the schemes in this study is a sizable task. So only the relevant aspects are briefly attempted in this chapter.

Cottage Industries

India attained a great reputation for her handicrafts in the past. The innate skill of our craftsmen was an unbeatable glory for ages. At a time when the rest of the world was far from the hues of the modern industrial system, Indian handicrafts displayed the highest artistic qualities, unsurpassed elsewhere. But British rule in India gave a

---

1. *First Five Year Plan*, p. 28.

death blow to these flourishing handicrafts. Our indigenous handicrafts could not withstand the competition of cheap machine-made goods of foreign countries. Besides, the disappearance of princely States meant the loss of patronage, in the absence of which the cottage industries could not thrive. In short, with the disruption of village economy and its consequent self-sufficiency, the cottage industries began showing signs of decay. The extinction of handicrafts rendered a vast majority of rural masses unemployed and poverty-stricken. The result was severe pressure on land in the wake of dwindling cottage industries.

The problem of Backward Classes is really the problem of rural India. The backwardness and appalling poverty of the masses are due largely to two centuries of foreign rule. The devastating assault on the old village economy hastened the disruption of rural life. The educational and industrial policy followed by the British attracted all available talent mostly from the upper classes to the urban areas and to Government service. Unrestricted competition of mills and factories and the import of foreign goods disorganized the once thriving rural industries and village handicrafts. With the decay of rural industries and domestic handicrafts, the artisans lost not only their gainful occupation but also their hereditary education, skill, and culture. They were driven to backwardness and despair.[2]

The hardships encountered by Scheduled Tribes are better described in the Report of the Scheduled Areas and Scheduled Tribes Commission:

No other class of people suffered as a result of the policy of callous disregard towards cottage and village industries and arts and crafts in the days of the British power as much as the tribals. They were denied the requisite incentives; an atmosphere was created which

2. *Report of the Backward Classes Commission,* 1956, Vol. 1, para. 16, p. 55.

made them feel that their arts were good for nothing. The restrictions imposed by the forest authorities, which denied them the raw materials for their arts and crafts, greatly contributed to the decline of the industry and is still a major obstacle to its development.[3]

After independence, the importance of resurgence of cottage industries in reconstructing rural economy is greatly realized. Cottage industries which form the subsidiary occupations of agriculturists are mostly traditional, hereditary in nature, professed by village artisans. These handicrafts were pursued mostly by the Backward Classes. It is befitting therefore, that any welfare scheme for the advancement of Backward Classes should lay special emphasis on the development of cottage industries. Statewise classification of Backward Classes, compiled by the Backward Classes Commission, throws ample light on this fact.[4] The fact that crafts were associated with castes was asserted by the Planning Commission also. The First Five Year Plan observed: "For the greater part, crafts were chosen on the basis of caste and skills were passed on from one person to another."[5]

The Five Year Plans have emphasized the significance of cottage industries as the only solution for unemployment in the country. The National Income Committee of 1950-51 estimated that these industries provide employment opportunities to nearly 11.5 million workers in contrast with the factory establishments, which with large investments employ only 3 million. So, cottage industries play a great role in India's rural economy.

The difficulties confronted by cottage industries are: lack of finance, absence of marketing facilities, and lack of training and literacy to cater to modern demands.

---

3. *Report of the Scheduled Areas and Scheduled Tribes Commission.* Vol. 1, 1960–61, para. 3.23, p. 26.

4. *Report of the Backward Classes Commission,* 1956, Vol. 2.

5. *First Five Year Plan,* para. 17, p. 320.

Lack of finance is one of the greatest drawbacks facing the village artisan. As the First Plan remarked:

> Village artisans have scarcely any financial resources of their own, nor have they any security to offer. They produce mainly for local demand and, if they manufacture for a market outside the village, finance is generally found by some middleman. Finance for the development of village industries has to be viewed as a problem inseparable from finance for agriculture.[6]

To meet the requirements of village artisans, it was proposed in the First Plan to establish a Handicrafts Board, to advise on problems of handicrafts and to set up technical training institutes to train artisans in different trades.

The First Plan allocation for the revitalization of cottage industries in the State sector was Rs. 120 millions. The target for the central sector was Rs. 150 millions. The village industries recommended for development were:[7] Village oil industry, soap-making with neem oil, paddy husking, palm gur, Gur and Khandsari, leather, woolen blankets, high-grade handmade paper, bee-keeping, and the cottage match industry.

It was further proposed that the Khadi and village industries board should take active interest in the promotion of handicrafts. A number of boards were set up, such as (1) the All India Khadi and Village industries Board, (2) the All India Handicrafts Board, (3) the All India Handloom Board, (4) the Small Scale Industries Board, (5) the Coir Board, and (6) the Silk Board.

The expenditure incurred on the development of small industries through various boards during the First Plan is given in Table 5-1:[8]

---

6. *Ibid.*, para. 18, p. 321.
7. More details in the First Plan, Appendix, p. 324.
8. *Ibid.*, compiled.

TABLE 5–1

(Rs. in crores)

	1951–55	1955–56 (budget)	1951–56
Handloom	6.5	4.6	11.1
Khadi	4.9	3.5	8.4
Village industries	1.1	3.0	4.1
Small-scale industries	2.0	3.3	5.3
Handicrafts	0.4	0.6	1.0
Silk and sericulture	0.8	0.5	1.3
TOTAL	15.7	15.5	31.2

Out of this general allotment, a sum of Rs. 7.417 millions was spent for the development of cottage industries on the Backward Classes by the State Governments.

The Second Plan provision for the development of small-scale and village industries was much greater than the First Plan target. The general outlay was Rs. 2,000 millions, in addition to which it was proposed to spend Rs. 110 millions for cottage and medium industries and Rs. 70 millions for vocational and technical training for the rehabilitation of displaced persons. The Second Plan outlay are recorded in Table 5-2:[9]

TABLE 5–2

Industry	(Rs. in crores)
1. Handloom	
Cotton weaving	56.0
Silk weaving	1.5
Wool weaving	2.0
	59.5
2. Khadi	
Wool spinning and weaving	1.9

9. Second Five Year Plan, compiled.

Decentralized cotton spinning and Khadi	14.8
	16.7

3. Village Industries

Hand pounding of rice	5.0
Vegetable oil (ghani)	6.7
Leather footwear and tanning (village)	5.0
Gur and Khandsari	7.0
Cottage match	1.1
Other village industries	14.0
	38.8

4. Handicrafts	9.0
5. Small-scale industries	55.0

6. Other industries

Sericulture	5.0
Coir spinning and weaving	1.0
7. General schemes (administration, research, etc.)	15.0
TOTAL	200.0

A sum of Rs. 54.73 millions was envisaged for the promotion of cottage industries on Backward Classes during the Second Plan, the pattern of expenditure being as stated in Table 5–3:[10]

TABLE 5–3

Category of Backward Class	Expenditure		
	Second Plan	1956–57	1957–58
Scheduled Castes	24,754,550	1,470,388	1,782,430
Scheduled Tribes	23,850,580	1,328,145	2,811,770
Other Backward Classes	3,522,450	270,383	765,210
Ex-Criminal Tribes	2,601,570	269,106	353,288
Total	54,729,150	3,338,022	5,712,698

10. *Report of the Commissioner for Scheduled Castes and Scheduled Tribes*, 1957–58, para. 48, p. 77.

This expenditure was incurred for benefiting 36,023 Backward Class members comprising 2,850 families.

A number of training-cum-production centers were established in the country to give a fillip to handicrafts. In spite of opening these centers the results obtained were not satisfactory. Production was found inadequate and the training schemes showed very poor response from the rural masses.

The recommendations made by the Committee on Plan Projects for achieving better results were:[11]

    i) For those who practice it as a subsidiary occupation, it must be related to their agricultural or forest operations and should enable them to supplement their earnings appreciably.

    ii) For others who take it as the main occupation, it must continue to be a profitable venture in the face of severe competition that is offered by purely commercial venture.

It is felt that the production of handicrafts should not be of an indigenous nature but they should cater largely to modern demands. For this the introduction of a commercial aspect is necessitated. The increase in the tempo of production would lessen the pressure of unemployment by creating more employment opportunities for the rural population.

The Third Plan allocation for the development of cottage industries in the State sector is indicated in Table 5-4.[12]

It has been recommended by the Commissioner for Scheduled Castes and Scheduled Tribes, that for rehabilitating trainees, the follow-up program should be well organized. He further suggested: "In order to enable the

11. *Report of the Study Team on Social Welfare and Welfare of Backward Classes,* Vol. 1, 1959, para. 7, p. 159.

12. *Report of the Commissioner for Scheduled Castes and Scheduled Tribes,* 1961–62, p. 73.

TABLE 5–4

(Rs. in millions)

| Category of Backward Class | Provision in the Third Plan | 1961–62 | |
		Allocation made	Expenditure incurred
Scheduled Tribes	23.193	3.609	1.847
Scheduled Castes	45.530	4.541	3.056
TOTAL	68.723	8.150	4.903

trainees to stand on their own feet after the completion of the course they should be given aid in the form of loans repayable on easy terms, instead of inadequate outright grants."[13]

To encounter the competition of cheap factory goods the Commissioner recommended:

A design centre experimenting in various uses to which the traditional products can be easily put to, should be started. All the Rest Homes and Dak Bungalows should be furnished with the products manufactured by the tribals and adequate publicity should be given to the places from where these articles have been procured. It is suggested that the welfare department should help the Scheduled Caste and the Scheduled Tribe artisans and ex-trainees in finding markets for their produce, procuring raw materials and developing special designs which may reflect the genius of the people, to attract sale of such products.[14]

Agriculture

India is primarily an agricultural country. Agriculture constitutes the pattern of livelihood for nearly 70 percent

13. *Ibid.*, para. 11.14, p. 77.
14. *Ibid.*, p. 78.

of our population. It forms the mainstay of Backward Classes in particular. According to the 1951 Census, out of 55.327 million Scheduled Castes, nearly 38.1 millions depend on agriculture. And out of a total population of 22.5 million Scheduled Tribes, 17.3 millions depend on agriculture. The same Census records that 295 millions or nearly 83 percent live in villages, while 62 millions or nearly 17 percent live in cities. Out of 83 percent, 29 percent are self-supporting, 12 percent are dependents, and the remaining are non-earning dependents. Self-supporting agriculturists are estimated at 68 millions and constitute about 80 percent. Besides, out of a total rural population of 295 millions, 249 millions were engaged in agriculture. The agricultural population was classified as:

1. cultivators of land, wholly or mainly owned;
2. cultivators of land, wholly or mainly unowned;
3. cultivating laborers; and
4. non-cultivating owners of land.

Thus, the pressure on agriculture is one of the major economic problems. Even though new avenues of employment have been created by starting industries, the Census figures record very little change in the occupational structure of the population, particularly the rural population. A comparative study of Census figures since 1911 to the present day reveal that industries in India are not capable of absorbing sufficient majority. Whatever may be the causes for such a state of affairs, the fact remains that a large section of our population is thrown on agriculture. It is observed that, in 1911, 17.5 percent were engaged in industries. In 1931, 16.3 percent and according to 1951 Census 10.5 percent. These figures speak for themselves the prevailing situation in the country.

Moreover, the uneven distribution of the population, with overcrowded villages and scanty urban population, is also responsible for the poor yield in agriculture. Too many people are engaged in agriculture, which is the least remunerative of all industries. The rural-urban population percentage from 1921 to 1951 throws light on this factor:

Year	Rural	Urban
1921	88.7	11.3
1931	87.9	12.1
1941	86.1	13.9
1951	82.7	17.3

The livelihood pattern of the Urban and Rural population of 1951 Census further proves the vast number engaged in agriculture, as recorded in Table 5-5.[15]

Agricultural progress is relative, depending on so many factors. Diminutive numbers engaged in agricultural operations, with economic holdings, coupled with the quality of the land and nature's bounty, go to make maximum yield. But unfortunately, in India none of these factors are efficiently grouped and the result is that ours is the poorest agricultural country in the world. The lopsided nature of our economy has further aggravated the situation.

Yet another fact causing anxiety is the preponderance of landless laborers. According to 1951 Census, out of 38.1 millions of Scheduled Castes and 17.3 millions of Scheduled Tribes depending on agriculture, nearly 4.8 millions among the Scheduled Castes and 2 millions among the Scheduled Tribes are landless laborers. The Scheduled Caste agriculturists constitute 15.3 percent of the total agricultural classes in the country, form 33 percent of the total landless-laborers. The concentration of Scheduled Caste landless-laborers in South India is 42.1 percent; Central India 34.2 percent; East India 31.3 percent; West India

15. Census of India, 1957, compiled.

TABLE 5-5

Cultivators of land wholly or mainly owned, and their dependents		Cultivators of land wholly or mainly unowned, and their dependents		Cultivating laborers and their dependents		Non-cultivating owners of land; agricultural rent receivers; and their dependents	
Males	Females	Males	Females	Males	Females	Males	Females
Livelihood pattern of the Rural Population, 1951.							
82,811,682	80,111,091	15,521,384	14,691,883	21,462,215	21,479,113	1,976,217	2,395,077
Livelihood pattern of the Urban population, 1951.							
2,303,795	2,119,993	734,824	691,711	933,647	936,968	462,101	491,159

19.2 percent; North West India 17.4 percent; and North India 17.2 percent. The Scheduled Tribes agriculturists form 7 percent of the total agricultural classes of India, but constitute only 6.3 percent of the total landless laborers, indicating that the incidence of landless labor is somewhat less among the Scheduled Tribes, than among the general population of India. The concentration of Scheduled Tribes landless laborers in South India is 27.2 percent; West India 21.1 percent; Central India 18.3 percent; East India 10.5 percent; and North India 1.7 percent.[16]

The All India Agricultural Labour Enquiry Report, 1950-51, has also made a reference to the striking growth of rural agricultural labor population. The percentage distribution of rural families categorywise is indicated in Table 5-6:[17]

TABLE 5–6

| | Agricultural land owners | Agricultural tenants | Agricultural laborers | | | Non-agricultural rists |
| | | | with land | without land | Total | |
			(Percent)			
North India	7.7	56.1	5.7	8.6	14.3	21.9
East India	16.3	29.9	19.0	13.7	32.7	21.1
South India	23.0	6.1	27.3	22.8	50.1	20.8
West India	44.8	18.4	8.8	11.6	20.4	16.4
Central India	25.0	22.0	14.6	22.1	36.7	16.3
North West India	42.2	25.0	2.7	7.1	9.8	23.0
All India	22.2	27.2	15.2	15.2	30.4	20.2

Efforts have been made by the Government to ameliorate the lot of Backward Classes. During the First Plan, State Governments undertook various schemes to benefit agriculturists at a cost of Rs. 30,363,925. Out of this amount, Rs. 26,598,852 was spent on Scheduled Tribes,

16. *Report of the Commissioner for Scheduled Castes and Scheduled Tribes,* 1956–57, para. 2, p. 43.
17. *All India Agricultural Labour Enquiry Report,* 1950–51, p. 9.

Rs. 658,485 on Scheduled Castes, Rs. 3,012,828 on Ex-criminal Tribes, and Rs. 93,760 on Other Backward Classes.

The expenditures incurred on schemes under the Second Plan was to the tune of Rs. 40,543,971. The details of expenditure are given in Table 5-7:[18]

TABLE 5–7

Category	State Sector (Rs)	Centrally sponsored schemes (Rs)	Total (Rs)
Scheduled Tribes	20,095,671	2,198,000	22,293,671
Scheduled Castes	3,245,000	4,384,000	7,629,000
Ex-Criminal Tribes	3,636,300	800,000	4,436,300
Other Backward Classes	6,185,000	—	6,185,000
TOTAL	33,161,971	7,382,000	40,543,971

The Third Plan allocation was Rs. 123.8 million under the State sector. During 1961-62 an expenditure of Rs. 13.247 millions was incurred as against the provision of Rs. 13.786 millions envisaged for the purpose on Scheduled Castes and Scheduled Tribes. Table 5-8 throws light on the plan provision and expenditure:[19]

TABLE 5–8

Category	Third Plan provision	Provision	Expenditure
Scheduled Castes	413.46	40.02	40.24
Scheduled Tribes	824.97	97.84	92.23
TOTAL	1,238.43	137.86	132.47

18. *Report of the Commissioner for Scheduled Castes and Scheduled Tribes*, 1956–57, p. 44.
19. *Ibid.*, 1961–62, p. 58.

Land Policy

A proper land policy for the economic betterment of Backward Classes is of utmost importance. As observed in the First Five Year Plan:

> From the social aspect, which is not less important than the economic, a policy for land may be considered adequate in the measure in which, now and in the coming years, it reduces disparities in wealth and income, eliminates exploitation, provides security for tenant and worker, and, finally promises equality of status and opportunity to different sections of the rural population.[20]

The problems concerned with land policy are the unit of economic cultivation, proprietary rights, security of tenure, and the consolidation of holdings. The First Five Year Plan has dealt with all these problems and suggested measures for the implementation of a just national land policy. To achieve better results in the interest of Backward Classes, the recommendations made by the Backward Classes Commission were:

> Land reform acts should be simple and easily understandable by the backward communities, in whose interest they are enacted. Otherwise, it will lead to endless litigation and exploitation. There should be no loopholes in legislation that might lead to social conflict in rural areas. Too many and frequent changes in land legislation create confusion and difficulty.[21]

The disparity between the vast number of landless laborers, and the limited areas of land at the disposal of the Government, renders difficult the settlement of Backward Classes on land who are mostly landless agriculturists. The three sources of providing land are:

---

20. *First Five Year Plan*, p. 184.
21. *Report of the Backward Classes Commission*, para. 32, p. 64.

(a) Cultivable waste and other lands with the State;
(b) Land released through the imposition of ceilings on land holdings; and
(c) Bhoodan and gramdan lands.*[22]

*"Bhoodan" and "gramdan" are land gift movements in India started by Vinoba Bhave. A person owning large areas of lands is asked to give a small portion of his land as a voluntary gift. The lands donated as gifts are distributed among the landless laborers.

The overall statewise settlement of Scheduled Castes and Scheduled Tribes on lands is indicated in the following Table:[23]

TABLE 5–9

| State/Union Territory | Land in acres alloted to | | | |
	Scheduled Castes	Scheduled Tribes	Other Backward Classes	Total
Bihar	44,867	44,350	13,970	103,187
Bombay	852,973	891,581	2,213,923	3,958,477
Madhya Pradesh (Madhya Bharat Region)	200,000	—	—	200,000
Orissa	10,985	35,364	8,240	54,590
Tripura	—	25,646	—	25,646
TOTAL	1,108,825	996,941	2,236,133	4,341,900

The introduction of agricultural colonies goes a long way in solving the land problem of Backward Classes. Among Backward Classes, the Scheduled Castes, the Scheduled Tribes, and Denotified Communities are greatly benefited by these colonies which offer all the basic amenities of life. A major development effected in the colonization scheme during the Third Plan period was the allotment of lands for individuals at different places for the hitherto group allotment. "It is hoped that with this modification in

22. *Report of the Commissioner for Scheduled Castes and Scheduled Tribes,* 1957–58, para. 6, p. 62.
23. *Ibid.,* para. 13, p. 64.

this scheme it will now be possible for the State Government to work this scheme more expeditiously."[24]

Shifting Cultivation

Shifting cultivation is a tribal agricultural system followed by tribals who live in hill slopes and forest region. According to the information gathered by the Commissioner for Scheduled Castes and Scheduled Tribes, this type of cultivation is termed variously in different States. In Assam and Tripura it is called "Jhum," "Bewar," "Dahiya" or "Penda," in Madhya Pradesh, "Podu," in Andhra and South Orissa, "Rama," "Dahi," "Koman" or "Brirga" in North Orissa, and "Gudia" or "Domgar Chas" in South Orissa.[25]

But shifting cultivation is generally regarded as the least economical method, for it involves deforestation, denudation of hill slopes, soil erosion, and other evils associated with it. Shifting cultivation has been the subject of great controversy. During the First Five Year Plan, an attempt was made to control this practice in the States of Assam, Andhra, Bihar, Madhya Pradesh, Orissa, and Tripura. The Second Five Year Plan undertook a more ambitious scheme in this direction.

The shortcomings of shifting cultivation have been discussed by several experts competent to make observations on such a practice. It has been generally felt that this tribal agricultural system cannot be considered an evil. On the contrary, it has its own validity. Modification rather than abolition has been suggested by various committees appointed to probe through the matter. It has been remarked by M. D. Chathurvedi, the then Inspector General of Forests, in 1953, that:

24. *Ibid.*, 1961–62, Part I, para. 9.14, p. 57.
25. *Ibid.*, 1956–57, para. 18, p. 49.

The correct approach to the problem of shifting cultivation lies in accepting it, not as a necessary evil, but
recognizing it as a way of life, not condemning it as an
evil practice, but regarding it as an agricultural practice
evolved as a reflex to the physiographical character of the
land.[26]

M. S. Shivaraman, adviser to the Program Administration of the Planning Commission, observed in 1957: "It
is a mistake to assume that *jhuming* (the word used in
Assam for shifting cultivation) in itself is unscientific land
use."[27]

According to the Scheduled Areas and Scheduled Tribes
Commission:

The most reasonable policy, therefore, is to develop
shifting cultivation on scientific lines so as to limit its
disadvantages and promote the fertility of the soil. For
this purpose we recommend the undertaking of research
in every area where jhuming cultivation exists on a wide
scale.[28]

But efforts have still been made to control this practice
in areas wherever possible. The three main measures that
are being undertaken for weaning away the tribals from
resorting to the practice of shifting cultivation are:[29]

1. Introduction of terrace cultivation;
2. Colonization; and
3. Pilot Project centers.

The allocation of Rs. 9.2 millions was made to the State
Government of Andhra Pradesh, Assam, Bihar, Bombay,
Kerala, Madhya Pradesh, Madras, Mysore, Orissa, and

26. *Report of the Committee on special Multipurpose Tribal Blocks,*
1960, p. 48.
27. *Ibid.,* p. 48.
28. *Report of the Scheduled Areas and Scheduled Tribes Commission,*
1960–61, Vol. 1, para. 13.23, p. 149.
29. *Report of the Commissioner for Scheduled Castes and Scheduled
Tribes,* 1957–58, para. 46, p. 76.

Union Territories of Manipur and Tripura, during 1957-58. These States and Union Territories were advised to formulate schemes for granting subsidies for reclamation of lands, terracing, irrigation, and all steps to encourage the tribals to settle down permanently.

The general pattern of schemes falls into three types:[30]

1. Opening of Demonstration Centers to demonstrate a more balanced land-use plan for these areas;
2. Colonizing shifting cultivators in permanent colonies for agriculture; and
3. Improving the methods of cultivation through demonstration, training, and subsidized agricultural programs.

In the Third Plan, schemes for settling shifting cultivators find place in the State Sector. Besides this, the Departments of Agriculture and Forest are also taking steps to control shifting cultivation and train the tribal people in better methods of agriculture.

Debt Redemption

Debt redemption occupies an important place in the economic amelioration of Backward Classes. The history of rural finance is one of indebtedness, the agriculturists falling prey to unscrupulous moneylenders. Hence, to prevent Backward Classes from being exploited by moneylenders and other unscrupulous agencies, it is necessary to take constructive measures. The magnitude of general indebtedness has been estimated by the Rural Credit Survey Committee of the Reserve Bank of India. But it does not contain any statistical data relating to the indebtedness prevalent among Backward Classes. However, it is observed that the incidence of indebtedness is very high among the Scheduled Castes and Scheduled Tribes. The Study Team on Social Welfare and Welfare of Backward Classes observed:

---

30. *Ibid.*, 1958–59, para. 23, p. 82.

Among the Backward Classes, the tribal communities have been increasingly impoverished by the nefarious activities of moneylenders, middlemen, and contractors. While each of them has worked to the detriment of the Backward Class interests, they are more formidable when they work in combination, or play multiple roles; the contractor being the middleman or the middleman a moneylender.[31]

The causes of indebtedness among the Backward Classes have been very aptly summarized by the Commissioner for Scheduled Castes and Scheduled Tribes as follows:

Even for subsistence requirements Scheduled Castes and Scheduled Tribes often need loans and because of landlessness their credit worthiness is so low that only village "Sahukars" who charge exorbitant interest are willing to advance them loans. The extravagant expenditures on social customs enhance their loan requirements. The inherited debt is another contributing cause of indebtedness. Innumerable people are "born in debt," live in debt, and die in debt, from generation to generation.[32]

Legislative and executive measures have been undertaken by the State Governments to curb this practice. Cooperatives have been started to substitute the moneylenders for purposes of financing Backward Class agriculturists.

In view of the vast indebtedness prevalent among the Scheduled Tribes, the Elwin Committee remarked:

The problem of indebtedness will not be overcome unless an all-sided attack is made through legislative measures, administrative enforcement and the develop-

31. *Report of the Study Team on Social Welfare and Welfare of Backward Classes,* para. 14, p. 162.
32. *Report of the Commissioner for Scheduled Castes and Scheduled Tribes,* 1957–58, para. 84, p. 90.

ment of public opinion. This should be responsibility of the development agencies and the Tribal Welfare Departments.[33]

Cooperation

The cooperative movement in India started in the closing decades of the nineteenth century. The Cooperative Credit Societies Act was passed in 1904, to meet the needs of the agriculturists, artisans and others. Since then, cooperative societies are established extensively in various fields—agriculture, industry, forestry, farming, etc. The importance of cooperative societies in a country like ours needs no emphasis. Cooperative societies are the only medium to educate villagers in self-help, economy, borrowing for productive purposes and in being thrifty.

The reasons for the failure of cooperative movement among the tribals have been enumerated by the Elwin Committee as follows:

i) The workers who took the program of cooperatives to the tribals did not know of their corporate practices and could not relate the formal program to them.

ii) The rules and regulations for the formation of cooperatives were far too complicated and unsuited to the understanding and the acceptance of the tribal people, with the result that even where they have become members of a cooperative, the management is generally in the hands of a non-tribal. In fact, the cooperatives have become one more way whereby the non-tribals control the economic and social interest of the tribals.

iii) The tribals find it difficult to pay the share capital, even though the minimum is as low as ten rupees. Many are unwilling to risk even a payment of one rupee.

iv) The value of the societies promoted by the co-

---

33. *Report of the Committee on Special Multipurpose Tribal Blocks,* 1960, p. 133.

operative worker is more a matter of his own convenience than an integral part of tribal life. This the tribal mind could not appreciate.[34]

Some progress has been made in the development of cooperative societies during the Five Year Plans. Under the First Plan, a sum of Rs. 5.36 millions was spent on cooperative societies, for the benefit of the Backward Classes. The details of the Second Plan allocations are given in Table 5-10.[35]

The total expenditure on cooperatives in the Second Plan was, Rs. 5.777 millions as against the Plan outlay of Rs. 21.543 millions.

In June 1961, a Special Working Group on cooperation for Backward Classes was set up by the Government of India to study the progress made by the Backward Classes in the field of cooperation during the first two plans. After a detailed study of the problem, the Group recommended several measures for the economic advancement of the Backward Classes through cooperatives. One of the suggestions was the establishment of a National Corporation of Cooperative Development for tribals at an estimated expenditure of Rs. 13.7 millions. Besides, the working Group also recommended a district organization set-up for fostering cooperation among the tribals.

The Third Plan allocation under the State sector for the development of cooperative schemes for Scheduled Castes was to the tune of Rs. 31.4 millions. The allocation for Scheduled Tribes under the centrally sponsored program was Rs. 2,730 millions.

But the glaring defects of the cooperative societies are recorded by the Study Team on Social Welfare and Welfare of Backward Classes:

34. *Ibid.,* p. 134.
35. *Report of the Commissioner for Scheduled Castes and Scheduled Tribes,* 1957–58, para. 58, p. 82.

TABLE 5-10

Category of Backward Class	Allocation made for the Second Plan period (Rs)		Expenditure incurred during 1956–57 (Rs)		Estimated expenditure for 1957–58 (Rs)	
	Centrally sponsored scheme	State sector	Centrally sponsored scheme	State sector	Centrally sponsored scheme	State sector
Scheduled Castes	1,955,000	4,694,800	17,500	46,533	—	109,958
Scheduled Tribes	5,312,000	8,659,025	1,111,870	195,905	811,820	1,053,360
Other Backward Classes	—	662,650	—	12,065	—	16,600
Ex-criminal Tribes	—	259,350	—	5,000	—	8,700
TOTAL	7,267,000	14,275,825	1,129,370	259,503	811,820	1,188,618

Social workers among backward classes have frequently expressed that the small farmers and the landless laborers benefit the least from the cooperative societies. This was tested in our field studies. Forty-four percent of 115 members spread over 8 States felt that the small farmers and landless laborers are not at all benefited by activities of the cooperative societies. The main reason for this is the lack of credit-worthiness of the landless and the small cultivator.[36]

The most popular among the cooperative societies are the Forest Laborers' Cooperative societies. These societies cater to the needs of the tribals and save them from exploitation by forest contractors. The credit for introducing such societies goes to B. G. Kher, who first opened them in Bombay during 1946-47. Since then these societies have gained popular support throughout India. The First Plan made provision for the establishment of 79 societies in the States of Andhra Pradesh, Bihar, Madras, Rajasthan, Saurashtra, and Kerala. During the Second Plan it was estimated to start 117 societies, 92 under State Sector, and 25 under Central Sector. In the Third Plan, an allocation of Rs. 27.3 millions was made under the Central Sector for Scheduled Tribes, and Rs. 20.8 millions, under the State Sector. No provision has been made for cooperative schemes for Scheduled Castes under the Central Sector. But in the State Sector, a provision of Rs. 31.4 millions was allotted for varied cooperative schemes.

The progress made in the development of forest laborers' cooperative societies during 1961-63 is indicated in Table 5-11.[37]

But these societies are not active throughout the year. So with a view to provide employment opportunities to

36. *Report of the Study Team on Social Welfare and Welfare of Backward Classes,* 1959, Vol. I, para. 30, p. 167.

37. *Report of the Commissioner for Scheduled Castes and Scheduled Tribes,* 1962–63, pp. 99–100.

TABLE 5–11

| | Physical targets achieved | | | |
| | 1961–62 | | 1962–63 | |
	Central Sector	State Sector	Central Sector	State Sector
Andhra Pradesh	—	—	—	—
Assam	N.A.	5 societies	N.A.	—
Bihar	N.A.	—	5 societies	—
Gujarat	6 societies	—	12 societies	—
Kerala	—	—	—	Grants for 10 paid secretaries
Madhya Pradesh	30 societies	—	40 societies	—
Maharashtra	44 societies	—	21 societies	6 societies
Rajasthan	N.A.	—	N.A.	—
Himachal Pradesh	—	—	—	6 societies
Manipur	—	12 societies	—	4 societies
Tripura	—	1 New society organized and 5 old societies maintained	—	6 societies maintained

the workers engaged in such societies, it has been suggested by the Commissioner for Scheduled Castes and Scheduled Tribes, to make them "forest-cum-labor" contract societies.

Another type of cooperative societies is Grain Golas. They are a sort of grain banks advancing loans in kind to Scheduled Castes and Scheduled Tribes. The scheme of Grain Golas originated in Bihar in 1902. They are functioning satisfactorily in many parts of India now, particularly for the benefit of Scheduled Tribes. During the First Five Year Plan, 391 societies were started in the States of Bihar, Orissa, and West Bengal. The Second Plan target was 1,183.

The Third Plan provision with details of targets achieved during 1961-63 is recorded in Table 5-12.[38]

Communications

Improvements in communications is an important requisite for the development of Backward Areas populated by Backward Classes. In view of its importance, it is given priority in the Five Year Plans. During the First Five Year Plan, an allocation of Rs. 41.2 millions was made for this purpose. Out of this amount, Rs. 33.1 millions was spent in Assam. Similarly, out of the Second Plan's provision of Rs. 88.7 millions, Rs. 41.2 millions was spent for the construction of roads, etc., in Assam. Under the Third Plan, Rs. 56.892 millions was allocated under State Sector. In addition, the Third Finance Commission recommended special grants of Rs. 360 millions for improvement of road Communications in the Backward Areas, which is stated in Table 5-13.[39]

---

38. *Ibid.,* p. 101.
39. *Ibid.,* 1961–62, p. 96.

TABLE 5-12

| | State/ Union Territory | Third Plan | | Targets achieved during 1961–62 | Allotment made | (Rs. in millions) 1962–63 | |
		Provision	Targets fixed			Expenditure incurred estimated	Targets achieved
State Sector	Bihar	7.3	60	5.2	0.55	0.32	54 opened, 72 maintained and 8 buildings constructed
	Mysore	N.A.	0.1	0.4	0.10	0.10	—
	Orissa	20.10	57.6	22 new and 31 old completed and 69 under construction	0.5	0.3	79 completed
Central Sector	Madhya Pradesh	N.A.	N.A.	3.5	N.A.	N.A.	90

TABLE 5–13

(Rs. in millions)

State	Per year	Total for four years 1962–66
Andhra Pradesh	5.0	20.0
Assam	7.5	30.0
Bihar	7.5	30.0
Gujarat	10.0	40.0
Jammu and Kashmir	5.0	20.0
Kerala	7.5	30.0
Madhya Pradesh	17.5	70.0
Mysore	5.0	20.0
Orissa	17.5	70.0
Rajasthan	7.5	30.0

Housing

The living conditions of Backward Classes, particularly the Scheduled Castes and Scheduled Tribes, are deplorable. Hence housing facilities to improve their dwelling is an urgent need. The First Plan allocation for this purpose was Rs. 21.7 millions. Under the Second Plan, a sum of Rs. 82.3 millions was spent. The Third Plan provision was Rs. 30 millions to be spent exclusively on Scheduled Castes. The pattern of expenditure was the construction of houses for sweepers and scavengers, granting of house sites to Scheduled Castes persons engaged in unclean occupations and allotment of house sites for landless laborers among the Scheduled Castes. Expenditure incurred on this scheme is recorded in Table 5-14:[40]

---

40. *Ibid.,* p. 118.

TABLE 5-14

(Rs. in millions)

State	Allocation for 1962–63	Expenditure incurred during 1962–63	Physical targets achieved during 1962–63
Andhra Pradesh	0.351	0.351	N.A.
Bihar	0.371	0.371	N.A.
Gujarat	0.020	0.010	39 house sites
Jammu and Kashmir	0.043	—	—
Madhya Pradesh	0.174	0.014	N.A.
Madras	1.063	1.049	5467 house sites
Punjab	0.011	0.011	60 house sites
Uttar Pradesh	0.400	0.399	281 house sites
West Bengal	0.200	0.094	322 house sites
TOTAL	2.633	2.299	—

Similarly, an expenditure of Rs. 1.3574 millions was incurred on the housing schemes for Scheduled Tribes. The details of expenditure are given in Table 5-15.[41]

Housing facilities offered to Backward Classes also provide for a slum clearance scheme launched in 1956 and a village housing projects scheme introduced in 1957. As regards slum clearance, 289 projects and an expenditure of Rs. 253.0 millions were sanctioned up to March 1963. In addition, a sum of Rs. 63.9 millions was spent for the implementation of the slum clearance scheme in Delhi. Similarly, the village housing scheme was spread over 5,000 villages in the country. Modifications have been made in the housing projects, on the deliberations of the village housing seminar organized at Mysore in 1962.

In addition to the aforesaid schemes, Scheduled Castes and Scheduled Tribes are given the benefit of subsidized industrial housing scheme, plantation labor housing scheme and low-income group housing scheme.

41. *Ibid.*, p. 122.

TABLE 5–15

(Rs. in millions)

State/Union Territory	Allocation made in the Third Plan	Physical targets proposed for the Third Plan	Allocation made for the year 1962–63	Expenditure incurred during 1962–63	Physical targets achieved during 1962–63
Andhra Pradesh	2.500	1950 houses	0.300	0.300	N.A.
Kerala	0.593	560 houses	0.159	0.1754	159 houses
Madras	1.000	1300 houses	0.200	0.200	266 houses
Maharashtra	1.000	N.A.	0.300	0.300	N.A.
Mysore	0.704	880 houses	0.167	0.167	184 houses
Orissa	0.800	13340 houses	0.100	0.136	85 houses
West Bengal	2.000	4000 families	0.350	0.354	834 families
Andaman & Nicobar Islands	N.A.	450 houses	0.010	0.0014	2 houses
Himachal Pradesh	0.330	7 inns	0.104	0.104	2 inns
Manipur	0.300	600 houses	0.060	0.060	N.A.
Tripura	0.150	500 families	0.030	0.039	180 families
TOTAL	9.377	—	1.780	1.8368	—

But the plan targets and schemes appear to be inadequate considering the vast problem that has to be tackled by the Government.

Tribal Development Blocks

The most significant program for the development of tribal areas is the establishment of Special Multipurpose Tribal Blocks, in consonance with Articles 46 and 275 of the Constitution. The object of these blocks is to bring about radical changes in the economic and social standards of the tribals. Forty-three Special Multipurpose Tribal Blocks were set up jointly by the Ministry of Home Affairs and the Ministry of Community Development and Cooperation in the most underdeveloped tribal areas. There was criticism on the work of these blocks, so a committee was appointed under the chairmanship of Verrier Elwin, in 1959, with the following terms of reference:

    i) To study the working of the Special Multipurpose Tribal Blocks; and

    ii) To advise the Government of India on how to implement the intensive development program of the Blocks more effectively and give the program a proper tribal bias.

The report was accordingly submitted in 1960.

These blocks are now called Tribal Development Blocks. A suggestion to this effect was recommended by the Elwin Committee in 1960. Besides, the Committee also recommended the opening of 300 new Tribal Development Blocks covering areas having 55 percent tribal population. But the Government of India has decided to start 330 such Blocks covering areas having 66.6 percent tribal population. The pattern of expenditure on these Blocks, during the Third Plan is Rs. 25,000 for vehicles, Rs. 75,000 for Project Office Personnel, Rs. 0.24 million

TABLE 5-16

State/Union Territory	Number of Blocks	Area covered	Number of villages covered	Total population covered	
				Total population	Population of Scheduled Tribes.
Andhra Pradesh	2	1,052 sq. miles	413 main villages and 93 hamlets	45,571	40,927
Punjab	1	1,764 sq. miles	172 villages	12,106	12,106
Himachal Pradesh	1	N.A.	251 "	13,379	13,379
Manipur	1	1,352 sq. miles	221 "	25,156	25,156
Tripura	1	492 sq. miles	184 "	20,944	17,429

for Economic development, Rs. 0.1 million for Communications and Rs. 60,000 for Social Services. A detailed account of the areas covered with their population is given in Table 5-16.[42]

Table 5-17 indicates the expenditure incurred on Tribal Blocks in 1961-62:[43]

TABLE 5–17

State/Union Territory	Number of new blocks sanctioned so far for the Third Plan period	Number of Tribal Development Blocks opened during 1961–62	Number of Special Multi-purpose Tribal Blocks continued during 1961–62	Expenditure incurred during 1961–62 on Tribal Development Blocks shown in Cols. 4 and 5 (Rs. in lakhs)
Andhra Pradesh	16	2	4	10.24
Assam	37	11	7	30.75
Bihar	49	5	8	17.87
Gujarat	41	4	3	1.98
Kerala	2	—	—	nil
Maharashtra	18	2	4	12.00
Madhya Pradesh	71	—	—	42.00
Madras	2	—	—	nil
Orissa	60	6	4	17.09
Punjab	2	1	—	1.50
Rajasthan	13	—	1	2.31
Himachal Pradesh	2	1	1	N.A.
Manipur	7	1	1	3.08
Tripura	4	1	1	5.16
Total	324	34	34	143.98

There are certain shortcomings in the scheme of Tribal Development Blocks. However, these inadequacies could be overcome by undertaking a survey of tribal areas on

42. *Ibid.,* 1961–62, p. 49.
43. *Ibid.,* p. 50.

scientific lines with greater emphasis on agriculture, health, communications, education, etc. The expenditure should be framed on the recommendations of the Elwin Committee as: Schemes for economic development, 60 percent; Communications, 25 percent; and Social Services, 15 percent. In spite of certain shortcomings, these blocks appear to be the best approach to the welfare of tribals. As the Committee has remarked: "The experiment has not failed, valuable experience has been gained."[44]

To conclude, "In the program of the Special Tribal Blocks, if it is planned wisely and implemented sincerely, India has an effective instrument to save her tribal people from poverty and fear, and develop them along the lines of their own genius."[45]

44. *Report of the Committee on Special Multipurpose Tribal Blocks,* 1960, p. 182.
45. *Ibid.,* p. 193.

6

CONCLUSION

THE PROBLEM OF BACKWARD CLASSES IS ONE OF DOING justice to the underprivileged sections of society. This problem could be better explained against the historical background. Hence, the correlation between backwardness and the socio-economic phenomenon of caste provides the starting point for the investigation of the problem. The caste system as perpetuating class distinctions in Hindu society stands out peculiar for its immutability and social isolation fostered among the people professing the same religion. However, the caste system was subjected to constant modifications because of practical necessities. Changes in the caste system were inevitable. To trace a few important modifications, caste as conceived by the Varna theory was dynamic. Guna, or nature, constituted the chief determinant of caste. But in the course of time this dynamism gave way to rigidity and subsequently resulted in social discrimination. This is how untouchability and unapproachability took root in Hindu society. Rigorous caste regulations were imposed on food habits, customs, ritual, social get-togethers, occupational mobility, etc. Thus the pollution complex rendered the caste system an institution of discrimination and segregation. This aspect of the Hindu social structure has been characterized as "the most thoroughgoing attempt known in human history to introduce absolute inequality as the guiding principle in social relationships."[1]

The next phase of the evolution of the caste system was the allotment of specific occupations to specific castes. The choice of occupations was restricted to lower castes of the social order. The caste system dictated the pattern of the economic set-up of society, by assigning superior jobs to higher orders and manual labor and unclean work activities to lower orders. Besides, there was a stigma attached to these lowly occupations which further accentuated the social isolation among different sections of society. As regards the mobility of occupations, Brahmans had the option of going in for any trade other than their specific allotment and meanwhile retain the same social status accorded to them. But mobility was carefully restricted in the case of lower orders. Rights and equality were denied to these underprivileged classes. Thus the caste system was largely responsible for the creation of privileged and underprivileged classes in society.

With the advent of the British rule, the caste system underwent radical changes. The universalization of education and the influence of English literature on liberty, freedom, and democracy stirred the intelligentsia of the lower orders to question Brahmanical supremacy. As a result of this, passive submission of lower orders to the dictates of caste rules ceased to operate. As Morris-Jones observed: "Social reform has often been anti-Brahmin actually to increase consciousness of caste on both sides."[2] Equally interesting was the tendency among lower classes to rise in social estimation of society, by attributing new designations implying a high social origin to their caste groups. This tendency was glaringly prominent among the artisans. This social imitation of the lower classes has

1. Kingsley Davis, *The Population of India and Pakistan*, 1951, p. 170.
2. W. H. Morris-Jones, *The Government and Politics of India*, 1964, p. 59.

been termed by M. N. Srinivas as "Sanskritization." Sanskritization, in short, means the cultural and structural changes of society.

The early periods of the British rule marked significant changes in traditional caste hierarchy. During this time, a revision of the old social ideal in the context of social transformation was urged. The socio-religious movements of the period made efforts for the establishment of society on the principles of catholicity and cosmopolitanism. The impact of the British rule, especially their policy of throwing open the doors of education to all classes irrespective of caste and the admission of candidates belonging to different communities into Government Service, produced marvelous effects. The Non-Brahman movement in South India was a natural reaction to the traditional social order. Western ideas, ideals, and institutions introduced in India shook the foundations of the old society. With the growth of the national movement, the country witnessed a new sense of unity. The progressive policies advocated by nationalist parties created a mental revolution, a new determination to do justice to Backward Classes. Gandhiji's entry into politics gave further shock to the rigidity of the caste system. He evinced keen interest in the welfare of Harijans in particular and fervently criticized the caste system for doing injustice to these sections of society. Similarly, efforts made by Harijan leaders like B. R. Ambedkar to fight casteism prepared the ground for the inauguration of a new society based on equality and justice.

With the dawn of independence a new chapter has commenced in the social history of India. The framers of the Constitution have not only devised a suitable Constitutional framework for the country but also conceived the remedies for social problems. The incorporation of provisions relating to the cause of doing justice to Backward Classes constitutes a glorious chapter in the Indian

Constitution. The imbalance in society caused by the caste system is sought to be corrected by doing justice to Backward Classes on the social, economic, and political plane. This aim of the Constitution finds expression in the preamble, Fundamental Rights and Directive principles. The term "Backward Classes" for whom special concessions are accorded in the Constitution includes the four categories: the Scheduled Castes, the Scheduled Tribes, Other Backward Classes, and Denotified Communities.

The Constitutional safeguards for Backward Classes are found in Articles 15 (4), 16 (4), 29 (2), and Part XVI of the Constitution, which deals with Special provisions for Scheduled Castes and Scheduled Tribes. Art. 15 (4) provides:

> Nothing in this article or in clause (2) of Art. 29 shall prevent the State from making any special provision for the advancement of any socially and educationally backward classes of citizens or for the Scheduled Castes and Scheduled Tribes.

Similarly, Art. 16 (4) guarantees:

> Nothing in this article shall prevent the State from making any provision for the reservation of appointments or posts in favor of any backward class of citizens which, in the opinion of the State, is not adequately represented in the Services under the State.

Article 29 (2) is a corollary of Art. 15 (4). Under Part XVI of the Constitution, reservation of seats in Parliament and Legislative Assemblies of States for Scheduled Castes and Scheduled Tribes are guaranteed in Arts. 330 and 332. Article 335 ensures the representation of the Scheduled Castes and the Scheduled Tribes in Services. Meanwhile, it is laid down in Art. 334 that reservation of seats in Parliament and Legislative Assemblies would cease to have effect on the expiration of a period of twenty years from the commencement of the Constitution, according to the Constitution (Eighth Amendment) Act, 1959. Lok Sabha (the Lower House of Parliament) passed the constitutional amendment bill on Dec. 9, 1969, seeking to extend the reservation of seats in the House and State Assemblies for Scheduled Castes and Scheduled Tribes for a further period of 10 years—that is, up to 1980. Similarly, Art. 335 provides a governing clause that the claims of the members of the Scheduled Castes and the Scheduled Tribes would be considered "consistently with the maintenance of efficiency of administration."

But the process of equalization effected through Constitutional safeguards for Backward Classes is beset with many difficulties. In view of the historical factors, Constitutional guarantee for the protection of Backward Classes was not only justifiable but also inevitable. The social conditions in India were such that they necessitated the incorporation of special treatment for Backward Classes. These classes were denied opportunities of education, which stood in the way of their general advancement. Besides, the principle of equality enshrined in the Constitution cannot be operated in vacuum. To build an egalitarian society special preference to Backward Classes is inevitable. To transform a social order based on inequality, special concessions to the victims of inequality are necessary. As observed in the case of *D. G. Viswanath* v *Chief Secretary Govt. of Mysore:*

> It is cynical to suggest that the interest of the Nation is best served if the barber's son continues to be a barber and a shepherd's son continues to be a shepherd. The limitations of the doctrine of laissez faire is now well known. We have pledged ourselves to establish a Welfare State; social justice is an important ingredient

of that concept. That goal cannot be reached if we overemphasize the merit theory.[3]

It is argued against special concessions for Backward Classes that it contradicts the principle of "equality of opportunity" envisaged in the Constitution. Criticisms are advanced that reservations for Backward Classes in services and educational institutions would bring down the quality and standards of the services and education. Then again, special preference for Backward Classes would create a psychology among non-Backward Classes that casteism is perpetuated. It has been charged by critics that Constitutional safeguards for Backward Classes have drawn caste into the political arena. Adult franchise and democratic decentralization have placed political power in the hands of numerically strong Backward Castes. It is felt that castes are becoming politically dominant and there are situations where they play an important part in the Constitution of cabinets in some States. This conflict between the privileged and underprivileged classes in the political field is pointed out in the States of Andhra Pradesh, Maharashtra, Kerala, Gujarat, Mysore, Madras, and Bihar. Hence it has been commented that: "Politics is more important to castes and castes are more important in politics than ever before."[4]

Caste loyalties are said to be prominent in political relations. Politicians aim at securing votes by winning caste loyalties. Critics have charged that "caste forms the strongest party in India."[5] A. R. Wadia observes: "The democratic method of voting has given a new lease of life to castes, for our democracy is still immature, political parties have yet to take roots, and so the masses of our illiterate voters find a safe guide in voting on the basis of

3. *The Mysore Law Journal*, Vol. 41, No. 21, November 10, 1963, p. 307.
4. W. H. Morris-Jones, *The Government and Politics of India*, 1964, p. 65.
5. Jayaprakash Narayan, *Deccan Herald*, October 31, 1960.

caste and religion and community."[6] This tangle of casteism in politics has been explained by Myron Weiner as
follows: "For most Indians, the great competition is not
between India and the West or even India and China, but
between social groups within India."[7]

The role played by caste in elections is recorded by
many case studies. These studies point out that the nu-
merical strength of castes plays a deciding role in politics.
"The role of caste in the elections in Poona can be understood from three independent sources—the reactions of
voters to the propaganda campaigns of various parties,
the press and the polling figures at certain booths."[8] These
case studies also point out that in the arena of politics it
its possible to expect intercaste alignments. Small caste
groups align with each other to offer competition to numerically dominant castes. But some election studies reveal
that political organization and leadership cut across caste
loyalties.[9] Thus the role played by caste affinities and caste
loyalties in the political field and their influence on the
conduct of the major political parties are advanced in
support of the caste set-up in politics.

It is interesting to note that controversial opinions and
contradictory interpretations are given regarding the part
played by caste in politics. It is held that when caste as-
sumes a political role and competes with different groups
it automatically results in its extinction. E. R. Leach has
observed that "competition between caste groups is in
defiance of caste principles." Similarly, Gough says that
when a caste group turns itself into a political faction it
ceases to be a caste.[10] F. G. Bailey admits that political
conditions are not completely swayed by caste and that

6. A. R. Wadia, *Democracy and Society*, 1966, p. 84.
7. Myron Weiner, *The Politics of Scarcity*, 1963, p. 71.
8. V. M. Sirsikar, *Political Behaviour in India*, 1965, p. 248.
9. Modasa Constituency in Gujarat, *Indian Voting Behaviour*, (eds.) Myron Weiner and Rajni Kothari, 1965.
10. Detailed discussion in *Aspects of Caste in South India, Ceylon and North West Pakistan*, E. R. Leach (ed.), 1960.

political parties cut across many other factors.[11] Commenting on casteism in politics, Panikkar remarked: "This accusation comes mainly from the higher castes whose privileged position in society, official life and politics is being threatened by the awakening of the new classes."[12]

But it has been explicitly stated by some that caste is continuing to be the dominant unit of social action. M. N. Srinivas finds that "the principle of caste is so firmly entrenched in our political and social life that everyone including the leaders has tacitly accepted the principle that, in the Provincial cabinets at any rate, each major caste should have a minister."[13] Many Western scholars hold similar views. Myron Weiner is of the view that "social changes accompanying modernization are facilitating the development and not the diminution of community interests in Indian politics."[14] A field study conducted by Lloyd I. Rudolph and Susanne Hoeber Rudolph, in Madras State, on the role played by "Vanniya Kula Kashtriya Sangam" is a pointer to the close association between caste and elections.[15] Similar observation has been made by Selig S. Harrison, in his investigation on "caste and the Andhra Communists."[16] By way of conclusion, Morris-Jones has remarked: "Caste (or sub-caste or 'community') is the core of traditional politics. To it belongs a complete social ethos. It embraces all and is all-embracing."[17]

An analysis of the case for and against the part played by caste in politics points to the conclusion that, in the absence of All India studies on this situation, it is difficult

---

11. F. G. Bailey, *Politics and Social Change,* 1963.

12. K. M. Panikkar, *The Foundations of New India,* 1963, p. 247.

13. M. N. Srinivas, *Caste in Modern India,* 1962, p. 72.

14. Myron Weiner, *The Politics of Scarcity,* p. 78.

15. Paper entitled "The Political Role of India's Caste Associations" appeared in *Pacific Affairs,* Vol. 33, 1960.

16. Selig S. Harrison, *India: The Most Dangerous Decades,* 1960.

17. W. H. Morris-Jones, Paper entitled "India's Political Idioms," published in *Politics and Society in India,* C. H. Philips (ed.) , 1963, p. 138.

to accept assertions and generalizations as basic realities. It is true that some sociological, anthropological, and political behavior studies are carried out, to examine the impact of the caste system on various factors, in the light of changed conditions of the country. But such inquiries have restricted value, as they relate to a few villages or cities of specific States. The facts recorded in one village or a district could not be taken as the basis for analyzing the prevailing conditions in a State as a whole. Elaborate investigations of this nature throughout India should be undertaken for an analytical study of the present impact of caste on social, economic, and political institutions of India. It could be said that the problem of casteism has arisen because of the emergence of "a new type of stratification in which caste and class are mixed up in an inextricable tangle. The desire to bring about an egalitarian society is no doubt there; but it needs a systematic program of action spread over a long period if inequalities are to be reduced appreciably. The task of transforming the most rigidly stratified society in the world into an egalitarian one is indeed Himalayan."[18]

It is true that India has not yet achieved the ideal of classless and casteless society, but the failure to achieve this ideal could not be attributed to Constitutional safeguards for Backward Classes as perpetuating casteism singularly. In the words of K. M. Panikkar:

. . . the emergence of labour as a political force and the position in national life achieved by the movement of the untouchables, no less than the doctrine of social equality enshrined in the new Constitution, are effective safeguards against any attempts to reinstate the doctrine of caste.[19]

---

18. *The Gazetteer of India*, Vol. 1, 1965, p. 568.
19. K. M. Panikkar, *The Foundations of New India*, p. 98.

The Constitution has provided for the reconciliation of the competing claims of Backward Classes and Non-Backward Classes by incorporating specific articles governing reservations. Article 334 clearly shows that preferential treatment accorded to the Scheduled Castes and the Scheduled Tribes in political representation is not a permanent feature of the Constitution. The reservations would expire in 1970, according to the Constitution (Eighth Amendment) Act, 1959. Lok Sabha (the Lower House of Parliament) passed the constitutional amendment bill on Dec. 9, 1969 seeking to extend the reservation of seats in the House and State Assemblies for Scheduled Castes and Scheduled Tribes for a further period of 10 years—that is, up to 1980. As regards the representation of these classes in Services, it is emphatically stated that their eligibility for special preference would be considered "consistently with the maintenance of efficiency of administration." (Article 335.) Besides, the special treatment of Backward Classes in Arts. 15 (4), 16 (4) and 29 (2) is not mandatory, but only the enabling provisions of the Constitution. The peculiar tangle of equality and special preference has become all the more crucial because of our scarce economy. The only solution that could be suggested is that advanced sections of society should temporarily forego absolute equality in the larger interests of Backward Classes. Constitutional problems relating to certain sections of society as Backward Classes are hard to solve with mathematical precision.

To evaluate Constitutional safeguards for Backward Classes, the problem of administering justice for these classes is tackled with many compromises and skillful adjustments. The Constitutional guarantee of justice for these classes is beset with difficulties because of the complexity of their disabilities. While educational and economic backwardness is a common feature of these sections, they differ widely in their social disabilities. The Scheduled Castes present a problem of their emancipation from untouchability. The problem of Scheduled Tribes is one of integration with the rest of the population. Other Backward Classes have no such marked disabilities. On the contrary, the administration of justice for these classes demands the evolving of a workable and satisfactory criterion to determine who are backward. The problem of Denotified Communities is chiefly their rehabilitation, weaning them away from their hereditary avocation of criminality. How these disabilities are eradicated by Constitutional safeguards is discussed in the forthcoming section.

For an examination of Constitutional provisions for the eradication of the social disabilities of Scheduled Castes, it is necessary to define who are Scheduled Castes. Article 366 (24) defines them thus: "Scheduled Castes means such castes, races, or tribes or parts of or groups within such castes, races or tribes as are deemed under Art. 341 to be Scheduled Castes for the purposes of this Constitution."

The stigma of untouchability is the declared criterion for classifying Scheduled Castes. Article 341 empowers the President to specify the lists of Scheduled Castes for purposes of guaranteeing special provisions for these sections envisaged in the Constitution. Since 1950, a number of orders were passed specifying the lists of Scheduled Castes. But wrong inclusion or exclusion of castes in these lists are frequently reported. Hence it is necessary that the lists of Scheduled Castes be scientifically scrutinized to ensure that only such castes are included in the lists who are in need of special assistance. The scrutiny of these lists demands an intensive investigation of the socio-economic conditions of these classes throughout the country. It is gratifying to note that the Lokur Committee is appointed to undertake this work. The Committee has finalized the work and the rescheduling and descheduling of Scheduled Castes would be reported shortly.[20] Another measure which demands urgent consideration is, persons belonging to specific regions where they are eligible to be enlisted as Scheduled Castes should not be denied concessions if they move to other regions for livelihood purposes and where their caste does not qualify for getting included in the lists of Scheduled Castes. To overcome certain discrepancies in this direction, it is necessary to prepare synonymous, generic, and sub-caste names of Scheduled Castes, with a view to prevent people other than Scheduled Castes from enjoying special concessions by virtue of synonymous caste designations.

Untouchability is the greatest social disability of Scheduled Castes. Legally this practice stands abolished in the Constitution under Article 17. Further, untouchability is made an offense under the Government of India by "The Untouchability (Offences) Act, 1955." Apart from social legislation and legislative enactment, the Government has realized the necessity of intensifying the work of voluntary agencies in eradicating this evil. States and Union Territories have been asked to maintain lists of villages which practice untouchability. Some of the measures adopted for the speedy removal of untouchability are: the institution of cash prizes to villages for the non-practice of untouchability; introduction of mixed hostels, mixed colonies, adoption of Harijan children; award of gold medals for intercaste marriages with Harijans; reform of scavenging by introducing wheelbarrows to remove night soil; attractive salaries for doing menial jobs, etc. But these measures have touched only the fringe of the problem. Untouchability is reported to be still prevalent in many parts of the country. Accepting the facts recorded by the latest reports, it could be asserted

---

20. *The Indian Express,* Dec. 2, 1966.

that basic social values of the caste-ridden society are remaining immutable, defying all attempts to transform them.

It could be suggested, therefore, that the economic basis of untouchability has to be tackled in the same degree as social basis. The only way to improve their economic status is by creating a new occupational structure by means of education. Their grievances concerning untouchability are purely economic. It is a well-known fact that the majority of them constitute landless agricultural laborers in villages or are engaged in menial jobs. As they are economically poor they depend mostly on high castes for their subsistence. Hence, these classes are incapable of asserting their rights and privileges by withstanding the economic boycott organized by high castes in villages. So it is necessary to take measures to provide employment opportunities to Scheduled Castes in factories and industrial concerns, to divert them from their present economic dependence on other classes. Lack of education is responsible for poor economic standards and their attendant consequences. Once their economic position improves it would automatically raise their social estimation. So the abolition of untouchability rests chiefly on the creation of a new socio-economic status for Scheduled Castes. In the absence of this measure, constitutional guarantee for the abolition of untouchability would not be effective.

Equally important is to stabilize the position of the Commissioner for Scheduled Castes and Scheduled Tribes. The Constitution provides for the appointment of a Commissioner to investigate and evaluate the problems of Scheduled Castes and Scheduled Tribes, under Art. 338 (1). But the recommendations of the Commissioner seem to be very poorly implemented, as is evident from the annual reports. Besides, the States evince very little interest in furnishing necessary information to the Commissioner for the compilation of these reports. For a proper evaluation of welfare schemes it is necessary that field research work should be emphasized. In view of this inadequacy, it could be suggested that the office of the Commissioner should be staffed with research personnel to carry out field research. To make the Commissioner more authoritative, the recommendation of the Study Team on Social Welfare and Welfare of Backward Classes that the following holds good and deserves to be implemented:

> The Report of the Commissioner may present a State-wise analysis and that the Government should issue explanatory Memoranda on the shortcomings and inadequacies pointed out in the Commissioner's Report. The Report and the Memorandum should be discussed in the Parliament and the State legislature every year.[21]

Besides, "The Untouchability (Offences) Act, 1955," should be made more rigorous if it is to be effective. The courts should expedite the cases registered under the Offences Act. At the lower level of administration, Panchayats should take the initiative in the eradication of untouchability. This problem has to be tackled on many fronts to "untwist successfully the thousand-year-old twist of the human mind."

Social justice for Scheduled Tribes demands "the fight for the three freedoms—freedom from fear, freedom from want, freedom from interference."[22] Before proceeding to the discussion of the measures undertaken to ensure social justice, it is necessary to define the term "Scheduled Tribes." It is defined in Art. 366 (25) as follows: "Scheduled Tribes means such tribes or tribal communities or parts of or groups within such tribes or tribal communities as are deemed under Article 342 to be Scheduled

---

21. *Report of the Study Team on Social Welfare and Welfare of Backward Classes,* Vol. 1, 1959, p. 185.
22. *The Tribal World of Verrier Elwin,* 1964, p. 291.

Tribes for the purpose of this Constitution." Article 342 provides for the specification of the lists of Scheduled Tribes by the President. But some discrepancies have been pointed out as regards the lists issued. It is generally felt that the overall view of all features distinguishing tribes is not taken into consideration in preparing the lists of Scheduled Tribes. These discrepancies have arisen as there is no specific criterion for classifying Scheduled Tribes, as is the stigma of untouchability in the case of Scheduled Castes. Factors considered relevant in the classification of Scheduled Tribes are tribal origin, primitive way of life, and general backwardness. But this basis of classifying Scheduled Tribes does not seem to benefit the lowest layer of tribals, who are extremely backward. In view of this situation, the Scheduled Areas and Scheduled Tribes Commission have specified the nonvocal section of tribes in different States for consideration, to be incorporated in the lists of Scheduled Tribes.[23] It is to be hoped that this recommendation of the Scheduled Areas and Tribes Commission would be implemented by the Government of India in the interests of tribals.

As regards the administration of tribal areas, the Constitution has provided for a minister for tribal welfare in the States of Bihar, Madhya Pradesh, and Orissa, under Art. 164 (1). The Fifth Schedule of the Constitution specifies clearly the pattern of administration and control of Scheduled Areas and Scheduled Tribes. The Sixth Schedule lays down principles for governing tribal areas in Assam.

One of the most significant measures in the direction of social justice is the prohibition of "forced labor," Art. 23 (1), which states: "Traffic in human beings and begar [forced labor] and other similar forms of forced labor are prohibited and any contravention of this provision shall be an offence punishable in accordance with law."

---

23. *Report of the Scheduled Areas and Scheduled Tribes Commission,* Vol. 1, 1960–61, Chairman's foreword to the President.

Forced or bonded labor is one of the worst forms of exploitation of Scheduled Tribes. It is termed *Sagri* in Rajasthan, *Vetti* in Andhra Pradesh, *Gothi* in Orissa, *Jeetha* in Mysore, and *naukri-nama* in Madhya Pradesh. This system of pledging people against a loan borrowed stands abolished in the Constitution. But it is reported that the system is still prevalent in many parts of the country. As it contravenes the principle of egalitarianism, it is necessary that the States investigate the problem and devise measures to free them from serfdom.

Besides, the Scheduled Areas are witnessing a rapid process of transformation. Hence it is important to study the impact of industrialization on tribals. So far three surveys have been conducted in this sphere:

(1) The Socio-Economic Survey of Tribal Labor in Tisco, Pilot Survey, on the basis of a 1 per cent sample, conducted by the Government of Bihar, 1958;

(2) Socio-Economic Survey conducted under the supervision of B. R. Misra, Patna University, Bihar, 1959; and

(3) Study of the Impact of Industrialization on the life of Adivasi Employees of Naumandi Iron Ore Mines, Tisco. (But these surveys are inadequate to ascertain the impact of industrialization on tribals. However, they reveal that tribals are displaced as a result of the location of power and irrigation projects in tribal areas, particularly in Bihar, Orissa, Rourkela, Durgapur, West Bengal, and Madhya Pradesh. It is necessary to launch schemes of rehabilitation to meet the economic and educational needs of tribals instead of cash compensation. In short, the welfare schemes for tribals should concentrate on a selected few programs having a vital bearing on the urgent needs of the people in view of inadequate finances.)

The most complex problem is the integration of tribals with the rest of society. As Nehru remarked: "What we ought to do is to develop sense of oneness with these people, a sense of unity and understanding. That involves a psychological approach."[24] Their integration is affected through voluntary agencies, Tribal Councils, and Cultural Research Institutes. As Tribal Councils are the keynote for preserving the cultural, religious, moral, and social standards of the tribals, it is necessary to retain them side by side with the statutory Panchayats. Voluntary agencies are evincing keen interest in the welfare of tribals by convening tribal conferences to focus attention on tribal problems, training of tribal welfare personnel, opening of educational institutions in tribal areas, publication of literature on tribals, etc. Equally important is the establishment of Cultural Research Institutes. These Institutes not only collaborate with State Governments in all matters relating to tribal welfare but prove extremely useful in outlining welfare schemes. But the research work of the Institutes should be more practical than academic. As suggested by the Elwin Committee, these Institutes should encourage research surveys on economics relating to Agricultural Schemes and Cottage industries in tribal areas. Besides, elaborate inquiries into the impact of industrialization on tribal psychology should be carried out, to assist the Government in formulating welfare schemes to cater to the needs of tribals.

Much has been done to safeguard tribal interests with a view to assimilating them with the rest of the population. This has been testified by the Elwin Committee: "Today there is a wide measure of respect for the tribal civilizations and a recognition that these fine people have a real contribution to make to the rest of India."[25]

---

24. *Ibid.,* p. 490.
25. *Report of the Committee on Special Multipurpose Tribal Blocks,* 1960, p. 20.

The Constitution has provided for special concessions in educational institutions and government service to Other Backward Classes, as these opportunities were denied to them in the past. But the framers have failed to define the term "Backward Classes," with the result that it has become one of the most controversial topics of discussion. In the absence of a precise definition, it is reasonable to look to different interpretations given by the Judiciary, Backward Classes Commission, and several committees constituted in States to investigate the problem. But no satisfactory criteria have been evolved to determine the Other Backward Classes. In view of the difficulties in evolving a positive and workable criterion for determining backwardness, there is a feeling in some quarters that the category of Other Backward Classes should be done away with. The criteria put under trial-and-error method so far were:

1. Caste criterion;
2. Criterion of Social Backwardness;
3. Criterion of Educational Backwardness; and
4. Economic criterion.

As the socio-economic status in India was determined by caste hierarchy, it was decided to emphasize the caste factor for determining backwardness. But the caste criterion came in for criticism as violating the egalitarian concept and non-discriminatory clauses of the Constitution. Besides, synonymous caste names, the tangle between well-organized and fairly advanced caste groups vying for special concessions, the non-record of caste in Census Reports, and the Judicial interpretation that it is not reasonable to place singular emphasis on caste have made the caste criterion inadequate to determine backwardness.

The need for considering the relevance of the criterion of social backwardness has arisen from the fact that a reference is made to this aspect in Art. 15 (4) . But the Constitution does not contain any definition of "Social Backwardness." A number of factors have contributed to social backwardness—caste, illiteracy, poverty, and occupation. But caste, illiteracy, and poverty are taken up in different sections of the discussion on criterion of "Educational Backwardness" and "Economic criterion." So under the criterion of social Backwardness, the "occupation test" to determine backwardness is examined. In India, government service is highly esteemed. Certain occupations are treated as inferior according to conventional beliefs, and people who profess these occupations are rated low in social esteem. But a detailed study of the occupational structure indicates the correlation between caste and occupation. The All India Federation of Backward Classes has urged for the consideration of the occupation test for classifying Other Backward Classes. It has been argued that people who traditionally earned their livelihood through manual labor constitute the Backward Classes. Therefore the issue of manual labor and backwardness should not be mixed up with that of the economic factor. Under such circumstances, the occupation test, however, seems to be objective as one of the criteria for determining Other Backward Classes.

The criterion of educational backwardness is another which deserves a thorough consideration in classifying Other Backward Classes. The problem of education in most of the States is chiefly the problem of Backward Classes, for it is they who are extremely backward in education. Census Reports, investigations carried out in Mysore State, and the studies on the social composition of students in universities and colleges conducted in Poona and Baroda reveal that the traditional privileged classes (Brahmans) are strongly represented in educational institutions, particularly at the higher levels of education. But there are certain inadequacies in this criterion also. The unit for measuring literacy presents contradictions. The two alternative units are family and caste. Statistical enumeration of literacy family-wise would be cumbersome in view of the unwieldy population of the country. But caste-wise enumeration, although it appears practical, contravenes the principle of non-discrimination on caste. In view of these difficulties, it could be suggested that "occupational groups" are to be taken as the unit for determining educational backwardness. It would serve the dual purpose of recording the literacy position of Other Backward Classes and also their occupational composition.

The economic criterion is another suggestion to determine Other Backward Classes. It is felt that reservation benefits should be given to those individuals who fall below a prescribed economic level. Economic backwardness should be made the index for purposes of special concessions and State protection. Economic disparities which resulted in the creation of Backward Classes could be got rid of by placing emphasis on economic conditions. Besides, the economic test would be in consonance with the spirit of the Constitution, as it does not create discrimination on grounds of caste, race, creed, etc. But it has been pointed out that backwardness should be judged by social and educational conditions of the people and not singularly by economic conditions. Besides, it is felt that social relief on income basis would be difficult to administer in an underdeveloped country like ours. Table 6-1 illustrates this difficulty.[26] Conditions in certain States are such that the economic test could not be applied as the chief determinant of backwardness. Kerala has shown that the classification of people below a certain economic level as Other Backward Classes does not appear to be workable in the circumstances of the State. Hence, the economic criterion is inadequate to determine backwardness.

---

26. Quoted in *Report of the Backward Classes Commission,* Vol. 3, 1956, p. 12.

TABLE 6-1

Number of Households in India Divided by Income Groups			
Range of income per household per annum	Rural (in lakhs)	Urban (in lakhs)	Total (in lakhs)
0 – 500	81	Neg	81
500 – 1,000	193	17	210
1,000 – 1,500	143	35	178
1,500 – 2,000	94	27	121
2,000 – 2,500	34	18	52
2,500 & above	29	14	43
TOTAL	574	111	685

In view of the complicated problem of classifying Other Backward Classes, we could only suggest a working hypothesis toward a satisfactory criterion. From the foregoing analysis it could be said that uniform criterion throughout the country is not workable. Any criteria suggested should be in consonance with Art. 15 (4) of the Constitution. The problem should be thoroughly investigated by the States for evolving a satisfactory criteria by taking the following factors into consideration:

(a) Traditionally neglected social classes
(b) Poor education
(c) Inadequate political power
(d) Economic backwardness (poverty), and
(e) Lack of white-collar jobs.

It has been suggested by the Commissioner for Scheduled Castes and Scheduled Tribes that random sample surveys should be undertaken in all States by committees consisting of an anthropologist, administrator, social worker, and member of Parliament. The following criteria suggested by the Commissioner are equally satisfactory:

Income-cum-merit is the only equitable basis for granting concessions to the underprivileged sections of the people, though in the case of certain castes which are not still vocal enough to take full advantage of the opportunities so far offered, criterion of caste-cum-occupation will have to be recognised for the present. For that purpose, lists of caste-cum-vocations considered very low in the social structure, will have to be drawn up and maintained for some time.[27]

Another working hypothesis could be to devise measures on the pattern of distribution of Congress tickets to contest elections in the political arena. In the distribution of Congress tickets quotas are fixed only for Scheduled Castes and Scheduled Tribes. But certain guidelines are followed as regards other sections of society. The Congress Working Committee issues certain general instructions, such as to safeguard special interests, minorities, and representation of women, etc. But ultimately practical considerations influence decision-making. What will be uppermost in the minds of the election committees is to secure adequate support of all sections to ensure success for the candidates contesting elections. So a similar policy may be followed for the determination of Other Backward Classes. Whatever is decided by the Legislature from time to time would be adopted. This would be in accordance with the changed demands of the time.

One more device is that the reservation policy should be in accordance with the necessities of the specific fields of reservation. For instance, reservations or special concessions are given as regards admission to educational institutions and entry to Government service. Just as scholarships are awarded to students on the basis of need or poverty, concessions regarding admission to educational institutions should be given to those students coming from a poor educational background, and preference in Government service should be given to those who have

27. *Report of the Commissioner for Scheduled Castes and Scheduled Tribes,* 1957–58, pp. 171–72.

poor representation in this field. Economic progress of
the country seems to be the only panacea for all the ills.

Of all the categories of Backward Classes, the least
benefited from Constitutional safeguards are Denotified
Communities. These people are grouped along with Other
Backward Classes for special concessions. They are not
accorded special quotas like Scheduled Castes and Scheduled Tribes, nor are they given representation in Parliament or Legislatures. While a special officer is appointed
in charge of Scheduled Castes and Scheduled Tribes and
a Commission was constituted to go through the problem
of Backward Classes, no such safeguards are provided for
Denotified Communities. As these people have certain
handicaps and maladjustments of a special nature, it is
necessary that the Union Government undertake a thorough investigation of this problem aimed at their rehabilitation. The neglect of this problem would endanger
the peace of the country if the traditional avocation of
criminality of these classes is to assert itself.

In recognition of the fact that Backward Classes are
educationally and economically underprivileged, they are
provided with special safeguards in these spheres to bring
them to a position of equality with the rest of the population. The essence of these safeguards is "justice" as guaranteed by the Constitution.

Education has been made a Constitutional guarantee
under Articles 29, 30, 45, and 46. Backward Classes are
provided with Inland and Overseas scholarships, reservations in educational institutions, exemption from payment
of tuition fees in most of the universities to candidates
from Scheduled Castes and Scheduled Tribes, and relaxation in age for admission to technical and professional institutions. Besides, basic education suitable to rural conditions is advocated for the liquidation of backwardness. It
is felt that basic education is the best method of providing
vocational training and guidance, besides teaching the

three R's to the rural masses. The Working Group on the Welfare of Backward Classes has recommended free education for Scheduled Caste and Scheduled Tribe Students at all stages. The need for the dissemination of training and employment information among the Backward Classes has been emphasized. It is advocated to start higher secondary schools on the pattern of multi-purpose schools with forestry and agriculture as the two main components.

The task before an underdeveloped country is not merely to get better results with the existing framework of economic institutions but to mold them to the needs of the community so as to offer the fullest opportunity to every section of society to grow and to contribute to the national well-being. With this objective in view, a number of economic schemes are designed for the betterment of Backward Classes. These schemes relate to the development of agriculture, cottage industries, forestry, cooperation, tribal development blocks, communications, housing, etc. The Five Year Plan outlay for the welfare of Backward Classes is recorded in Table 6-2:[28]

TABLE 6-2

(Rs. in millions)

Category of Backward Classes	First Plan outlay	Second Plan estimated expenditure	Third Plan estimated cost of programs
Scheduled Tribes	198.3	430.0	604.3
Scheduled Castes	70.8	276.6	404.0
Denotified Communities	11.0	28.9	40.0
Other Backward Classes	20.3	58.6	90.4
TOTAL	304.0	794.1	1138.7

Of the total amount of Rs. 2,110 millions spent during the first three plans, Rs. 1,150 millions have been devoted

28. Compiled.

to Scheduled Tribes, about Rs. 720 millions to Scheduled Castes, about Rs. 220 millions to Denotified Communities and Other Backward Classes, and Rs. 20 millions to aid voluntary organizations.

The Fourth Plan provides for an outlay of Rs. 1,800 millions, of which Rs. 1,000 millions are for Scheduled Tribes, Rs. 660 millions for Scheduled Castes, and Rs. 140 millions for other schemes. The tentative breakdown of the allocation is given in Table 6-3:[29]

TABLE 6-3

Category of Backward Classes	Education	Economic development	House sites water supply and other schemes	Aid to voluntary organizations	Rs. in millions Total
Scheduled Tribes	220	680	100	—	1,000
Scheduled Castes	300	150	210	—	660
Denotified Tribes	20	20	10	—	50
Other Backward Classes	60	—	—	—	60
Common Provisions	—	—	—	30	30
TOTAL	600	850	320	30	1,800

In short, the Government has assumed a great responsibility for the well-being of Backward Classes. If this responsibility is cautiously discharged with an emphasis on the qualitative aspect of development schemes and their speedy implementation, "justice" assured for the Backward Classes would acquire full meaning and significance in the Constitution.

---

29. *Fourth Five Year Plan,* a draft outline, p. 372.

APPENDIX

*The Untouchability (Offences) Act, 1955**

An Act to prescribe punishment for the practice of "untouchability," for the enforcement of any disability arising therefrom and for matters connected therewith.

Be it enacted by Parliament in the Sixth Year of the Republic of India as follows:

1. Short title, extent and commencement—

    (1) This act may be called The Untouchability (Offences) Act, 1955.

    (2) It extends to the whole of India.

    (3) It shall come into force on such date as the Central Government may, by notification in the official Gazette, appoint.

2. Definition—In this Act, unless the context otherwise requires,

    (a) "hotel" includes a refreshment room, a boardinghouse, a lodging house, a coffeehouse, and a café;

    (b) "place" includes a house, a building, a tent, and a vessel;

    (c) "place of Public Entertainment" includes any place to which the public are admitted and in which an entertainment is provided or held.

Explanation—"Entertainment" includes any exhibition, performance, game, sport, and any other form of amusement;

    (d) "Place of Public Worship" means a place, by whatever

---

* Came into force on June 1, 1955.

name known, which is used as a place of public religious worship of which is dedicated generally to, or is used generally by persons professing any religion or belonging to any religious denomination or any section thereof, for the performance of any religious service, or for offering prayers therein; and include all lands and subsidiary shrines appurtenant or attached to any such place;

(e) "shop" means any premises where goods are sold either wholesale or by retail or both wholesale and by retail and includes a laundry, a haircutting salon, and any other place where services are rendered to customers.

3. Punishment for enforcing religious disabilities—whoever on the ground of "untouchability" prevents any person—

   (a) from entering any place of public worship which is open to other persons professing the same religion or belonging to the same religious denomination or any section thereof, as such person; or

   (b) from worshiping or offering prayers or performing any religious service in any place of public worship, or bathing in, or using the waters of, any sacred tank, well, spring or water-course, in the same manner and to the same extent as is permissible to other denominations or any section thereof, as such person; shall be punishable with imprisonment which may extend to six months, or with fine which may extend to five hundred rupees, or with both.

Explanation—For the purpose of this section and section 4 persons professing the Buddhist, Sikh, or Jaina religion or persons professing Virashaivas, Lingayats, Adivasis, followers of Brahma, Prarthana, Arya Samaj, and the Swaminarayan Sampraday shall be deemed to be Hindus.

4. Punishment for enforcing social disabilities—Whoever on the ground of "untouchability" enforces against any person any disability with regard to—

   (i) access to any shop, public restaurant, hotel or place of public entertainment; or

   (ii) the use of any utensils, and other articles kept in

public restaurant, hotel, dharmasals (place of charity), Sarai or musafirkhanta (tourist place) for the use of the general public or of persons professing the same religion, or belonging to the same religious denomination or any section thereof, as such person; or

(iii) the practice of any profession or the carrying on of any occupation, trade or business; or

(iv) the use of, or access to, any river, stream, spring, well, tank, cistern, water tap, or other watering place, or any bathing ghat, burial or cremation ground, any sanitary convenience, any road, or passage, or any other place of public resort which other members of the public, or persons professing the same religion or belonging to the same religious denomination or any section thereof, as such persons, have a right to use or have access to; or

(v) the use of, or access to, any place used for a charitable or a public purpose maintained wholly or partly out of State funds or dedicated to the use of general public, or persons professing the same religion, or belonging to the same religious denomination or any section thereof, as such person; or

(vi) the enjoyment of any benefit under a charitable trust created for the benefit of the general public or of persons professing the same religion or belonging to the same as such person; or

(vii) the use of, or access to, any public conveyance; or

(viii) the construction, acquisition or occupation of any residential premises in any locality whatever; or

(ix) the use of any dharmashala, sarai or musafirkhana which is open to the general public, or to persons professing the same religion or belonging to the same religious denomination or any section thereof, as such person; or

(x) the observance of any social or religious custom, usage or ceremony or taking part in any religious procession, or

(xi) the use of jewelry and finery;

shall be punishable with imprisonment which may extend to six months, or with fine which may extend to five hundred rupees, or with both.

5. Punishment for refusing to admit persons to hospitals, etc.—Whoever on the ground of "untouchability"—

   (a) refuses admission to any person to any hospital, dispensary, educational institution or any hostel attached thereto, if such hospital, dispensary, educational institutional or hostel is established or maintained for the benefit of the general public or any section thereof; or

   (b) does any act which discriminates against any such person after admission to any of the aforesaid institutions; shall be punishable with imprisonment which may extend to six months, or with fine which may extend to five hundred rupees, or with both.

6. Punishment for refusing to sell goods or render services—Whoever on the ground of "untouchability" refuses to sell any goods or refuses to render any service to any person at the same time and place and on the same terms and conditions at or on which such goods are sold or services are rendered to other persons in the ordinary course of business shall be punishable with imprisonment which may extend to six months, or with fine which may extend to five hundred rupees, or with both.

7. Punishment for other offences arising out of "untouchability"—

   (i) whoever—

   (a) prevents any person from exercising any right accruing to him by reason of the abolition of "untouchability" under Article 17 of the Constitution; or b bb

   (b) molests, injures, annoys, obstructs or causes or attempts to cause obstruction to any person in the exercise of any such right or molests, injures, annoys or boycotts any person by reason of his having exercised any such right; or

   (c) by words, either spoken or written, or by signs or by visible representations or otherwise, incites or encourages any person or class of persons or the public generally to practice "untouchability" in any form whatsoever; shall be punishable with imprisonment which may extend to six months, or with fine which may extend to five hundred rupees, or with both.

Explanation—A person shall be deemed to boycott another person who—

(a) refuses to let to such other person or refuse to permit such other person to use or occupy work for, hire for, or do business with, such other person or to render to him or receive from him any customary service, or refuse to do any of the said things on the terms on which such things would be commonly done in the ordinary course of business; or

(b) abstains from such social, professional or business relations as he would ordinarily maintain with such other person.

  (2) whoever—

  (i) denies to any person belonging to his community or any section thereof right or privilege to which such person would be entitled as a member of such community or section, or

  (ii) takes any part in the excommunication of such person, on the ground that such person has refused to practice "untouchability" or that such person has done any act in furtherance of the objects of this Act, shall be punishable with imprisonment which may extend to six months, or with fine which may extend to five hundred rupees, or with both.

8. Cancellation or suspension of licences in certain cases— When a person who is convicted of an offence under section 6 holds any license under any law for the time being in force in respect of any profession, trade, calling or employment in relation to which the offence is committed, the court trying the offence may, without prejudice to any other penalty to which such person may be liable under that section direct that the licence shall stand canceled or be suspended for such period as the court may deem fit, and every order of the court so canceling or suspending a licence

shall have effect as if it had been passed by the authority competent to cancel or suspend the license under any such law.

Explanation—In this section, "license" includes a permit or a permission.

9. Resumption or suspension of grants made by Government—
   Where the manager or trustee of a place of public worship which is in receipt of a grant of land or money from the Government is convicted of an offence under this Act and such conviction is not reversed or quashed in any appeal or revision, the Government may, if in its opinion the circumstances of the case warrant such a course, direct the suspension or resumption of the whole or any part of such grant.

10. Abetment of offence—
    Whoever abets any offence under this Act shall be punishable with the punishment provided for the offence.

11. Enhanced penalty on subsequent conviction—
    Whoever having already been convicted of an offence under this Act or of an abetment of such offence is again convicted of any such offence or abetment, shall, on every such subsequent conviction, be punishable with both imprisonment and fine.

12. Presumption by courts in certain cases—
    Where any act constituting an offence under this Act is committed in relation to a member of a Scheduled Caste as defined in clause (24) of Article 366 of the Constitution, the court shall presume, unless the contrary is proved, that such act was committed on the ground of "untouchability."

13. Limitation of jurisdiction of civil courts—
    (1) No civil court shall entertain or continue any suit or proceeding or shall pass any decree or order or execute wholly or partially any decree or order if the claim involved in such suit or proceeding or if the passing of such decree or order of such execution would in any way be contrary to the provisions of this Act.
    (2) No court shall, in adjudicating any matter or executing

any decree or order, recognize any custom or usage imposing any disability on any person on the ground of
"Untouchability."

14. Offences by companies—
   (1) If the person committing an offence under this Act is
   a company, every person who at the time the offence
   was committed was in charge of, and was responsible
   to, the company, for the conduct of the business of the
   company, shall be deemed to be guilty of the offence
   and shall be liable to be proceeded against and punished accordingly:
   Provided that nothing contained in this sub-section
   shall render any such person liable to any punishment,
   if he proves that the offence was committed without
   his knowledge or that he exercised all due diligence to
   prevent the commission of such offence.
   (2) Not withstanding anything contained in sub-section
   (1), where an offence under this Act has been committed with the consent of any director or manager, secretary or other officer of the company, such director,
   manager, secretary or other officer shall also be deemed
   to be guilty of that offence and shall be liable to be
   proceeded against and punished accordingly.

Explanation—For the purposes of this section—

(a) "Company" means any body corporate and includes a
firm or other association of individuals; and
(b) "Director" in relation to a firm means partner in the
firm.

15. Offences under the Act to be cognizable and compound-
able—
   Notwithstanding anything contained in the code of criminal
   procedure, 1898—
   (a) every offence under this Act shall be cognizable; and
   (b) every such offence may, with the permission of the
   court be compounded.

16. Act to override other laws—
   Save as otherwise expressly provides in this Act, the provisions of this Act shall have effect notwithstanding any-

thing inconsistent therewith contained in any other law for the time being in force, or any custom or usage or any instrument having effect by virtue of any such law or any decree or order of any court or other authority.

17. Repeal—
The enactments specialized in the Schedule are hereby repealed to the extent to which they or any of the provisions contained therein correspond or are repugnant to this Act or to any of the provisions contained therein.

The Schedule

1. The Bihar Harijan (Removal of Civil Disabilities) Act, 1949 (Bihar Act XIX of 1949).
2. The Bombay Harijan (Removal of Social Disabilities) Act, 1946 (Bombay Act X of 1947).
3. The Bombay Harijan Temple Entry Act, 1947 (Bombay Act XXXV of 1947).
4. The Central Provinces and Berar Scheduled Castes (Removal of Civil Disabilities) Act, 1947 (Central Provinces and Berar Act ZZIV of 1947).
5. The Central Provinces and Berar Temple Entry Authorisation Act, 1947 (Central Provinces and Berar Act XLI of 1947).
6. The East Punjab (Removal of Religious and Social Disabilities) Act, 1948 (East Punjab Act XVI of 1948).
7. The Madras Removal of Civil Disabilities Act 1938 (Madras Act XXI of 1938).
8. The Orissa Removal of Civil Disabilities Act, 1946 (Orissa Act XI of 1946).
9. The Orissa Temple Entry Authorisation Act, 1948.
10. The United Provinces Removal of Social Disabilities Act, 1947 (U.P. Act XIV of 1947).
11. The West Bengal Hindu Social Disabilities Removal Act, 1948 (West Bengal Act XXXVII of 1948).
12. The Hyderabad Harijan Temple Entry Regulation, 1938 F (No. LV of 1358 Fasli).
13. The Hyderabad Harijan (Removal of Social Disabilities) Regulation, 13587 (No. LVI of 1358 Fasli).

14. The Madhya Bharat Harijan Ayogta Nivaran Vidhan, Samvat 2005 (Madhya Bharat Act No. 15 of 1949).
15. The Removal of Civil Disabilities Act, 1943 (Mysore Act XLII of 1943).
16. The Mysore Temple Entry Authorisation Act, 1948 (Mysore Act XIV of 1948).
17. The Saurashtra Harijan (Removal of Social Disabilities) Ordinance (No. XL of 1948).
18. The Travancore–Cochin Temple Entry (Removal of Disabilities) Act, 1950 (Travancore-Cochin Act VIII of 1125).
19. The Travancore-Cochin Temple Entry (Removal of Disabilities) Act, 1950. (Travancore-Cochin Act XXVII of 1950).
20. The Coorg Scheduled Castes (Removal of Civil and Social Disabilities) Act, 1949. (Coorg Act 1 of 1949).
21. The Coorg Temple Entry Authorisation Act, 1949 (Coorg Act II of 1949).

SELECT BIBLIOGRAPHY

Books On Indian Constitution

Aggarwala, O. P. *Fundamental Rights and Constitutional Remedies*. Vols. 1–4. Metropolitan, Delhi: 1953, '54, '56 and '58.

Aiyar, A. K. *The Constitution and Fundamental Rights*. Madras: 1955.

Banerjee, A. C. *Indian Constitutional Documents*. Vol. III, 3rd ed. Calcutta: Mukherjee, 1961.

Banerjee, A. C. and Chatterjee, K. L. *Survey of the Indian Constitution*. Calcutta: 1957.

Banerjee, D. N. *Our Fundamental Rights*. Calcutta: World Press Pvt. Ltd., 1960.

————. *Some Aspects of the Indian Constitution*. Calcutta: World Press Pvt. Lt., 1962.

Basu, D. D. *Commentary on the Constitution of India*. Vols. 1–2, Calcutta: S. C. Sarkar and Sons Pvt. Ltd., 1955, '56.

Basu, D. D. *Cases on the Constitution of India*, Vol. II. (1952–54), Calcutta: S. C. Sarkar and Sons Pvt. Ltd., 1956.

Chaplain, H. L., and Joshi, G. N. *Readings in Indian Constitution and Administration*. Delhi: Hindustan Electric Printing Works, 1925.

Chaudhri, A. S. *Constitutional Rights and Limitations*. Vol. I, Allahabad: 1958.

Coupland, R. *Constitutional Problem in India*. Madras: Diocesan Press, 1944.

Dicey, A. V. *Introduction to the study of the Law of the Constitution*. London: Macmillan and Co., Ltd., 1950.

Dowling and Edwards. *American Constitutional Law.* The Foundation Press, Inc., 1954.

Gledhill, A. *The Republic of India.* London: Stevens and Sons, Ltd., 1951.

Gledhill, A. *Fundamental Rights in India.* London: Stevens and Sons, Ltd., 1956.

Gwyer, M., and Appadorai, A. *Speeches and Documents on the Indian Constitution.* Vols. 1–2, 1921–47, London: Oxford University Press, 1957.

Jain, M. P. *Indian Constitutional Law.* Bombay: 1962.

Keith, A. B. *Constitutional history of India.* Allahabad: Central Book Co., 1961.

Pylee, M. V. *Constitutional Government in India.* Bombay: Asia Publishing House, 1960.

Pylee, M. V. *India's Constitution.* Bombay: Asia Publishing House, 1965.

Ragavachariar, N. R. *Constitution of India with Commentaries.* Madras: 1951.

Ramachandran, V. G. *Fundamental Rights and Constitutional Remedies.* Vols. 1–2, Lucknow: Eastern Book Co., 1959, '60.

Ramaratnam, N. *Quinquennial Digest.* Vols. 1–2, 1956–60, Madras: 1962.

Sharma, B. M. *The Republic of India.* Bombay: 1966.

Shukla, V. N. *Commentaries on the Constitution of India.* Lucknow: Eastern Book Co., 1960.

Government of India Act, 1935. Govt. of India Publication.

The Constitution of India. Delhi: Govt. of India Press, 1963.

General Books

Ambedkar, B. R. *Annihilation of Castes.* Bombay: Bharat Bhusan Publishing Press, 1937.

————. *Communal Deadlock and a Way to Solve it.* Bombay: All India Scheduled Castes Federation, 1945.

————. *Pakistan or the Partition of India.* 3rd ed. Bombay: Thacker and Co., 1946.

————. *What Congress and Gandhi Have Done to the Untouchables.* Bombay: Thacker and Co., 1946.

————. *Who were the Shudras.* Bombay: Thacker and Co., 1947.

————. *States and Minorities.* Bombay: Thacker and Co., 1947.

————. *Untouchables.* Delhi: Amrit Book Co., 1948.

Anderson, J. N. D. *Changing law in Developing Countries.* London: George Allen and Unwin, 1963.

Bailey, F. G. *Caste and Economic Frontier.* Bombay: Oxford University Press, 1958.

————. *Tribe, Caste and Nation.* Bombay: Oxford University Press, 1960.

————. *Politics and Social Change.* Bombay: Oxford University Press, 1963.

Beteille, A. *Caste, Class and Power.* Bombay: Oxford University Press, 1963.

Bhattacharya, J. N. *Hindu Castes and Sects.* Calcutta: 1896.

Blunt, E. A. H. *The Caste System of Northern India,* 1931.

Brandt, R. B. (ed.). *Social Justice.* Englewood Cliffs, N. J.: Prentice-Hall, Inc., 1962.

Buhler, G. *The Laws of Manu.* London: Clarendon Press, 1889.

Chirol, V. *India.* London: 1925.

Cox, O. C. *Caste, Class, and Race.* 1948.

Davis, K. *The Population of India and Pakistan.* Princeton, N.J.: Princeton University Press, 1951.

Desai, A. R. *Social Background of Indian Nationalism.* Bombay: Oxford University Press, 1948.

Dutt, N. K.: *Origin and growth of Caste in India.* London: Kegan Paul, 1931.

Elwin, V. *The Tribal world.* Bombay: Oxford University Press, 1964.

————. *A philosophy for NEFA.* Bombay: 1960.

Gandhi, M. K. *Hindu Dharma.* Ahmedabad: 1950.

————. *Removal of Untouchability.* Ahmedabad: Navajivan, 1951.

Ghoshal, A. *A history of Indian Political Ideas.* Bombay: Oxford University Press, 1959.

Ghurye, G. S. *Caste and Class in India.* Bombay: Popular Book Depot, 1957.

————. *The Scheduled Tribes.* Bombay: Popular Book Depot, 1959.

Gunther, J. *Inside Asia.* London: Hamilton, 1939.

Haimendorf, C. *Caste and Kin in Nepal, India and Ceylon.* Bombay: 1966.

Halappa, G. S. *History of Freedom Movement in Karnatak.* Government of Mysore, 1964.

Havanur, L. G. *Backward Classes.* Bangalore: 1965.

Hayek, F. A. *The Constitution of Liberty.* London: Routledge and Kegan Paul, 1960.

Hocart, A. M. *Caste: A Comparative Study.* London: 1950.

Hutton, J. H. *Caste in India.* Bombay: Oxford University Press, 1951.

Isaacs, R. *India's Ex-Untouchables.* Bombay: Asia Publishing House, 1965.

Jatava, D. R. *The Social Philosophy of B. R. Ambedkar.* Agra: 1965.

Karunakaran, K. P. (ed.). *Modern Indian Political Tradition.* 1962.

Keer, D. *Dr. Ambedkar: Life and Mission.* Bombay: Popular Prakashan, 1954.

Kogekar, S. V., and Park, R. L. *Report on the Indian General Elections, 1951-52.* Bombay: Popular Book Depot, 1956.

Krishna Rao, M. V. *The Growth of Indian Liberalism in the Nineteenth Century.* Mysore: 1951.

Laidler, W. *Social-Economic Movement.* London: Kegan Paul, 1953.

Laski, J. *Grammar of Politics.* London: George Allen & Unwin, Ltd., 1950.

Leach, E. R. (ed.). *Aspects of Caste in South India, Ceylon and North West Pakistan.* Cambridge: 1962.

Mackim, M. (ed.). *Village India.* Chicago University Press, 1955.

Majumdar, D. N. *Caste and Communication in an Indian Village.* Bombay: 1958.

Maheswari, S. R. *The General Election in India.* Allahabad: Chaitanya, 1963.

Mason, A. T., and Leach, R. H. *In Quest of Freedom.* Englewood Cliffs, N. J.: Prentice-Hall, 1959.

Mayer, K. B. *Class and Society.* New York: Random House, 1961.

Morris-Jones, W. H. *The Government and Politics of India.* London: Hutchinson and Co., Ltd., 1964.

Max Weber, *The Religion of India.* Free Press of Glencoe, Ill.: 1958.

Mitra, S. *Resurgent India.* Bombay: Allied Publishers, 1963.

Nehru, J. *The Discovery of India.* Calcutta: Signet Press, 1948.

————. *The Unity of India.* London: Lindsay Drummond, 1948.

————. *Speeches 1949-53.* New Delhi: Publications Division, Government of India, 1954.

————. *Speeches 1953-57,* Vol. 3, 1954. New Delhi: Publications Division, Govt. of India, 1958.

Nanavathi, M. B., and Vakil, C. N. (eds.). *Group Prejudices in India.* Bombay: Vora, 1951.

O'Malley, L. S. S. (ed.). *Modern India and the West.* London: Oxford University Press, 1941.

Panikkar, K. M. *Hindu Society at Cross Roads.* Bombay: Asia Publishing House, 1961.

————. *The Foundations of New India.* London: George Allen & Unwin, Ltd., 1963.

Park, R. L., and Tinker, I. (eds.). *Leadership and Political Institutions in India.* Madras: Oxford University Press, 1960.

Poplai, S. L. (ed.). *Select Documents on Asian Affairs,* 1947-50. Bombay: Oxford University Press, 1959.

Philips, C. H. (ed.). *Politics and Society in India.* London: George Allen & Unwin, Ltd., 1963.

Radhakrishnan, S. *The Hindu View of Life.* London: George Allen & Unwin, Ltd., 1948.

————. *Eastern Religions and Western Thought.* London: Oxford University Press, 1940.

————. *The Philosophy of Sarvepalli Radhakrishnan.* New York: 1952.

Rajendra Prasad. *Speeches.* New Delhi: Government of India, Publications Division, 1955.

————. *Speeches 1952-56.* New Delhi: Publications Division, Government of India, 1958.

Rein Court, A. D. *The Soul of India.* New York: Harper and Brothers, 1961.

Risley, H. *People of India.* London: W. Thacker and Co., 1915.

Salvadori, M. *Liberal Democracy.* London: Pall Mall Press, 1958.

Sanjana, J. E. *Caste and Outcaste.* Bombay: Thacker and Co., 1946.

Schunpeter, J. A. *Capitalism, Socialism, Democracy.* 1947.

Senart, E., and Ross, E. (tr.). Caste in India, London: 1930.

Sherring, M. A. *Hindu Castes and Tribes,* Calcutta: 1872.

Sheen, V. *Nehru,* London, 1960.

Sirsikar, V. M. *Political Behaviour in India,* Manaktalas, Bombay: 1965.

Smith, D. *India as a Secular State.* Princeton: Princeton University Press, 1963.

Sovani, N. V., and Dandekar, V. M. (eds.). *Changing India* Bombay: Asia Publishing House, 1961.

Social Welfare in India, 1955.

Selections from Swami Vivekananda.

Spitz, D. *Democracy and the Challenge of Power.* New York: 1958.

Srinivas, M. N. *Caste in Modern India.* Bombay: Asia Publishing House, 1962.

Tagore, R. *Nationalism.* London: Macmillan and Co., Ltd., 1920.

Tinker, H. *Reorientations.* Bombay: Oxford University Press, 1965.

Thurston, E. *Castes and Tribes of Southern India,* vols. 1–9. Madras: 1909.

Tawney, R. H. *Equality.* London: George Allen & Unwin, Ltd., 1951.

Unnithan, T. K. N. *Gandhi and Free India.* Bombay: 1956.

Weiner, M. *The Politics of Scarcity.* Bombay: Asia Publishing House, 1963.

————. *Political change in South Asia.* Calcutta: Firma K. L. Mukhopadhyay, 1963.

————, and Kothari, R. (eds.). *Indian Voting Behaviour.* Calcutta: Firma K. L. Mukhopadhyay, 1965.

Wadia, A. R. *Democracy and Society.* Bombay: Lalvani Publishing House, 1966.

Zinkin, T. *Caste Today.* London: Oxford University Press, 1963.

Reports

Report of the Backward Classes Commission, vols. 1–3. Delhi: Government of India Press, 1956.

Report of the Constitutional Proposals of the Sapru Committee, 1945.

Report of the Committee on Special Multipurpose Tribal Blocks, Ministry of Home Affairs. Government of India Press, Nasik Road: 1960.

Report of the First General Elections in India, 1951–52, Vol. 1. New Delhi: Government of India Press, 1955.

Report of the First General Elections in India, 1951–52, Vol. 2. New Delhi: Government of India Press, 1955.

Report of the Election Commission of India, Second General Elections. New Delhi: Government of India Press, 1957.

Report of the Indian Statutory Commission, Vol. 1. Calcutta: Government of India Central Publications Branch, 1930.

Report of the Indian Statutory Commission, Vol. 2. Calcutta: Government of India Central Publications Branch, 1930.

Report of the Indian Franchise Committee, Vol. 1. Calcutta: Government of India Central Publications Branch, 1932.

Indian Constitutional Reforms. Calcutta: 1919.

Report of the Joint Committee on Indian Constitutional Reform, Vol. 1, Part II (1933–34). New Delhi: Government of India Press, 1934.

Report of the Joint Committee on Indian Constitutional Reform 1933–34, Vol. 1. New Delhi: 1934.

Report of the Proposals for Indian Constitutional Reform. London: 1933.

Report of the Study Team on Social Welfare and Welfare of Backward Classes, Vol. 1. New Delhi: Govt. of India Press, 1959.

Report of the States Reorganisation Commission, 1955.

Report of the Scheduled Areas and Scheduled Tribes Commission, Vols. 1–2, 1960–61. Simla: Government of India Press, 1962.

Memorandum on the Report of the Backward Classes Commission, Ministry of Home Affairs. Government of India.

Report of the University Education Commission, Vols. 1–2. Simla: Government of India Press, 1951.

Report of the Commissioner for Scheduled Castes and Scheduled Tribes, 1951-63. Government of India Press.

Constituent Assembly Debates, vols. 1–10. Government of India Press.

Mysore Backward Classes Commission: Interim Report. Bangalore: Govt. Press, 1960.

Mysore Backward Classes Commission: Final Report. Bangalore: Govt. Press, 1961.

Report of the Administrative Reforms Committee, Vol. 1, Government of Kerala. Trivandrum: Govt. Press, 1958.

Report of the Commission for Reservation of Seats in Educational Institutions, Kerala, 1965. Trivandrum: Govt. Press, 1966.

Imperial Gazetteer of India, 1907.

The Gazetteer of India, Vol. 1. Nasik: Govt. of India Press, 1965.

India Reference Annuals 1956-64. Delhi: Publications Division, Govt. of India.

The Times of India Directory and Year Book, 1965-66. Bombay: Times of India Office, 1966.

Law Reports

The All India Reporter, Vol. 38, 1951.

The All India Reporter, Vol. 38, 1951 (Mysore, Nagpur, Orissa).

The All India Reporter, Vol. 38, 1951 (Bhopal, Calcutta, Bombay).

The All India Reporter, Vol. 39, 1952.

The All India Reporter, Vol. 40, 1953.

The All India Reporter, Vol. 42, 1955.

The All India Reporter, Vol. 43, 1956.

The All India Reporter, Vol. 45, 1958.

The All India Reporter, Vol. 45, 1958 (Madras, Manipur, Mysore).

The All India Reporter, Vol. 45, 1958 (Andhra Pradesh, Assam).

The All India Reporter, Vol. 47, 1960.

The All India Reporter, Vol. 48, 1961.

The All India Reporter, Vol. 49, 1962.

The All India Reporter, Vol. 50, 1963.
Mysore Law Journal, Vol. 38, August, 1960.
Mysore Law Journal, Vol. 39, February, 1961.
Mysore Law Journal, Vol. 41, October, 1963.
Mysore Law Journal, Vol. 41, November, 1963.

Census Reports

Census of India, 1921.
Census of India, 1931.
Census of India, 1941.
Census of India, 1951.
Census of India, Special Groups 1951 Census.
Census of India, 1954, Paper VIII.
Census of India, 1957, Paper No. 1.
Census of India, 1957, Paper No. 2.
Census of India, 1961.
The Mysore Population Study. New York: United Nations
    Publication, 1961.

Five Year Plans

First Five Year Plan ⎫
Second Five Year Plan ⎪   Government of India
Third Five Year Plan ⎬   Planning Commission
Fourth Plan Outline ⎭

Encyclopedias

Encyclopaedia Britannica, Vol. 4, U.S.A., 1910.
Encyclopaedia of the Social Sciences, vols. 3–9. New York: Mac-
    millan Co., 1935, 1949.
The Columbia Encyclopedia. New York: Columbia University
    Press, 1947.

Periodicals

Eastern Economist

Man in India
Journal of the National Academy of Administration
The Economic Weekly
Indian Journal of Political Science
Indian Journal of Social Research
Indian Law Institute Journal
American Political Science Review
American Sociological Review
Vanyajathi (A Journal on Scheduled Tribes)
Political Scientist

Newspapers

The Times of India, Bombay
The Hindu, Madras
The Indian Express, Bombay
Deccan Herald, Bangalore
Blitz, Bombay

INDEX

357